A HISTORY OF

WESTFIELD INDIANA

Published by The History Press
Charleston, SC 29403
www.historypress.net

First published 2015

Manufactured in the United States

ISBN 978.1.62619.402.1

Library of Congress Control Number: 2014953439

Contents

Preface

The story is in the records, an array of written sources created for specific uses beginning in 1835 and accumulated, in many forms and for many purposes, during more than a century and a half. The story is of the succeeding decades and generations after the arrival of the founders of Westfield and Washington Township, Hamilton County, Indiana.

The records are found in fascinating groups, as created by religious and governmental organizations, personal letters, journals, diaries, news reports, works of other authors, civic organizations, photographs and other illustrations.

Close focus on these sources rekindles the liveliness of the people spoken of in their lifetimes and can inform, enlighten and even move readers, particularly those for whom this is the story of their own or adopted heritage.

The specific knowledge gathered from what historical records have been preserved includes tactile interstices, intervals of utter silence and unrecoverable information. Bridging these gaps—and there are many—requires viewing many more sources of many different kinds. And what emerges is necessarily episodic: select periodic narratives over more than a century and a half, as if visiting the general scene at intervals.

As for expression of gratitude, the first and foremost is to Frances and Dr. Howard Lee for sponsoring another work, the 178-year history of the Westfield Monthly Meeting of Friends, which set the course for this work as well. The Lees' beneficence reminds of the sponsoring "angels" of another long-ago age when the similarly enlightened gave freely of their resources for works in all branches of the humanities and the arts. I am truly fortunate to be in their debt.

A story of this length is never complete within the knowledge of one person. Many others have contributed information of absolute importance. The following have contributed appreciably in that manner.

The few extant issues of newspapers published in Westfield are mostly those preserved by Joe and Leanna Roberts of Westfield. And the voluminous transcriptions by their son Tom Roberts of sources in their truly impressive family archives, and many additional sources, have amplified the following study remarkably. The collection of monthly meeting minutes of the Westfield Society of Friends, particularly regarding the initial wave of founders, has been provided graciously by the Westfield Friends Monthly Meeting, their accessibility arranged by Frances Lee. These have been augmented by similar records at the Friends Archives, Earlham College. The collections of the Westfield Washington Historical Society, and the access given by that organization led by WWHS president Bruce Hansen, has been of absolute importance. The donations of primary and other source materials by members and others to the WWHS have created a fascinating archive of truly significant record groups, of which the organization and member donors can be proud and from which scholars can benefit greatly. All images are courtesy of the Westfield Washington Historical Society; photos relating to members of the Horton family are courtesy of Don Horton.

My wife, Barbara, has contributed endlessly her expertise in computer usage to prepare this work for publication. Throughout the project, the young lives of Eva and Ryan (in age order, very important) have enriched my own in mysterious and wonderful ways, easing the effect of the perpetual craquelure of aging by reminding me that any such historical narrative can have lasting value. Greg Dumais, commissioning editor for The History Press, the nation's premier publisher of textual local histories, has guided the work to publication with the personable expertise of those who held similar positions among the best independent publishing houses of the past. Project editor Elizabeth Farry has also done copyediting that well serves that essential function while retaining the writer's voice, a balancing act only the best can perform. To all who have helped, as in contributing oral history interviews, I give my thanks and continuing appreciation. Finally, the work in its final form is my own to claim and for which to be totally responsible in all facets of its creation.

Introduction

Westfield and Washington Township, Hamilton County, Indiana, came to be as it is today in the same manner as other local scenes in the Midwest where the first few settlers arrived, followed by many more, until all the land in the township had been purchased for farming and for a few villages, and that combination came to support a growing population in production and consumption.

The story begins with fewer than a dozen people of a "peculiar" distinction (their own word), who purchased their land claims from the federal land office in Indianapolis from 1831 forward. Others followed, the majority, like the first arrivals, from the nation's Southland, most commonly from North Carolina and of the Quaker religious faith and practice (the Society of Friends). By 1837, much of the land in the township had been purchased, but more settlers acquired the remaining acreage within the following few years. All those who arrived throughout the 1830s and '40s are distinguished herein with the term "founders."

Then, with farms established and towns set in place, the residents continued their chosen occupations, chiefly farming, absorbing changes (slowly at first) from within and from without, both those of their own doing and those offered or pressed upon them. And so all across the woodland Midwest was the "filling out" of the former "Old" Northwest Territory, eventually becoming the states of Ohio, Indiana, Michigan, Illinois and Wisconsin. (Even then, in the mid-1840s, another Northwest Territory in the far West was gaining interest as settlers ventured toward the West Coast, drawn largely by the similar chance to claim land and create livelihoods in what would become the states of Oregon, California and Washington.)

But instances of uniqueness do occur within the confines of a locale wherever it is situated geographically. And Westfield and Washington Township, Hamilton County, Indiana, became what it was at any one point in time and what it is today by the efforts of individuals and the natural resources gifted on the fifty-six square miles of this township, with Westfield always the largest of the close-knit total of four towns whose footprints remained small for many decades in the extensive surrounding farm fields. Westfield attained its singular growth by the crossing of two early roads that became the very center of town and the later coming of two railroads, which crossed at the southwest corner town.

The founders brought the spark of ambition that changed their physical environment dramatically within their own lifetimes, and that was continued over the following decades by the generations that succeeded them. There are yet those in the town (recently officially designated a true "city") and township who trace their family histories to the founders who began arriving in 1831.

Before long, in the settlement of the town and township, newcomers began to add to the evolving character of the town, though the town and township remained an unhurried, neighborly and largely harmonious community.

Over the years, other religious denominations have made their contributions to the social development of this locale—Methodists in the 1840s and Wesleyan Methodists who joined Friends in the fabled Underground Railroad to protect escaped slaves. Westfield would become well known by both slaves and slave hunters as a safe station along the long escape route, a place where peaceful resistance to recapture took creative forms but always prevailed.

Another distinguishing local characteristic was established here early, that of the promotion of education of area children. The Quakers' Union High School was a widely known prized presence from 1860 to the early years of the twentieth century. Before that, the first meetinghouses of Friends were also schools beginning in 1835. The promotion of education has remained a priority for most of the locale's history.

By the third generation, the founders' offspring were enjoying success in a region that they helped make famous for its abundant crops of corn, wheat and other grains and beef and dairy herds and hogs for the busy pork market. From the beginning, the farm families supported the development of a town, while the townspeople, the merchants, tradespeople and others supplied essential needs of the farm families.

Within recent decades, growth has dominated municipal oversight remarkably and continually, so much so that the former rural environment is largely gone except for a relatively few farming operations. This place has become well known for the quality of life for raising families and for high-tech employment. And most recently, city officials have established a family sports tourism center ("our new industry," Westfield mayor Andy Cook says), a complex of many playing fields, clinics in sports medicine and hotels and other accommodations for tourists. The local antislavery heritage and the retaining of an attractive remnant of the small-town atmosphere has also created a modern vibrancy for Westfield and the township located close to major transportation routes and to the capital city Indianapolis and its many tourist attractions. Remarkable residential and commercial growth in the past decade have changed this place phenomenally, putting Westfield in the top tier of nationally recognized places to live. And another characteristic is an active appreciation of the historical perspective.

The following shows some of that passing milieu.

1

The Founders Assemble in the Wilderness

He listened to that inward voice.
—James Greenleaf Whittier, "The Quaker of the Olden Time"

The first telling glimpse of them all together is on a deep winter Thursday (they call it "Fifth Day"), December 10, 1835. They are gathered in a new log "meetinghouse" amidst the stumps of freshly chopped trees deep in the immense, enveloping forest. The simple log structure, with minimally made, newly hewn benches without cushioning, sits on a small plot of ground in the northwest corner of section six of Washington Township, the westernmost of the three townships of the center tier of Hamilton County, Indiana. Within sight to the north, an ancient east–west trail used earlier by Native Americans and a few traders crosses Range Line Four East, the primary reference for the first ever land survey done here in 1820. The range line is marked merely with the surveyor's "blazes" on trees at measured distances north and south for six miles through the township.

Most of those in the new meetinghouse today are from North Carolina (they say simply "Carolina" or "Caroliny"). Most have not seen winters this cold before coming to Indiana, a new state as of 1816. They have come hundreds of coarse miles in the past year or so for two reasons. First, to avoid daily scenes of human slavery (their long-standing efforts to aid, educate and gain the freedom of slaves has largely been outlawed by Southern states). And they have come to buy land claims here in the "New Purchase," nearly the entire central portion of the state, all lands south of the Wabash River, acquired in 1818 from Native Americans, and extending to the northern boundaries of the first large counties originating along the Ohio River. The settlers have purchased 80 or 160 acres at the set price of $1.25 per acre plus a survey fee. The land cannot be bought on credit anymore, but the land taxes have been delayed for five years in the place of credit purchases.

They are "Quakers," so named in derision long ago in England, but their forebears transformed the spiteful moniker into one of considerable respect widely recognized in Europe and America. They are the most recent of the "Quaker Migration," the only such for conscience sake in American history. Their predecessors settled first in southwest Ohio; others came soon into the White River Valley of eastern Indiana and still others to Morgan and Hendricks Counties near the center of the state, and now these few have come to the newly named Washington Township, Hamilton County. The mass emigration has been occurring for three decades and has included many hundreds of families and thousands of individuals. Over this time, throughout the Carolinas, Virginia and Georgia, Friends have left, often selling out at a substantial loss to join the migration.

The Northwest Ordinance of 1789 forbade slavery (Article Six) in the new territories, but that provision has been ignored by some who instead apply the indenture laws to their liking. Slave hunters chase after escapees well into Indiana and often are aided by whites and even government officials and officers of the law. The unconscionable pretension by some to ownership of fellow human beings will die hard. To these people, slaves are chattel, their value figured alongside any beast of burden. When runaways are caught, they are labeled troublemakers and treated even more brutally. Legally free former slaves are also being kidnapped and sold back into slavery.

Before venturing here, most of these settlers stopped briefly at Fairfield Meeting in Hendricks County, established in 1826. Every other community of Friends in central Indiana is similarly composed largely of Southerners who have come for the same two basic reasons.

Two among them today are writing in new record books. Deborah Rich sits in one of the two equally partitioned and shuttered spaces with women and young children on one side; men and older boys are on the other side. In "First Day" (Sabbath) silent worship services, the shutters will be removed to create one room. Inside the new log structure still aromatic of freshly chopped timber, Deborah Rich is recording the minutes of the women's gathering. Beyond the partition, Zenas Carey writes minutes of the men's meeting. These two are "recording clerks."

They are all considering the same administrative matters; they will pass messages through the partition when needed, seeking "unity." The "presiding clerk" of each group is one acknowledged for discerning when unity has been achieved. There are no women's- or men's-only matters; instead, the responsibilities of the meeting are shared. Friends insist on equality of the sexes.

Friend Rich has written at the top of page one, "Westfield Monthly Meeting of Women Friends, branch of White Lick Quarterly Meeting, opened and first held the 10th of 12th month, 1835." Friend Carey has written, "The minutes of the Westfield Monthly Meeting of Friends, 12th month, 10th, 1835". They write in neat cursive, fine examples of practiced penmanship without errant ink blots.

The term "Monthly Meeting" is key to the gathering today. It signifies official recognition by the Indiana Yearly Meeting of Friends at Richmond, in Wayne County on the Ohio-Indiana state line, of group worship "in the manner of Friends" and with permission to conduct their own administrative matters for which local Friends will gather here each month. They have been preparing for this announcement for four years, and now the "privilege" has been granted to add the name "Monthly Meeting" to the title of the collective membership.

They have been assembling on each "First Day" (Sunday) for four years now for "silent worship" in the log cabin homes of members, often that of Friends Ambrose and Elizabeth Osborn, whose cabin is nearest the crossroads. There is no single minister in charge; each Friend is considered his or her own minister, as well as minister to the whole gathering when sharing from the urging by the Holy Spirit. During worship, the respectful silence is broken only when one rises to relate what has been suggested to her or him personally by the Holy Spirit, for which they "wait expectantly" for an hour or more each worship service.

Temporarily, this is a combined assemblage of Washington Township Friends and visitors from "Richland Meeting," another new group of Friends who have settled in Clay and Delaware Townships nearby to the south. Richland Friends built their log meetinghouse two years ago, a half mile north of their village of Bethlehem developing at another strategic crossroads along the same surveyor's range line, and are in preparation to become their own Monthly Meeting.

Both recording clerks use Friends' own calendaring terms rather than the pagan Roman names for months and days: Friends number the months consecutively, first through twelfth; the seven days of the week begin with "First Day" (the Sabbath) through "Seventh Day."

The meetinghouse serves also as a primary education school during the week, another characteristic of Friends, their active support of education; literacy among adults and children is expected. They welcome children of non-Friends to their school. Friends are asked regularly, "Are schools encouraged for the education of our young children under the tuition of teachers in membership with us?"

They are farm families mostly, hard at work clearing trees for small fields of grain crops. There is at least one mercantile entrepreneur among them so far; the energetic Asa Bales has opened a small store in addition to his farm work. There have been two other firsts: a newborn to the Harmon and Nancy Cox family in 1832 and the marriage two years earlier of William Hiatt and Mary Moon.

They are also establishing the first village in the township; they expect many more Friends to come. Friends will likely be the majority population for the foreseeable future. And now, as at many places in the movement westward of the nation's frontiers, a place name has traveled along with its former residents. For many of these few families, this will be their second "Westfield." The first was in Surry County in northwest North Carolina, hard against the boundary of western Virginia. They have left family members laid to rest in the graveyard there at that meetinghouse built, it is said, in 1787 in the "west field" of settlement, after the coastal plain and the piedmont plateau of North Carolina had been settled and their pioneering forebears entered the yet-higher Blue Ridge country. That original Westfield Meeting has now been "laid down" because nearly all its members have come north.

For the gathering today, these transplanted southerners have come from their own recently and quickly built cabins nestled in chosen spots in the surrounding deep forest, each with its own pyre of felled trees smoldering in the process of clearing land. Those who arrived early enough to plant have a stubble field or two of "Indian corn" and garden vegetables they have thankfully watched rise from the rich soil now plowed for the first time.

For the first two families to arrive here, their land office documents are dated 1831, when they purchased their claims. Asa Bales and wife, Susannah, and the Coxes with five children are the first of that particular record to arrive here. The Baleses' eighty acres, one-half of a quarter section, purchased on January 25, 1831, is on the east side of the township, up against the neighboring Noblesville Township line.

On May 23, 1831, Harmon Cox paid for 76 acres and another 80 acres on December 31, totaling the entire southwest quarter of section eighteen on the Delaware Township line (quarter sections are usually 160 acres in size; some vary because of surveying technicalities). The Coxes' claim is on the east side of the range line.

As found in the minutes of other Monthly Meetings, the Cox family—wife, Nancy, and children Alexander, born 1816; Isaac, 1818; Hannah, 1820; Enoch, 1822; and Aaron, 1830—had come to the White River Valley to the Driftwood Meeting "held at Sand Creek" in Bartholomew County, then on to Fairfield Meeting in Hendricks County and now here to Washington Township, Hamilton County.

Asa and Susannah Bales had arrived by another circuitous route common to Friends at the time: beginning at the Westfield Meeting in Surry County, North Carolina, and then the long trek to Springfield Meeting in Wayne County, Indiana, arriving on January 15, 1823, and then on to White Lick Friends Meeting in Morgan County. By mid-November of that year, they had moved to Fairfield Meeting in next door Hendricks County and now to the new Westfield in Hamilton County by late January 1831.

The next year, 1832, twenty-six more settler families, and possibly single individuals, arrived. In January: Benjamin Wheeler (80 acres); February: Sarah Hawkins (80); April: Isaac Wells (80, and 80 in October and 80 in December), Enich Yates (40); May: Ira Cook (80); August: Francis and Phillip Stultz (each 160); September: Jesse Rice (80), Charles Davis (80), Eli Rees (80), Simon Moon (70), William Anthony (160), Charles White (80), Isaac (80) and David Baldwin (76); October: Henry Mover (80), Benjamin Wagaman (80), Timothy Summer (160), Frederick Brandel (160), Eli Rees (80); November: John Stout (80), William Reynolds (200), Isaac Williams(157), Abner Barker (80); December: Ambrose (146) and William (80) Osborn and Thomas Reynolds (40). These new landowners have located mostly within two and a half miles of the crossroads; five are in the far southwest corner of the township, one in the far northeast corner and others in the far southeast corner.

In 1832, Asa Bales purchased another 160 acres along the range line, the southeast quarter of section thirty-six (in the rectilinear survey system, range lines are considered good routes for the first roads to be made, just as are each side of each mile-square section, eventually giving each claim access to a road).

Simon Moon typifies many of the new settlers in bringing a family here. He and wife, Hannah Stout Moon, brought six children—Joseph, Mary,

John, William, Riley and Sabina—to Indiana, first to near Richmond in late 1820, and then they transferred membership to the Sugar Grove Meeting near Plainfield, Hendricks County. (A son, Jonathan, died before the family left the Cane Creek Meeting in Guildford County, North Carolina.) The Moons are said to have arrived here near sundown on September 29, and their cabin, near the crossroads, was up by the next evening. Three children have been born to the Moons in Indiana: Simon Jr., daughter Hannah and son Elihu. Simon's ancestors had lived in Pennsylvania and then Virginia and North Carolina, common to Quakers in that order of locations. Simon Moon represents a long Quaker generational history: an ancestor is said to have come to America from England with William Penn in 1682, fleeing religious persecution.

Most of the new settlers brought families except for the Baleses. Harmon Cox and wife, Nancy, brought six children; David Baldwin, five; Isaac Baldwin, five; Simon Moon, nine; William Osborn, four; Zachariah Rees, seven; William Reynolds, four; Timothy Summer, four; Isaac Wells, five; Charles White, three; Charles Davis, six.

Until 1833, the land claim documents had only a county designation. But in November, the county commissioners set the boundaries of Washington Township. This year, seventy-three others purchased claims.

During 1834, 126 new Friends families bought land, spreading out to the central and northeast sections of the township mostly, with some in the center of the southern half of the township and some along the east side of the township. This year, at the crossroads, Bales and two others, Simon Moon and Ambrose Osborn, whose claims all corner at that point, platted a total of forty-eight town lots from their own claims to be the beginning of the village of Westfield.

The three submitted their plat at the courthouse in neighboring Noblesville on May 6, 1834. The plat shows forty-eight lots, 82½ feet across the front and 156¾ feet long, set aside to make this a proper town. The plat has two "Main" Streets (one will be called "Main Cross Street") and Walnut and Cherry Streets and the alleys Oak, Vine and "Moulberry." Now tradesmen and others providing useful items and services will come knowing that a township of promising farmers will support their commercial efforts. The farms will generate an economy in which the town will share by supplying the farm families with what they do not make themselves.

The year 1835 is the date on the claim parchments of 136 more landowners who have chosen acreage of 40 to 160 acres among the diminishing claims yet unsold in a circle farther from the crossroads.

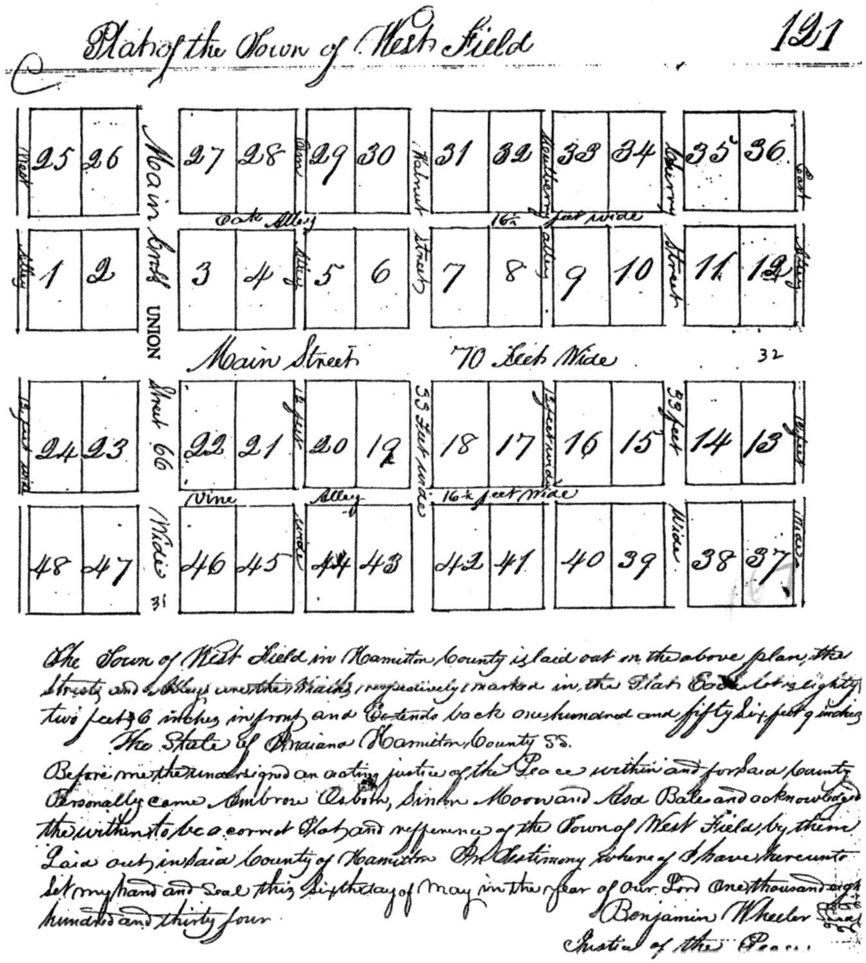

First plat of Westfield, 1834, by Asa Bales, Ambrose Osborn and Simon Moon, all Quaker emigrants from North Carolina beginning in 1831.

William Young has purchased 320 acres, a full half of section fifteen up north joining the Adams Township line. At this time, he is the largest landowner of record in the township.

In fact, by the end of this year, all sections of land are either totally or partially claimed except for acreage in section twenty in the northeast corner, section sixteen near the southwest corner and another section numbered sixteen near the northwest corner.

All the new landowners who have arrived in the past five years are busy turning their "wild" land, as it is referred to, into "improved" land, increasingly valuable real estate. (Land claims, even if "worked" two years, double and triple in value.) So far, 288 families or individuals (not all Friends) call Washington Township home when the Westfield Monthly Meeting of Friends received its official designation in December 1835.

Surveying the Wilderness

The county was surveyed by contract surveyors William L. Laughlin and Charles H. Test a decade ago in the spring of 1820, using the required rectilinear system of survey.

The invisible lines they ran are marked by "blazes" ("notches," "chops," "markers") on hardwood trees of a precise diameter likely to be around for the duration of the first land purchasers to arrive and lay out boundary fences. The bark was stripped for branding or carving the range, township and section numbers and directional abbreviations on these "witness," "bearing," "station," "line" and "sight" trees where survey lines run and intersect.

They had outfitted themselves, as required by the surveyor general in Washington, D.C., with "a good compass of Rittenhouse's construction, having a nonius [highest professional quality] division and moveable sights, and a two pole chain of 50 links" in addition to "tally rods," "marking irons" and their camp equipment. They were prepared to live outdoors throughout the survey. They used traverse trigonometry to run the "offsets" around ponds, swamps, rivers, creeks and the like.

The surveyor and his small crew of chainmen and axe men have trod on more land than anyone so far except the recent Native American occupants. For the benefit of those who would buy land, the surveyors had instructions to note "the kind of timber and undergrowth" that covered the land and to describe the land briefly, with notes such as "flat" or "1st [or 2nd] rate," "level," "inclining to swampy." They were also to note "rich land," "dry" or "wet prairie," and near streams and rivers perhaps "1st rate bottom" land. Also important were notations such as "spring [fed] branch"; settlers might pass up good land if there was not a spring within reasonable reach.

Also noted was the species of each tree marked and the diameter for easy finding. Poplar trees are particularly sought out for cabin logs for their supposed resistance to boring insects.

The species of each of the more than four hundred trees marked in the township include beech, ash, box elder, buckeye, burr and white oak, cherry, dogwood, elm, hackberry, hickory, hornbeam, ironwood, locust, lynn, maple, mulberry, poplar, "spice," "sugar" (perhaps maple), sycamore, "thorn" and white and black walnut. Walking through the forest was often rough; one pioneer says the spice "threw out arms and smaller sprouts in the center, and there were nettles and wild pea vines waist high. And woe to any one 'traipsin' through just after a rain. He'd get as wet as a drowned rat."

The two surveyors made all this important, hard-earned information available at the land office as a large plat map, scale two inches to the mile, with a compass in one corner.

The new landowners have come to a region from which the native population has been removed recently, many by local militias. Friends have not had the chance to reimburse the Indians as Friend William Penn had done even though the ownership of what is now Pennsylvania was granted to him by the king of England. But Friends in general have been aiding Indians for a long time, as is called for in their "Testimony" of equality for all. (In the South, Friends aided Indians in regard to their remaining land rights among other ways.) Yearly meetings in Ohio and Indiana have now joined those in eastern states in sending volunteer teachers and farming instructors, equipment and food supplies to the woodland Indians relocated west of the Mississippi on land much different than what they left in Indiana.

A panoramic view from high above the little settlement marked by the rising smoke spirals of numerous cabin chimneys and smoldering heaps of fresh-cut timber sees far to the west about eighteen miles into Boone County, established in 1830. On a northwest angling line is a strip of cleared land from Indianapolis to Lake Michigan acquired by the state from the Potawatomie Indians in 1826, along with tracts of land south of Indianapolis all the way to Madison on the Ohio River. This still-developing road will run the length of the state—an ambitious concept. The plan has been to clear a path one hundred feet wide, with the middle thirty feet "grubbed and graded." The work was interrupted by the Black Hawk War two years earlier, and settlement was delayed in the northwest portion of the state. The road has been in the making for ten years,

SERIOUS WORK

The survey work was taken seriously by most surveyors and their crews. Two chain bearers of surveyor Laughlin's crew wrote in one of the field notebooks, "We, James Doyle and Cicero Laughlin [a son or nephew] do solemnly swear in the presence of Almighty God, that in all measurements in which we shall be employed as chain carriers in this public survey, we will faithfully and impartially execute the duties of the trust reposed in us, to the best of our skill and abilities, and that as we shall so answer to God at the great [Judgment] day." Serious business, indeed. (Cicero reportedly fell into a creek running across Jackson and Noblesville Townships, hence "Cicero Creek" on the plat.)

promised to open fully in two years. This "internal improvement," as such ventures by the federal and state governments are called, is the "Michigan Road," the state's first grand effort to aid long-distance travel. The road is meant to encourage commerce and travel between the cargo-bearing flatboats and other craft tied up at Madison on the Ohio River and the deep-water ship traffic on Lake Michigan ("Michigan City" was platted there in 1832). If the removal of the Potawatomie Indians in northwest Indiana by state militia goes as planned, those refugees may be marched along a portion of the very ground they have given up for building the road.

Another, fainter line of passage, an earlier trading trail, though hidden in the dense forestation and not so easily seen, leaves the Michigan Road and comes east through the emerging village of Westfield. Here, the trail crosses the north–south surveyor's range line, a strategic crossroads, a good place to start a village.

The aerial view to the south of Westfield shows the short distance to Bethlehem. There, the range line divides Clay and Delaware Townships, the former on the west side of the line and the latter off the east side. That village is taking form at another crossroads where another east–west trail crosses the range line.

The old trail through Westfield and to the east about seven miles, give or take, leads to Noblesville and its trappings of a county governing center established in 1823. The major waterway in the county, the White River, runs by Noblesville. While a route of water travel in earlier years for canoes or flatboats smaller than those behemoths plying the major rivers, this river has not proven navigable for larger craft that would make for significant commercial traffic.

Coming full circle, the heady view north from the high perch is yet another deeply forested horizon across the seven-mile width of neighboring Adams Township, the county line as its northern boundary, and across another sixteen miles to the nearest boundary of the Great Miami Reserve.

It is, to be sure, a wilderness to which these first settlers have come to transform into a farming community. The clearing of land for fields continues, ground is being plowed for the first time and ownership boundaries are being marked with fences of homemade "rails." Plans are already being made for additions to living quarters for man and beast. And much thought and conversing is being given to the creation of roads, still with stumps standing but cleared well enough to get a few farm products to market, though impassable gullies of mud much of the year. The farther farmers have to drive hogs to market, the less the hogs weigh, making for lighter purses on the way back home. But if choosing to avoid driving hogs on hoof, there are the high prices charged by the few freight haulers available who will hire out for that purpose.

Those whose claims of purchase are dated 1836 and 1837 number another fifty-eight families. Their claims are tucked in among the claims of those who arrived earlier. Several of the 1836 arrivals have located close to one another—the majority in the north-central and west-central portions of the township. Those with claims dated 1837 have chosen from the few remaining.

By 1837, eighth month, there had been four schools the past year, one for six months and three for three months, totaling 124 children, 21 in schools not under the Monthly Meeting, 54 not in attendance of any school "but not entirely destitute of education." One neighborhood was "destitute of a Friends school."

In 1838, three schools—Richland, Westfield and Hinkle's Creek—existed, and one "small neighborhood was destitute of any school." There were 138 students enrolled in Friends schools, 34 in schools not under control of Friends and 46 not in schools "yet not entirely destitute of literary instruction."

For the school year of 1839–40, the Monthly Meeting's Committee on Education counted a total of 312 students, none being educated exclusively in Friends schools. The number of Friends children of a suitable age to go to school but who are growing up without instruction is 10, and 130 children have not been going to school but most are receiving some instruction. In three years, the number of school-age children had nearly tripled.

The township is filling up. On March 7, 1837, Asa Bales submitted another plat, this time for an addition of sixteen more lots on the north side of the new Penn Street and four lots opposite on the south side of the street. Several hundred families have arrived during the past six years, and Bales and some of those arriving choose to live in a village where they can practice some useful occupation other than farming.

2

Read It in the Paper

Though working hard clearing land and other farming chores, the founders may be curious about people in the other townships of the county and beyond who are working at the same tasks. The work is time consuming and exhausting, but the occasional trip to Noblesville can be necessary at times if required for taxes or other official transactions at the courthouse. And there are stores and makers of things in Noblesville that are not available here yet.

By the end of 1837, with few claims in the township remaining for sale and much wilderness remaining, a newspaper has been published in Noblesville for the entire previous year. Editor F.W. Emmons, a printer recently from the East, has titled his entry into the fourth estate the *Newspaper*. The first issue came out on January 12, 1836.

Readers in Westfield and the surrounding farms can scan the four brimming pages of each weekly issue not only for views outside their daily boundaries but also for practical reasons, such as announcements of auctions of household goods and tools, items they had to leave behind for want of space in the wagon or two-wheeled cart driven here from the Southland.

The public sale announced for January 21, 1837, to take place "near the court house door," offered "lumber, a lot of carpenter's tools consisting of bench planes, saws, bench screws, molding, augurs, chisels, brace and bits, gouges, one set of clamps with iron screws, one grindstone, a large lot of nails, hardware and many other things beside." The terms of sale were for "cash on all sums of three dollars and under, and six months credit where approved security is given on sums over three dollars."

Other advertisers include the W.A. Emmons emporium, the stores of Conner & Stephenson and F.B. Cogswell ("north side of square, seasonable, fashionable and cheap goods on short approved credit") and the J. Mann & Co. They can also obtain the services of the few tradesmen such as blacksmiths Fitch & Coon; shoe and boot maker Jabez W. Ross ("in his little small red shop east side of square"); cabinetmaker William A. Gilman; and hatters Daubenspeck & Pattison ("silks, beaver, castor & wool"). James A. Groves has just opened a "public house" to be called the "Mansion House," where he "is now erecting extensive stables large enough to accommodate the horses of all who patronize him." The Union Inn and the Exchange Hotel are already open for public accommodations. A new law office has just opened by an attorney named, coincidently, W. Quarles, one of the first specifically criminal lawyers in the state, according to Calvin Fletcher, with whom he often worked. An Indianapolis lawyer and civic leader, Fletcher owned land in Hamilton County, and he was a state senator for Hamilton and Marion Counties from 1826 to 1833.

The article "Our Village" in a late January 1837 issue of the *Newspaper* reports "heated" buildings numbering "seventy-five smokes" and that "more than thirty new buildings were erected here during the past summer." Similarly, in a nod to the fairly recent past, the "very tree which shades our humble hen house has…sheltered among its boughs many a fat wild turkey not more than fifteen years ago."

Letters to the editor are signed with noms de plume from mythology or classical literature. Occasionally one will sign his or her initials; a few sign their full names. A letter to the editor in the February 23 issue complains that only the northeast corner of the town square has been built on; the other three corners "have been suffered to remain so long unoccupied," that "people living near…have cows and pigs…pasturing on that land." The January 3, 1837 issue contains a letter from a reader in Washington Township signed only "J— M—," asking readers to "vote for James B. Ray as the next governor."

The news printed is a hodgepodge. Many articles first appeared in eastern papers. (The editor did travel to Cincinnati to hear a debate and reported on it in the paper.) The paper is like most—much print taken up by articles of little immediacy and lengthy descriptions of the actions of European governments and potentates, along with some local happenings and editorials and letters to the paper about events and subjects closer to home. There are long transcriptions of political speeches, sometimes taking an entire page or more and even continued in a subsequent issue, such as President Andrew Jackson's final annual address, first installment in the January 9 issue and concluded in the issue of March 23. Local and state politicians are occasionally quoted at length. There is also the occasional statistical compendium on taxes, election results, local and national markets and land sales.

There are illustrated ads for traveling entertainments; sometimes their performances are critiqued in the next issue. These might be traveling menageries, small circuses or performances by professional thespians better trained and equipped than the local amateurs. Individuals with some professed talent are also announced, such as lecturers, musicians and phrenologists, one of whom skipped town without paying his bills, described by the editor as obviously having the "bump of dishonesty" on his head. These occasional events occur in Noblesville, of course, for the larger audiences, but never in staid Westfield, where Friends, the majority population, discourage attending such "diversions."

The editor has a knack for making the paper seem chatty by including just enough passages in quotation marks to give some articles a conversational tone, so that reading the newspaper can seem a little like conversing with those quoted. For some readers who do not leave the farm for weeks at a time, this might be more like listening than just reading. Whatever the conversations are about, the reader can assume that others are reading and agreeing (or not) as a kind of socializing, for want of the real thing.

Some of the subjects written about at length are topics of interest to Westfield residents and those in the surrounding farms. The *Newspaper* of January 9, 1837, contains an extract from state legislator "Mr. Dumont's report on the subject of education," particularly concerning the "common schools." Dumont noted that all important matters of state government have some "supervisory authority to watch and direct its operations." All, that is, except for a statewide school system. The editor of the *Newspaper* has written about the advantages, the necessity, of education for farmers and "mechanics" to equip them to be successful at their occupations and to keep up with new ideas, equipment, machinery and other related products.

In Westfield, though, the opportunity for a basic education has been the concern of the Monthly Meeting's Education Committee, as mentioned in the first minutes recorded in the first authorized Westfield Monthly Meeting, including a directive to use the meetinghouse as a school for the primary grades. Friends are asked on a regular basis if all their children are getting a basic education. School fees and books will be provided to those who cannot afford them. (The editor stated in the March 16, 1837 issue, "Few parents know of the importance of a newspaper to their children.")

The newspaper is a good way to give notice of "Astrays" (January 1837), spreading the word about a horse, cow or other livestock that has wandered off the farm or town property and is still missing. Horses are stolen occasionally, and the crime and the apprehension of the guilty are fit news. Local horse theft associations are formed occasionally to aid communication among stock owners.

In the early summer of 1844, the paper tells of "county orders" being paid out for, in particular, two diverse expenses: bounties on wolf scalps and paying for the care of the poor. Though not connected beyond being county expenses, the two payments reflect the overall condition here regarding the settlement of this locale: with virgin wilderness still surrounding, local government is assuming a responsibility such as arises when people form a specific and extended community.

The common bartering relied on for many transactions includes the notice that the W.A. Emmons store, "in exchange for goods" stocked, wants "a quantity of otter, beaver, deer, fox, mink, muskrat, 'coon, wolf and bear skins." ("Also feathers and country produce" and, as of March 16, 1837, will trade also for "mole skins.")

The editor often includes articles and other information about the chief occupation here: farming. The June 15, 1837 issue of the newspaper notes the election of Asa Bales as the first president of the Hamilton County Agricultural Society, which met to organize on Saturday, May 27. (The same issue announced the next meeting of the society for the last Saturday in June at the courthouse.) Bales had called for such an organization to be formed in Washington Township if the county did not follow the state legislature's recommendation for counties to charter such organizations statewide. Before organizing, many of the members had read Calvin Fletcher's mid-January remarks to the Marion County Agricultural Society at their most recent fair. For Fletcher, the primary goals for any such organizations are to improve farming practices and to lobby for more convenient access to the larger markets. And already there is talk in Westfield of hosting a county agricultural fair to exhibit local farm production and the best cattle.

But most of the farmers are lagging behind the wishes of an active few. In the fall of 1837, "Farmer" writes to the editor: "Some months since there was a county agricultural society formed. We adopted a constitution, we signed it. But death seems to have overtaken it in its 'earliest infancy.' The state legislature has wisely provided for the formation of township Agricultural

THE NEWSPAPER

Reading the sole newspaper is a list lover's treat. For example, the issue of February 2, 1837, informs that W.A. Emmons & Company has just opened a store of "goods" that includes an impressive array of cloth materials and finished clothing items (spelled thusly): broadcloths, black, blue and mixed; cassimers, drab, blue and mixed; sattinets, black, blue, drab, mixed and striped; pershams; pillow cloths; blanket cloths; flannels, red, white and canton; linseys; bombazines and bombazetts; brown, green, orange, purple, blue, crimson and scarlet merinos; circassians; silks; velvets; cambrics; muslins; laces; footing; ginghams; shawls; dress and pocket handkerchiefs; calicoes; shirtings; sheetings and tickings; drillings; veils; gauze; lace; harage; hose; gloves; thread in linen and cotton; sewing silks; tapes; braids; cords. Other available goods include hats and caps, boots and shoes, glass, china and crockery ware, tin and wooden wares, groceries "such as" spice, cloves, nutmegs, cinnamon, ginger, pepper, mustard, raisins, figs, starch, sal aeraatus, imperial tea, gunpowder tea, old and young hyson and fancy teas.

In hardware the store has a current stock of Sheffield cutlery and table service, common knives and forks, Spanish dirks, pen and pocketknives, butcher and shoe knives, locks, mortise, chests and trunks, butts and screws, files, rasps, drawknives, hammers, handsaws, candlesticks, snuffers and trays, cast steel axes, shovels, spades, hoes, nails bar and rod iron and castings, as well as dye-stuffs and "almost any article found in a variety store."

In the months of February to April, Emmons promises to pay (barter) eight cents a bushel "in goods" for clean house ashes and six cents a bushel for field ashes. Some say it is possible to recoup some of the cost for the land claim by selling the large piles of ashes from the perpetual pyre of felled trees. Ashes are used for making homemade soap, but on a much larger scale, to make potash, which in the aggregate is figured in tons.

Societies if it is neglected at the county seat; any township may form a society the first of which then becomes the county society. It is said that the people

Value of Coins.

Eagle, - - - -	$10 00
Sovereign, - - - -	4 84
Napoleon, - - -	3 85
Doubloon, Spanish, - -	15 53
———, Patriot, - -	15 53
V Thalers, - - - -	3 93[illegible]
X Thalers, - - -	7 85
X Guilders, - - - -	4 00
Frederick d'Or, - -	3 82[illegible]
Forty Francs, - - -	7 00
Georgia $5 branch mint, -	5 78
Guinea, - - - -	500
Ducat, - - - -	2 00
German Crown, - - - -	1 00
French Crown, - -	1 00
Louis d'Or, - - -	3 80

"Value of Coins" ad in Noblesville newspaper, 1830s.

of Westfield intend to avail themselves of this advantage if we of Noblesville much longer delay our support of a society in this place. Furthermore, I…suggest…that we have a meeting…for the purpose of making preparations for an agricultural fair this autumn."

Of particular interest to all of any means is the alarming news about the financial conditions of the banks nationwide. The June 1, 1837 issue of the *Newspaper* contains a message for immediate notice from the Indiana State Bank, signed by S. Merrill, president, and J.M. Ray, chief cashier. The bankers tell of the suspension of specie payment by some banks outside the state and how some of them are trying to raid the state bank of Indiana to prop up their dwindling reserves. But Merrill and Ray assure that "your money, fellow citizens, is in our vaults, and we are solemnly bound to protect it." But the state bank had itself suspended specie payment "in self defense" and would resume payment "the hour we learn that neighboring banks have done so." They promise that "every dollar will be redeemed."

The *Newspaper* in February 1837 provides a description of "counterfeits of the five dollar notes of the Franklin bank of Columbus" with details needed to identify the phony notes. "No genuine notes of this plate have ever been issued," and the fakes are "shorter and narrower than the genuine bills." There are also engraving mistakes to notice.

The public debate about canal building is continuing voraciously. Some see canals as the answer to the entire region's economic welfare, if not the outright survival; others disagree vehemently. Readers in Westfield likely have received letters from Friends in the southeastern counties where canal fever is rampant and growing and canal construction is well underway, giving opinions about how farmers are or are not benefiting from the canal system there from Lawrenceburg on the Ohio River (and from there to Cincinnati) north and across the National Road west of Richmond and on north.

Speaking of agriculture, in particular the successful use and sustaining of the soil, the *Newspaper* of December 7, 1837, acknowledges that the common method of farming by those who are settling new regions is detrimental to the soil, with far-reaching consequences. Pioneers "go on living upon the patrimonial wealth of Providence, till its value becomes seriously impaired or is wholly gone. They do not consider that land, like everything else, will wear out by bad husbandry."

Of interest also to readers in Westfield are the regular listing of prices paid in Noblesville for produce and other food and grain products. The *Newspaper* usually includes "Noblesville Prices Current" for apples, dried and fresh; per pound price for bacon, cheese, fresh pork, sugar, butter, beeswax, candles, ginseng, hides, lard and feathers; and per bushel price for corn, beans, oats, potatoes, rye and wheat. Eggs and chickens are bought by the dozen, wild game skins by the pelt, turkeys by the head, linseed oil and whiskey by the gallon, flour by the hundredweight and venison as hams. The prices for each item listed by weight or volume are corrected weekly.

Another matter of interest, rather a traditional "concern" to Friends (the term for the "sufferings" of those being oppressed in some fashion), is anything in the paper about Native Americans, almost always stated in the popular "Indian problem" attitude. The article "Indian War" in the February 23, 1837 issue, told of the U.S. Army routing the Seminoles from Florida. Already, "one hundred negroes and Indians have been captured." The writer continues to bluster, "We wish they had two real Kentuckians...with Gen. Jackson's breeches."

Friends' traditional "Indian Concern" for these oppressed, impoverished, besieged and constantly swindled victims of extreme prejudice and even violence is being informed with dependable and regularly updated sources of information from Friends engaged in education and instructional farming among the Indians in their new location, services requested by the Indians. (Some Friends have told of Indians in the South asking to help carry their baggage as they were leaving. "Them's Penn's people," the Indians were quoted as remembering.)

Friends, while still in the South, had aided Indians particularly with the federal government regarding land rights and, of course, the often forestalled payments long overdue, promised assiduously and in writing but remaining unpaid even when the Indians were desperate for food.

Each meeting has a committee on the "Indian Concern," as does each Quarterly and Yearly Meeting, where most aid and funds are directed for transport to Indian refugees now being removed to land that is strange to them across the Mississippi River. (Indiana Friends have already succeeded in asking the president to return to their new home west of the Mississippi some Indian braves whom the government sent to Florida to fight the Seminoles. One brave had been killed in battle there.)

In February 1838, readers in Westfield and Washington Township read what they most likely already knew—that Asa Bales, acting on behalf of deceased Friend Simon Moon, is offering some land for sale "located adjoining town, and 3 lots in town." (Simon Moon was reportedly buried in September 1835 in Westfield in a graveyard for which he had donated the land earlier when a child died and there was no place designated for burials.)

Another important function of county government is the probating of wills, and the records created in this charge are an informative read. For example, at the estate sale for Friend Thomas Chappell on September 12, 1838, Asa Bales purchased a set of match planes, a rabbit plane, a reed plane and a square. That bit of business was recorded dutifully in the probate office's "Will Book B" at the courthouse.

The *Newspaper* ceased publication with the March 22 issue in 1838. The editor had stated that 500 subscribers were necessary to keep it afloat. There were only 140 subscribers counted when the final issue was printed.

One of the first proofs of material progress made so far in Washington Township is a single item, which in the right supply will form the next building phase here. Unremarkable as that is alone, it is a traditional symbol of relative permanence, an indication of personal initiative. Someone in the township was bound to create this item, and in 1838 (some say 1839) Arnold (Aaron?) Lindley is said to be the first to find the right molding composition, construct a form for its shape and size and manage to fire it to the degree needed to produce a true brick. And he made many more—enough to build a brick house for his family north of Westfield.

3

The 1840s: The Promise Up Close

The Founders Enter a New Decade

The next ten years of that eternal ambiguity, the future, now begin with the portal year 1840. But that future in the short run seems poised for disturbance. Friends, Methodists, Wesley Methodists and others, though being several hundred miles from the daily sight of the enslaved "these our brethren," have already adopted different tactics in aiding escaped slaves. Some are openly considering becoming lawbreakers and liable for heavy fines and worse if caught giving direct aid to those who have miraculously slipped the bonds of terror and degradation but still fear for their very lives this far north, across the storied Ohio River, which was supposed to be the firmament of true freedom.

Most local Friends are wary of the bombast, and threat of violence even, of the vociferous abolitionists from a few abolition strongholds in this state and others in the East. The word "abolition" occurs for the first time in the minutes of the Westfield Monthly Meeting for ninth month, 1840, in regard to the current "commotion and excitement of the public mind at present agitated in this country on the subject of slavery."

Beginning mainly at the third month meeting in 1843, those who separate with the "body friends" are referred to as those "who have identified themselves with those who have separated themselves from us…not abiding in that meekness and patience which the Gospel recommends" and for "setting up a meeting contrary to our discipline."

The differences of opinion on how to react to the vestiges of slavery that have come close to home with the arrival of escapees on their very doorsteps have caused some prominent Friends (Asa Bales and his wife and Simon Moon and family, for example) to separate and establish their own Anti-Slavery Friends Meeting. These "separatists" are willing to thwart the fugitive slave laws and other restrictions of the federal and state governments. They are also equipping to host those freedmen still in danger of kidnap by slave hunters and even escaped slaves who choose to stay in the county to work the land and see their children educated by Friends teachers. Now Bales and the others can plan, fund, arrange and carry out secret acts of shelter and transportation to aid former slaves on an "underground railroad," as one

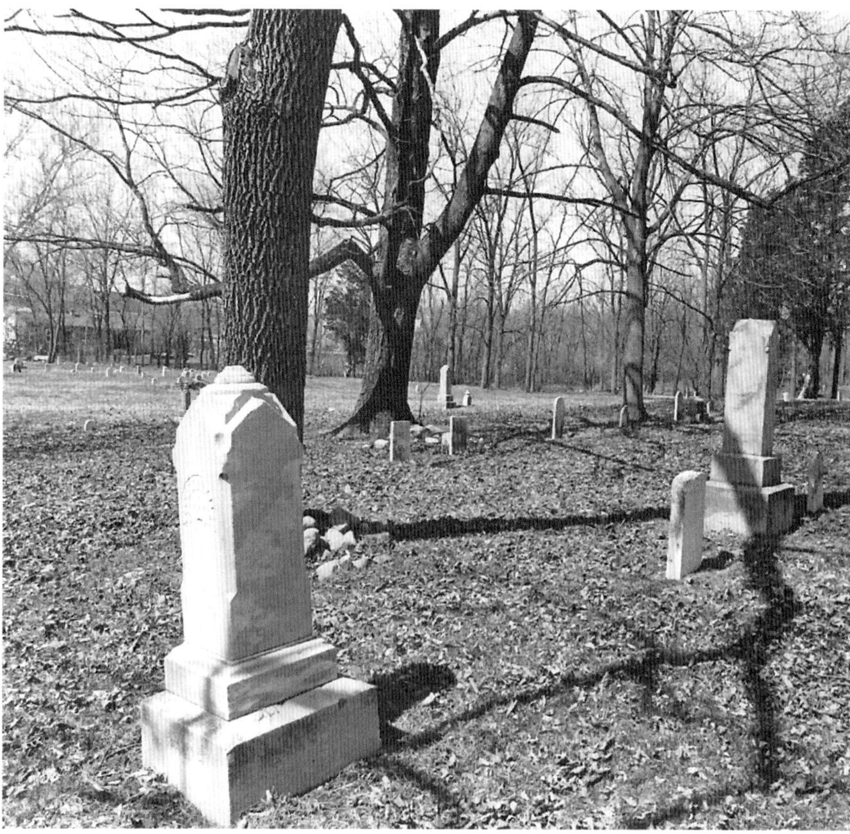

Grave markers in the Anti-Slavery Friends Cemetery on North Unions Street in Westfield, established in the mid-1840s.

TO THE

PROFESSORS OF CHRISTIANITY THROUGHOUT THE SLAVE STATES:

DEAR FRIENDS:—In gospel love we feel free to address you on a subject against which we have long maintained a calm and we believe a righteous testimony. We allude to slavery. Being now convened in a meeting capacity, we hesitate not to unfold to you our minds on a point so important to us all. Your candor, friends, will, no doubt, induce you to acknowledge that slavery, has so far, been attended with many evils: and we propose not, in this address, to throw one mite of excitement into the mind; but as friends to all men, as professed followers of the meek Messiah, as seekers after eternal happiness, we hope to be permitted to approach you in the true spirit of christian feeling.

When our Creator made man, it seems to us that it was not his design that one individual should avail himself of the unremunerated services of another; but that all were intended to experience equal rights and privileges. Now, if this position be correct (and can any one doubt it?) how then can we hold our fellow creatures in bondage, and at the same time enjoy the blessings resulting from the Divine approbation of our course? This question we respectfully desire may command your serious consideration. If slavery were extinct, the favors enjoyed, we feel assured, would fully equal the good work of its destruction; but while it remains in existence, we believe that evils must continue to flow therefrom. God is certainly *just* as well as merciful: and if we act not agreeably to his *known* will we cannot expect to enjoy his love. We feel no disposition whatever to reproach you; but only solicit a careful religious examination of the important subject upon which we are treating, in order that your minds by being favored by the Divine Being, may see clearly and distinctly the impropriety of continuing to retain those in servitude on account of their color, whom their creator hath invested with equal privileges with ourselves, and designed to enjoy the blessings of liberty. There is a peace, a joy, a diadem to be experienced as the reward of good deeds, which far surpasses all temporal possessions; and it is this which no man or any earthly power can take away, that we desire you may possess.

We do not recognize the right of any individual or any body of men whatever, who are aside from slavery, to take any unlawful means to effect its extinguishment; and it is our earnest desire that all who approach slave-holders on the subject, may do it either through the medium of sympathetic vocal utterance or addresses written in a friendly manner.

Finally, endeared friends, suffer us to entreat you by your regard for your own happiness, by your love for the peace and welfare of our common country, and by your profession of christianity, to let the enslaved go free *in such way* as you may see proper; and may the God of peace bless you with his unspeakable love.

Given forth by direction of the Meeting for Sufferings of Indiana yearly meeting of Friends, held at White Water 6th month 4th, 1842.

WILLIAM PARRY, Clerk.

P. S. Persons into whose hands this may come will please to circulate it amongst their friends, *if they feel a freedom to do so.*

Broadside printed by the Meeting for Suffering of Indiana Yearly Meeting in Richmond, Indiana, sixth month, fourth, 1842, to persuade "professors of Christianity throughout the slave states" to free their slaves.

slave catcher assumed when those he hunted disappeared impossibly as into the earth. In doing so, they and others in the admirable effort have already put Westfield on the map in that regard. Asa Bales separated on October 21, 1843; his wife, Susannah, separated the next month on the ninth, as did a few others.

For their part, Friends holding to the peace testimony orthodoxy continue to help the runaways and those who have been freed with financial and material aid. They have set up schools for the children of the escapees, one or two with former slaves as teachers. Each Friends meeting has an "African Committee" to address the ongoing succor these Friends continue to give. These committees collect donations regularly given from the membership for buying the freedom of those in bondage and those freed or escaped but who have been kidnapped back into slavery. In the Friends traditional practice of "publishing the Truth," they address slaveholders in person, often about what a corrosive effect slavery has on the slaveholding families, and they point out the potential fragility of the Southern economy based largely on slave labor. Friends also discourage the purchase of products derived from slave labor.

Editor Emmons had left Noblesville shortly after the demise of the *Newspaper* but has returned and is now publishing the *Little Western*, another weekly county paper distributed on Saturdays at the rate of two cents per week. This time, there is a declared political leaning, toward the Democrats, rather than the generally apolitical stance of his previous paper. The first issue of this new venture is June 4, 1842.

Some of the local Wesleyan Methodists are willing to help in aiding runaways. Their first full-time pastor arrived in January 1844. Reverend J.L. Pfaff, who is also a medical doctor, came to minister to that congregation, which, as had Friends when they first arrived, had been meeting in private homes. It is said of the Wesleyans that they are "warm in their advocacy of the anti-slavery cause" and who, like Friends, despise the detestable fugitive slave laws and will actively thwart the laws.

Local Friend Martha White, unmarried (though "seeing" Dr. A.T. Talbert on special occasions), is the niece of Levi and Catherine Coffin and occasionally visits the Coffins in Newport, where her uncle Levi has the reputation as, some say, "the president of the Underground Railroad." While she does not divulge information that would endanger her relatives or the movement, she does note in her diary when she visits antislavery and abolition meetings in Westfield, Carmel and Noblesville; at public halls; and in schools and other places.

Friend Martha White (born 1826 in Guilford County, North Carolina) had just returned to Westfield on September, "third day" (the ninth), 1845, from Newport. In her diary that day, she wrote, "Asa Bales very low with the fever." She heard that he died the next morning about four o'clock: "Oh what a treasure has the community lost in the death of this good man!" On "fifth day" (the twelfth), she wrote, "The much lamented Asa Bales was buried today." Burial was in the new cemetery of the Anti-Slavery Friends Meeting a few blocks north of the original meetinghouse. Martha Talbert wrote again on "second day, 27th" of October, "Susannah Bales died at 7 o'clock p.m. being about seven weeks from the time of her husband's death." The community had lost two founders whose contributions to its development have been unmatched. Asa had a store business in town and was active in the Underground Railroad and the local agricultural society, continually urging farmers to learn progressive ways to work. He had been a schoolteacher when they were members of the Fairfield Meeting. Their son Riley would carry on after his parents' deaths in hiding, feeding, clothing and transporting escaped slaves on their way north.

Near the end of the decade, the United Brethren build a church after meeting in homes, as had the Friends and the Methodists. More Friends from North Carolina arrive, though far fewer in number. Far less land is available for clearing and farming. But Friends here do leave, usually for Iowa and Kansas, so farms are available for sale occasionally

On June 24, 1848, Westfield gained the distinction of being incorporated.

4

The 1850s: The Promise on Display

The First Ever Federal Agricultural Census

The first official comprehensive statistics for a full four seasons on the nation's farms have been compiled by the late summer of 1850 by local township census enumerator Elam J. Brown, writing in the cumbersome census book provided by the federal government. This is a close count of farm production from June 1849 to June 1850. The numbers recorded show the amount of effort invested in the daily care of the livestock and the plowing, planting, cultivating and harvesting of each crop reported on in bushels, tons for the hay cut, pecks of orchard produce and pounds of butter churned and more.

There are thirty-one oxen in the whole township. They likely pulled wagons or two-wheeled carts from the South that contained household and a few other items brought after selling the farms in the Carolinas. That is fifteen yoke and a single ox on Robert Tomlinson's farm. Isaac Williams and Benjamin Smith each own one of the only two mules listed for the township. Williams had worked as a clerk in Asa Bales's store and then opened one of his own after Bales died in 1845.

There are 678 draft and buggy horses in the township and 457 milch cows (currently giving milk), from which 24,430 pounds of butter have been churned in the previous twelve months. That number is impressive not only in aggregate but also when considering the butter consumption of each family and pounds of butter taken to town to trade for other food items not made at home. Molasses, 1,303 gallons, was made in the township and 3,343 pounds of honey or beeswax reported.

The farms still have more acres of woods than of cleared fields. There are a total of 5,173 acres "improved" (cleared) for crops or planted meadows for the township. But a total of 11,735 acres are still wooded in somewhat the same condition that the new arrivals saw when they first looked for the trees blazed by the surveyor in 1820. The remaining wooded acreage is money of its own kind. Much firewood is consumed each year, and some trees produce foods such as nuts or wild fruit. Trees are felled also for cutting rails for fences, and those left standing serve as cover for wild game. So the remaining timber along with the woodland meadows, sweeps of prairie tall grass and even the swamps on the lowest ground not yet drained appear much as they did fifteen years ago.

The primary field crops grown throughout the township are Indian corn (120,240 bushels), wheat (13,360) and oats (10,327). The 3,092 sheep listed account for the wide use of wool for a variety of daily needs and as yet another farm product to sell, and the great popularity of swine show the large consumption of pork. Much of the pork can travel long distance to market as smoked hams or salted.

When Elam Brown sat with Friends David and Elvira Stalker at their farm three miles northeast of town, the numbers he recorded in the large census book were not unlike what he wrote when visiting other farms in the township. The Stalkers have cleared a similar number of acres as their neighbors all across the township, and their harvest figures are also among the most common of figures for other farms of the "neighborhood." (The numbers David gave can be counted on as true; he once bought a cow and, finding that it was a better cow than he had thought, returned to the seller and gave him more money befitting the cow's true found value. The story is told by Friends and non-Friends alike.)

The Stalkers purchased their claim on October 14, 1843—160 acres in section twenty, to which David and Elvira brought sons Ezra, born in 1841, and Aaron, born in 1842. Now there is also Eli, born in 1844, and Mary Ellen, born in 1845. And after six years of clearing and working the land, the result of all phases of their most recent harvest have been recorded all on one line across two large pages of a forty-six-column heading, a year's hard facts accomplishment.

David has cleared 45 acres so far; 115 remain "unimproved," their portion of the surrounding deep forest. He values the farm at $1,200 (cash) and has $120 worth of "farming equipment and machinery." The Stalkers have three horses, five milch cows, eight head of "other cattle," twenty-six sheep and ten swine, all together valued at $221. The tillable acres have produced 25 bushels of wheat, 400 of Indian corn and 200 of oats. The sheep have been sheared of one hundred pounds of wool. They have dug 15 bushels of Irish potatoes and 5 bushels of sweet potatoes. They report no "value of orchard products in dollars." (Of the thirty-nine other farms listed on the same pages, twenty reported cash value for these products, ranging from $7 to $50.)

Nine tons of hay have been cut. They produced or found thirty pounds of beeswax and honey; Elvira reports one hundred pounds of butter churned. They figure $20 is the value of their "homemade manufactures." The "value of animals slaughtered" is $41. The other farms listed on the two pages with David's figures have cleared acreage of a similar amount, a few as much as fifty acres. Only seven farmers put a dollar figure on their farms more than David, with most ranging from $800 to $1,000. Three farmers claim a value of farm equipment and machinery more than David's $120, with most in the $30 to $100 range.

Two farms have five horses to David's three. Most others have at least two. One farm has one more sheep than the Stalkers; there is a wide range of numbers below David's twenty-six. For swine, David has somewhat fewer than the others with ten; many have twenty or more. Only seven dollar amounts for "value of livestock" are reported above David's $220. David's wheat harvest is on the low end of the scale. David's corn harvest is bested by eleven other farms. Only two other farms have matched David's oat harvest at 200 bushels, with most well below that. Several factors figure in this data for acreage cleared and the other totals, strength of manpower most decidedly.

By far the most popular of the stock animals are the hogs, showing the number born to the common litter and the ongoing market for salt pork. Of the nine farms with honey and beeswax for sale, three produced more (one hundred, fifty and fifty pounds to the Stalkers' thirty pounds).

This year there was also a census taken of the "manufactures for the preceding year." Throughout the township and in town, four businesses are listed that made "products of industry." Cook Lomlindor's steam sawmill had eight hundred logs on the grounds valued at $800. Nathan Barker, blacksmith, had five tons of iron and three thousand bushels of "C Coal," all worth $545. White & Co. sold lumber, with $75 worth on hand, of which

"I own" $25 worth. J. Jackson, cabinetmaker, had a $200 stock of lumber and "sundries" valued totally at $400.

The sawmill employed three hands (at an annual labor cost of $45); the blacksmith, four ($8.50); the pump maker, two; and the cabinetmaker, three. The sawmill had produced 182,000 feet of lumber for a total of $1,365; the blacksmith, for "various kinds of work," earned $1,100. Ninety-five pumps had sold for a total of $500.

In two more years, with the passage of the Free Banking Act in 1852, private "banks of issue," local banks that could issue their own script, can begin operation. In 1854, the Farmers Bank of Westfield opened with W. Robson, president, and J.F. Reeves, cashier. The bank closed in 1858, the reason not entirely clear.

But during its short run, the Farmers Bank of Westfield issued bills in three denominations, one dollar, two dollars and five dollars. The bills, printed by the Baldwin, Adams & Company of New York, were profusely illustrated. On the one-dollar bill were drawings of, from the left, two boys and a wagonload of hay drawn by two oxen. Below this is the prominent numeral "1." The state seal is in the center with an eagle to the right and the number "1" above and the word "ONE" below.

The two-dollar bill is adorned with a woman blowing a horn and three men on the left with a load of hay. Above this active panorama is the word "TWO." The state seal is in the center between two engravings: a farmhouse on the right and a small herd of cattle on the left. The right portion has "TWO" with the numeral "2" above it.

The five-dollar bill shows an Indian kneeling with a long gun with the numeral "5" above on the left. The center portion shows a farmer carrying corn, a boy with a sled, a horse nearby and a stack of corn. On each side of this engraving is the word "FIVE." On the right is the state seal with the numeral "5" above it.

During the bank's brief existence, some "spurious" bills were afloat, no source readily known. These fakes had far less artwork: the two-dollar bill merely showed cattle under a tree, and the five-dollar bill had a child feeding corn to a horse. There has also been a fake ten-dollar bill, a denomination that the bank never issued; the fake replaced the "5" with "10," and a stock corn-gathering scene was added. (Illustrations are given for the face side only of the bills.)

For a report to the state as of January 25, 1857, the bank had had a total of 16,000 notes printed in the three denominations, and as of that date, 7,704 of this variety had been issued, 6,000 were on hand and 2,296 had been burned. When the bank ceased operation, its engraved plates for the three denominations were deposited in the state auditor's office. On October 31, 1875, the bank, closed now for seventeen years, still had $1,406 outstanding in circulation.

5
The 1860s: The Recent War

War and Aftermath

With the bombing of U.S. Army Fort Sumter off the shore of Charleston, South Carolina, on April 12, 1861, by troops of the new secessionist government, the fight was on to test the will of two divergent halves of the nation to settle long-standing disputes that had stymied Congress for some time. Though the "question" of slavery is paramount, there are other seriously divisive issues. The Southern states have majorities in Congress based on counting the millions of slaves as fractional citizens, thereby defeating any measure proposed by the Northern states that those in the South do not like, causing rancor and worse in the halls and chambers of Congress.

When the first act of war is heard about in Hamilton County, some men in Noblesville, determined to know more, are said to have borrowed a handcar from the Indianapolis, Peru and Chicago Railroad and manned the seesaw handles to ride to Indianapolis to hear more of the facts of the matter. These self-appointed representatives of the men of Hamilton County reportedly offered the services of the "Hamilton Continentals," a local militia unit beefed up recently as the fight for power in Congress reached its boiling point. The governor of Indiana was an adamant supporter of President Abraham Lincoln, and when the call came for troops to assemble quickly,

Governor Oliver Morton intended to be the first or among the very first in his position to commit as many troops as the state could produce and as fast as that could be done. He determined that troops from Indiana would be among the best trained, equipped and supplied for the coming war.

The governor gladly accepted the offer of the Hamilton Continentals as ready troops, and that unit was among the first to arrive in the city for hurried training. They were quickly named Company I of the hastily formed Sixth Regiment of fellow Indiana Volunteers.

Seventy-four county men were in these first ranks for three months of service. They were quickly sent to that western portion of the state of Virginia that was leaning toward allegiance to the Union cause, and on June 3, they were in the first battle of the war, at Philippi, Virginia. After this engagement, a select few of the regiment were given an odd scouting assignment: to mingle with the residents of a few towns during a seven-day assignment to explain the retaliation of the "Federals" for the attack on Fort Sumter.

Some of the men who had given their post office addresses as Westfield when mustering in served in this first call for service from April 21 to August 2, 1861. The Hamilton County Continentals returned to Indianapolis in the latter part of July a little ahead of schedule.

A few other men from Westfield joined the Thirty-ninth Indiana Regiment (later the Eighth Cavalry) that was mustered in August 1861. Before being discharged in July 1865, these troops were on duty for a while in North Carolina. They had marched through Kentucky and Tennessee and later Mississippi, Alabama, Arkansas, Georgia and South Carolina. One of their number, Daniel Burris of Company B, was killed at Gallatin, Tennessee, in February 1863. This regiment was furloughed in April 1865. Returning to active duty, the regiment continued on long marches and engaging the enemy in pitched battles. There were 30 officers and 547 men in the Thirty-ninth. Their total number included a regimental band. Of these Hamilton County men, 98 were killed or died in service.

Several other men from Westfield and Washington Township joined the 101st Indiana Volunteers, organized in August 1863 and returning home on June 25, 1865. These infantry troops were among the most well traveled in the conflict, having covered some 3,507 miles on foot, plus 959 by railroad and 650 on steamboats.

Others from Washington Township were assigned to the 130th Volunteers. They left Indianapolis on March 16, 1864, and returned home on December 13, 1865. On May 3, they marched to the front at the Battle of Resaca and then to Kennesaw Mountain, engaging in many skirmishes on the way. During the fall of 1865, with the surrender of the Confederacy at Appomattox, the regiment was mustered out at Charleston, South Carolina, on December 2, 1865, and arrived in Indianapolis on the thirteenth. Twenty-five local men had served with this regiment. Local physician J.B. Pettyjohn served as a contract surgeon with rank of acting assistant surgeon, U.S. Army.

A few other Hamilton County men served in the 147th as one-year troops, mustered in March 1865 and serving for one month before the end of the war. They served in guard and garrison duty. Of the two officers and eighty-one men from Hamilton County, thirty-one had given Westfield as their home post office. These troops were mustered out on August 4. One Westfielder in this call-up who enrolled on March 1, 1865, succumbed to disease (not otherwise described for the record) and died on the fifteenth.

Near the end of the war, two regiments made up largely of Indiana men were assembled on forty-eight hours' notice, equipped and sent to southern Indiana to stop General John Hunt Morgan, whose large raiding party had just crossed the Ohio River and into the town of Newburg, Indiana. The 109th served from the tenth to the seventeenth of July 1865. They had traveled as far as Cincinnati before Morgan was apprehended and his raid stopped.

Eleven of those from here who were killed or died in the war were buried in the Anti-Slavery Friends Cemetery. Burials at the other graveyards in the township included those at Friends meetings: Chester (nine), Eagletown (eleven), Greenwood (one), Lamong (Hammock, three), Thomas B. Moore (three), Little Eagle Creek (thirty-six, showing the strong antislavery sentiment at that meeting), Pleasant View (two), Sugar Creek (four), Summit Lawn (fifty-seven), Westfield (thirteen), and one grave at Gray Friends Meeting. Friends who complied with the military drafts or joined voluntarily were named individually in the minutes of the meetings throughout the war, as they were disowned for failing to uphold the ancient Quaker antiwar tradition. Most of those who requested reinstatement as members were received back into their respective meetings. Except for references to those "disowned" for military service, the minutes of the Westfield Monthly Meeting include no other references to the war.

THE COUNTY'S FIRST MAP, 1866

An inset on the Hamilton County map published in the year following the war shows the town and township to which the soldiers returned after the nation's severing and its fitful reuniting. This small plat can suggest a leisurely saunter through town, beginning by approaching along the range line from the south along the west side of the eighty acres Zachariah Rees purchased on September 3, 1832, about a third of a mile south of the center of town. Strolling north, one sees a truly impressive architectural achievement, that of Union High School (UHS), opened in the year before the war. This landmark structure is surrounded by a picturesque and popular grove of trees called "the school grove." The small brick cottage to the right of the large two-story school is the home of school superintendant L.A. Estes and family.

The school houses a Friends concept of higher learning for high school and beyond in the four large rooms, two on each floor. The school has already obtained a deserved reputation for educational excellence and secondarily has become a boarding school to accommodate its popularity.

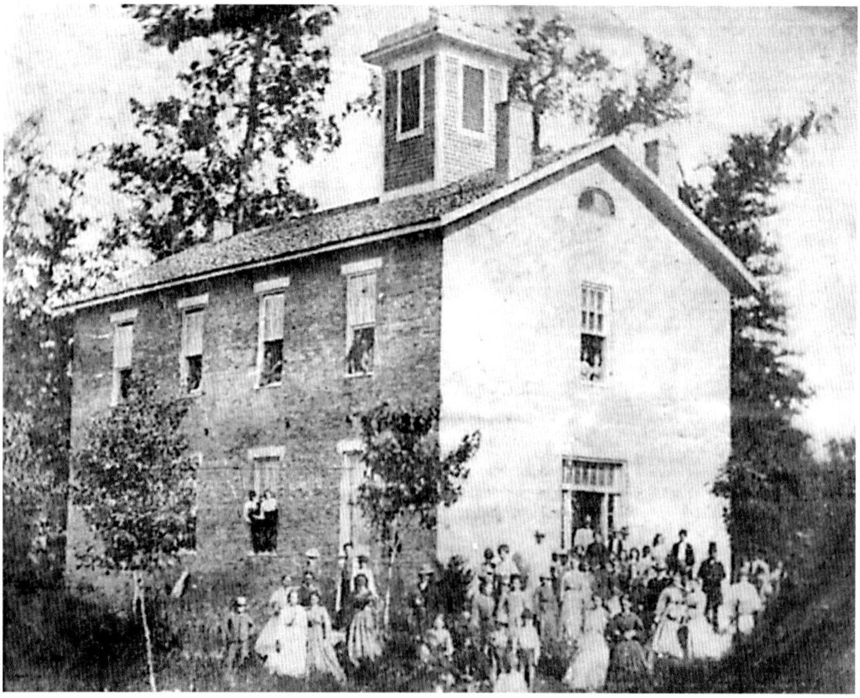

Union High School, built in 1860 and administered by the Westfield Monthly Meeting of the Society of Friends (Quakers). The Friends "Academy" was noted throughout the Midwest for the excellent curriculum and well-educated teachers.

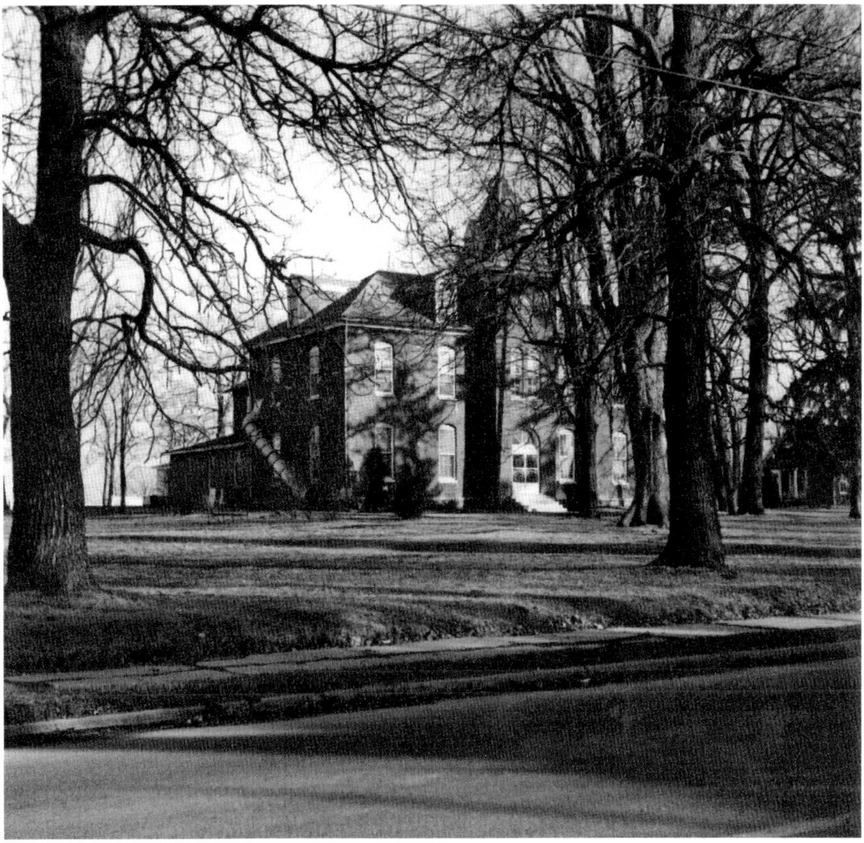

Former Union High School, showing the new front addition to the original 1860 building, on grounds adjoining those of the Westfield Friends Church.

Across the street to the west is the home and office of Dr. Embree, and his next neighbor north is the boardinghouse of Mrs. Losey, who has been housemother for as many UHS scholars as she can accommodate. Just beyond Mrs. Losey's is the home and office of Dr. Coffin.

Back across the road to the east is the Meetinghouse of the Society of Friends. This is the third structure here; the initial log cabin was replaced by a frame structure that burned in 1847. The meeting graveyard occupies the ground north of the meetinghouse that was donated in 1835 by founding Friend Simon Moon, who, as the vagaries of life would have it, was buried here later in the same year.

Directly to the east of the meetinghouse is the home and large land area of prominent Friends John D. and Lucinda M. Edwards. Next is the crossing of Cold Creek (some call it Cool Creek) passing under Range Line

Road flowing from left to right. A few feet north of the creek are the first of the forty-eight town lots set off by Asa Bales, Simon Moon and Ambrose Osborn thirty-two years ago, lots forty-seven and forty-eight on the left side of the road and all the others to the right, except for numbers twenty-three and twenty-four back on the west side of the road. These two front on Main Street. Those on the right are numbered thirteen through forty-six and arranged in two rows, lots thirteen through twenty-two fronting on Main Street.

At Main Street is the intersection with the Range Line Road and shops on the south side of the street; to the west a meat market, general store and millinery; and across a feeder creek flowing south are three buildings of a tannery. To the right is East Main with a shoe store, a wagon shop and a blacksmith shop on the south side with residences in between.

On Main Street to the west is a store on the northwest corner, then a drugstore on the northeast corner and then the post office, the Pfaff Hotel, a shoe shop, another tannery and a warehouse with other structures interspersed. East Street is the eastern boundary of town, with J.L. Seaman's steam gristmill and woolen factory just outside town.

Lots numbered one through twelve and sixty-five and sixty-six form the north side of Main Street. Another row of lots adjoins on the north, numbered twenty-five through thirty-six, and sixty-three and sixty-four front on Penn Street—named, of course, for the most famous early Quaker in America, William Penn, founder of Pennsylvania. These lots contain two harness shops, a tin shop, a wagon shop and several other structures including several residences.

Four blocks of lots form the north side of Penn Street, with two lots, numbers twenty-five and twenty-six, on the west side of Main Cross Street and the rest east of the street, one with a pump shop. A row of lots, numbered one through eight (number two the home and office of Dr. S.C. Dove) and forty-nine and fifty (the Wesleyan Methodist Church), forms the west side of the street. The Anti-Slavery Friends Cemetery sits along here also. On the east side of the street are two numbered lots, fifty-seven and seventy-six, the latter with a blacksmith shop. The lots on the north side of those forming Penn Street are much longer, and some are wider than those along the street. They are occupied by a blacksmith shop and the town school but otherwise empty, awaiting more growth of the town.

The inset on the map shows buildings of various sizes and shapes marked as black squares, rectangles and combinations of both. The town business directory in the inset includes merchants I.H. Brown; H.G. Kenyon; Coffin &

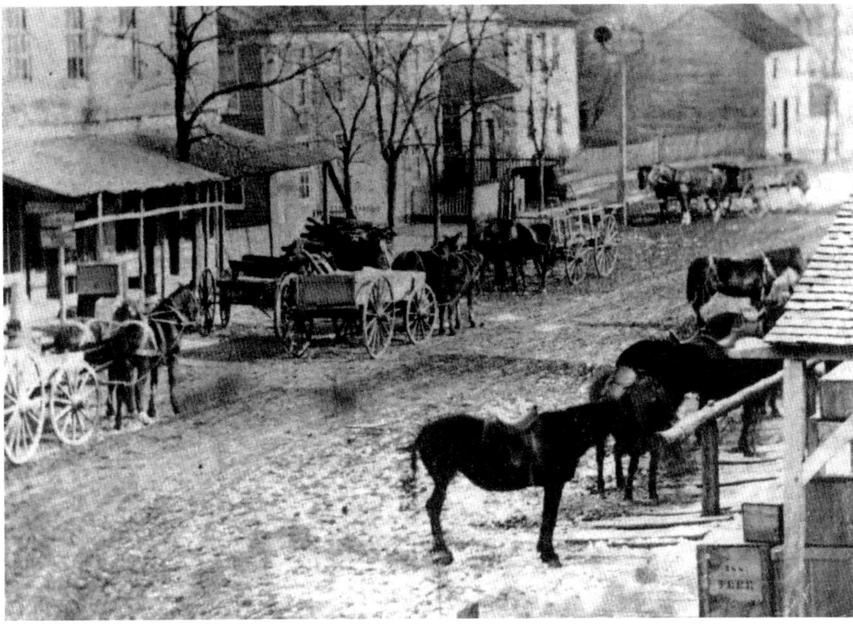

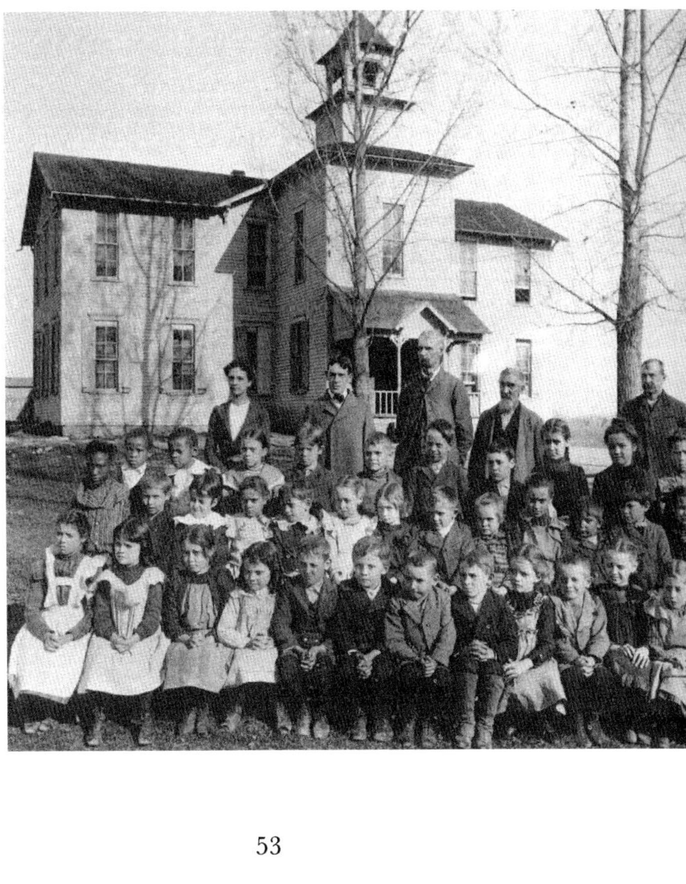

Above: East Main Street in Westfield (circa 1860s) serves as the east–west road through town.

Right: The first public school in Westfield, built in 1858 and destroyed by fire in 1904.

Howe; Carey & Co., druggists; Joel Demming's grocery and produce business; and Drs. J.S. Benson and S.C. Dove. The leading "mechanics" in town are J.N. Wells, blacksmith; R.C. Hollis, shoemaker; W.G. Stout, "plow & road scrapper shop"; the two shops of S. Dempey and J.H. Dempey, both "brick makers"; and the double-duty gristmill and woolen factory of J.L. Seaman.

These are the businesses that the townspeople and the surrounding farm families support with their "trading" and other shopping, as well as by getting repairs done or some new item handmade at a blacksmith's forge. The basics for reasonable well-being are here: foodstuffs, a drugstore dispensing what medicines the doctors do not provide, shoes, the skills of blacksmiths for shoeing horses, resetting wagon wheels, new special-order products and repairs. This is not a railroad town, so other things can be acquired in Noblesville, a ride of about an hour at a trot.

The last half of the 1860s passes in the aftermath of a war formerly unimaginable for its colossal death and destruction. The "house divided," as

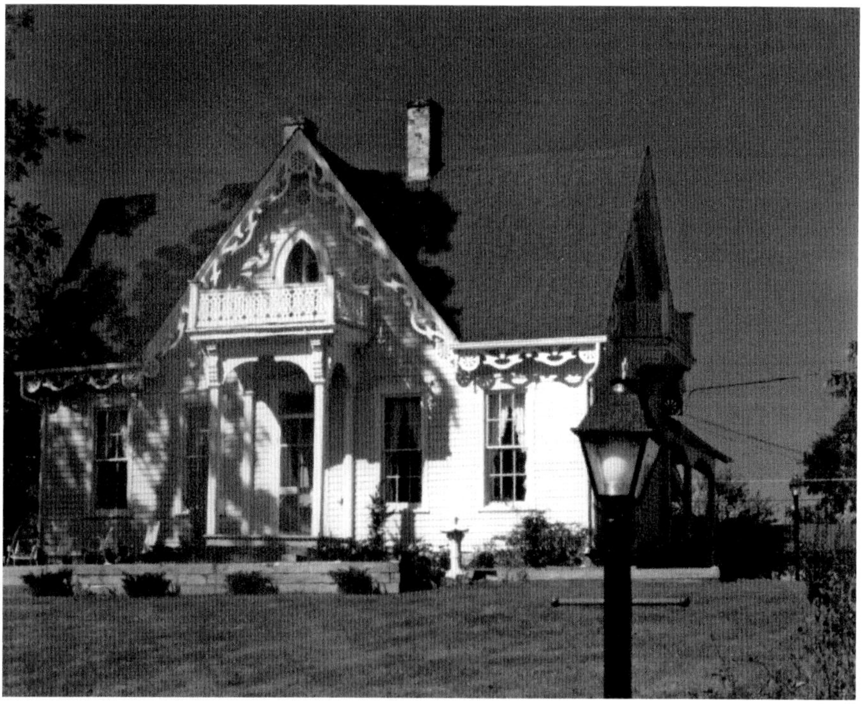

The Westfield home built about 1867 for Dr. Julius Benson and his wife, Margaret, on East Main Street (later State Route 32), the primary east–west street in town.

the now-martyred President Lincoln feared, has been rejoined, though with much bitterness and with a conflicted "reconstruction" in the South. There is an abiding, palpable winner-loser sense in the nation, and yet there is the occasional instance of a Confederate veteran moving to a northern town and marrying a Yankee sweetheart.

The county newspaper prints announcements of veteran reunions. One brief item inquires for the address of a war widow due a small pension. If any other mention is made, a simple reference to "the recent war" suffices. There is much space now given to serialized fiction gaining great popularity, mostly for those fans of romantic sagas, the "pernicious" novels against which the Friends advise.

One of the subjects of particular interest in Westfield is "woman's rights." The focus usually is on the movement for women attaining "the vote." And there is still the broadly discussed matter of temperance now in a time when the consumption of alcoholic beverages has risen, in part the result in notable proportion to the continuing physical pains of war. If women could vote, the problem with intemperance would abate as a matter of course. And when either subject, temperance or woman's rights, comes up, Westfield is often the center of the activity noted, well known as a place where organizational spirit is abundant and leadership abounds.

The local volunteer, amateur author "D.S.," writes for the paper, "It is a conceded fact that about one third of the voters in this county are in favor of temperance," but with "two thirds against you, in hopeless opposition to you, what are you to do?" Some believe there is "tenfold more vehemence" against women "having the vote." No supportive canvassing of this attitude is reported here, or supposed reason given.

Local women meet in a room offered by the Westfield Masons on July 14, 1869, to form the countywide Woman's Rights Association. They will meet "each Tuesday evening at 6½ o'clock" in the Westfield Town Hall upstairs over one of the stores to hear assigned essays, a sharing of select readings and the ongoing "discussion of Woman's Rights." Mrs. Clara Kenyon is president and Miss Mollie Baldwin secretary pro tem. There is an initiation fee of sixty cents. The group's succinct constitution is printed in the same news article about this first gathering. The association determines to spread temperance information at every opportunity. The charter members, in addition to the president and secretary, are Mrs. Melinda Campbell, Mrs. Emma Hedgcock and Mrs. Ella Conklin. The other members are Miss Mattie Coffin, Mrs. Julia Harvey, Mrs. Lydia Phelps and Miss Hattie Brown (coincidently a ladies' hat maker in town). On September 28, 1869, a Mrs. Livermore lectured on the

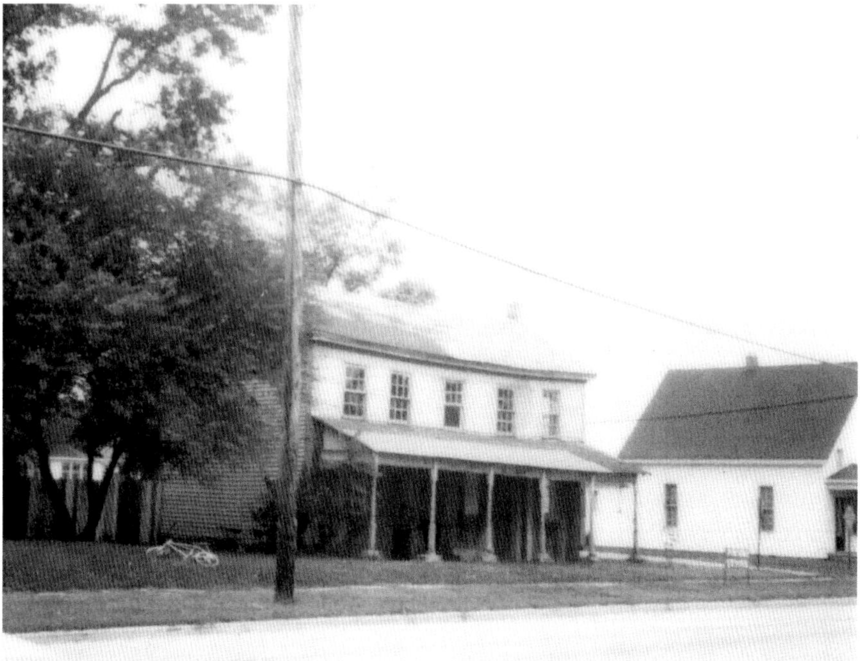

The Masonic Hall, Westfield, built in 1853 and shown in the 1960s.

issue at the Wesleyan Church in Westfield. The event notice stated, "Those in favor of women's suffrage should hear her while those who oppose it should by all means hear her. A gold ring will be drawn for."

Some of the apparently original comments in the paper compare with jibes from the classics of literature. One woman writes, in response to a letter in a previous issue of the paper, "I think that ebullition of hers contained enough concentrated hatred to poison a regiment."

In late October, a "woman's rights convention" was held at the Westfield ME Church. Forty-nine people were present, including Dr. J.D. Garner and a few other men. The officers reviewed the main purpose of the organization's constitution: to gain the vote for women. The editor of the paper reported that "Mrs. L. has that manlike strength which every woman must admire." The editor's wife was "completely captivated," though perhaps not with his comment that women naturally admired male characteristics in other women. At the meeting on Saturday, May 14, it had been "resolved, that a vote in Congress on the proposed amendment would not be presently expected." The voting rights amendment has been exhumed and reburied by every Congress since its first introduction.

Local businesses advertise in the Noblesville paper. W.H. Conklin's drugs, "south side of Main Street, opposite the Pfaff House," boasts a merchandising mix of wide appeal: groceries, "notions," toys, candies, oysters "raw or cooked," quails, chickens and turkeys, alive or killed and dressed. The store owner is "sole agent of Love Goods Bitters"; Linneus wine, made in Thorntown; and patent medicines, paints, oils, varnishes and dye stuffs.

The commercial activity in town shows a common lifestyle with a variety of commercial transactions. Funderburg and Yow, "pay cash for bark and hides." The ad for A.F. and C. Hess states inducements to their trade in boots and shoes. Some advertisers take a very direct approach, such as "READ THIS."

"We are now prepared to card spin and weave and do all kinds of work in our lines of business at the Woolen Factory at Westfield. Cash paid for wool." J.M. Kane is "wagon and carriage maker" and "ironer."

The number of millineries in Westfield from time to time indicates that while the plain Quaker bonnet is quite prevalent, many women wear uniquely designed and colorful hats. The town milliners each offer something a little different. Mrs. Julia A. Harvey advertises a "large selection of hats, bonnets, trimmings, ribbons, thread." Mrs. E.H. Arnett's ad, smallest of all, is quite concise, simply stating her name and occupation. Of a more general nature, Miss Amanda Phaff will do "all kinds of work, located in her house on north side of Main Street." At their new millinery store, Mrs. Julia Barvey and Miss Creagan "are prepared to make, bleach or repair all styles of hats and bonnets on Main Street one door east from Conklin's store."

The term "cornucopia" is well applied to the stock of the town grocery stores: "Jas. A. Williams, Grocery Dealer," lists "good brown sugar, light sugar, white A sugar, speckled trout, white fish, good coffee, prime Rio, Kegg soda, Dwight's soda, dried peaches, white coal oil gives better light that yellow. I also keep on hand a choice variety of fish and bacon, and everything kept in a country grocery and dry goods store." In this manner, these kinds of stores try to be all-purpose, one-stop enterprises.

Each advertiser promises that his or her establishment is the best around at what they do and sell, and all for the most reasonable price even outside of the township. One typical example reads, "New shoe store, Hess & Bro. Westfield, dealers in all kinds of boots and shoes."

Some ads are directed specifically to farmers: "The Kirby Harvester, with Self-rake and Mowing attachment sold here. Repairs for old machines. Abel

Doan, Agent, Westfield." J.M. Kane has five good wagons for sale and will make buggies to order. Ice-cold soda water is available at the establishment of W.H. Conklin. The local tanner has animal hair for sale for plasterers. Hiatt & Pennington offer "wood planing" at their chair factory and also have "pumps, horse hay, hay rakes (the Butler patent) broom handles, etc."

O.H. Brown calls his business "the old corner drug store," where he offers "paints, oils, varnishes, cut glass, putty, white lead, books and stationery, slates, school books, looking glass plate, lamps, foreign and native medicated wine and liquors, tobacco, perfumery, confectioneries, cigars, cosmetics, knives, pencils, pocket books, prescriptions" there on the "southeast corner of Main and Cross streets."

Late in the year, the editor of the *Hamilton County Register* published in Noblesville announced "four more subscribers from Westfield last week, now have over fifty names. Will have over a thousand by Christmas [countywide], and be rid of all nonpaying subscribers." The *Register* prints the occasional tinge of deprecation for any physical altercation in "the town of peace," such as this example from June 1, 1869:

> *Lively this week in the way of fights in Westfield. A little "mill" between Senor D'Anguelime the hot-blooded Castilian and husband of the "Blind Poet's" and a Bill Jackson. When the senor drew a revolver, Jackson seized, broke it and jammed the Senor's head up against Hess and Co.'s shop, pulled some hair out of the "Doctor's" beard. Jackson then went to house of old Isom Smith who ran him off with a shovel.*

And: "Pratt Willis gave himself up for whopping Perry of Deming. Pratt had a hole in the top of his head about three inches long, said that was nothing to what he did for Perry. Perry is trying to make it assault with intent to kill, the constable is summoning his witnesses."

And another: "George Hoskins jumped on Cam Slater's boy yesterday and Cam's boy raised a Fourth of July over his eye. Bunk [Funderburg] parted them and old Jeannie came down and gave him one of the worst tongue lashings he ever had."

The flour and cotton mill in Westfield is known for frequent new management and legal gambits: "The firm of Harvey and Stout is dissolved, Stout having disposed of his interest. The mill now belongs to Harvey alone, who assumes all liabilities of the firm." The factory connected with the mill belongs to the firm of Harvey and Musgrave. The case found its way into the Common Pleas Court, "the gentleman giving bond. Conclusion no man can foresee."

Many references are made to teachers' "institutes…held by county examiner" at Westfield. The event has been held in Westfield "for the last two years and will probably be held there again this year." And a statement of unusual insight: "Washington and Clay Townships furnish nearly all the teachers for the county."

In the issue of March 20, 1869, the writer from Westfield who signed as "Progress" issues a strong call to press the state legislature to allow "colored" children education. "Let us give the poor, benighted colored children equal chances to improve that we claim for ourselves." He praises black troops in the war: "Soldiers, did you ever meet a black face when in the late war you wanted a friend and find that black face unwilling to help you? Let us then repay them by giving them an equal claim to education, suffrage and protections." One news item from Westfield is particularly telling: "The man who struck the negro with the whip on Sunday last will do well to remember that slavery is extinct and that Indiana is not Old North Carolina."

"Progress" chides fellow townspeople in a May 25 missive telling of "Rev. I.N. Williams, a black man, who spoke May 15th in Westfield." A former slave for thirty-five years, Williams has been conducting a school for black children near Indianapolis for the last sixteen months. After the preacher spoke, there was a requested collection, which found a mere $2.08 in pocket change available. "Great liberality, was it not?" He is embarrassed for Westfield, where people have been very liberal in the past for the black children "south of the Ohio River." Apparently, he chides, "distance lends enchantment to the view." It's the children much closer home who need assistance now. (A state law of July 26, 1869, calls for colored children to be enumerated along with white children for schools. The state attorney general, however, decides that there will be separate schools but similar funding.)

Any news about railroad construction, or even the promise of it, is popular fare. In early February 1869, one citizen writes that a "cross railroad" is needed from Pendleton to Lebanon, passing through Westfield, to compete with the Peru and Indianapolis Railroad running through Noblesville. "A rail road which has no opposition will always put up the tariff so high that as to compel people to travel in wagons." About this time, it has also been written that the "town of Westfield is well provided for in some respects. They have six life insurance agents and six doctors and are looking for a new doctor every day."

There is more mill news: "Mr. Atkins sells out interest in the mill, S.H. Canard takes his place as miller. Musgrave succeeds Purcell as foreman.

Musgrave, the wool puller understands his business thoroughly." Indeed, Westfield has acquired a new medical professional: dentist Dr. Jay "late of Anderson" has just moved here and is "prepared to pull, plug, fix and clean teeth." Alfred Hiatt and Hull have opened shop on Penn street, making chairs and "other work demanded in that latitude."

In July 1869, "Dr. Collins sold his stock of goods to R. Fisher, and Mrs. Dr. Coffin has sold [her] millinery [business] to Missus George. Both will remain in the market at the old stand, southwest corner Main and Cross streets." Also: "M.H.G. Kenyon received a carload of Lake salt. Mr. P.T. Williams did not move his harness shop as reported." And for those alert to matters of education, it is "rumored that professor Howe of Westfield will go to Zionsville this fall to support the seminary of learning there."

At the troubled mill in August, "Mr. Stephen Harvey of the first Harvey Kerr, Musgrave, etc. got writ of replevia for books and the key of Woolen factory. Mr. Musgrave could not find that, said they must be stolen from the vehicle used in conveying fuel." That month also, Dr. Henson should be called to "the mill and factory as they are both dead. And their affairs want settlement." Stephen Harvey and Moses Musgrave continue to battle for possession of the wool factory.

Dr. J.B. Pettyjohn treated over thirty cases of diphtheria in four weeks. He "hasn't lost any." "Bascom" writes in and "wants to know who hit Billy Patterson, did he hurt him very bad. Also, will he hit him again, and if so, when?"

Westfield residents are always ready for a temperance debate. In late September, a letter by "Darius" to the *Register* contains some damning comment about the subject and Westfield's reputation as a "dry" town. According to this writer, "The whiskey traffic has been carried on here to a greater or less extent for a number years." And "to answer the question how can any man who has any claim to respectability sell whisky in Westfield, when it is known that the people are so much opposed to it? Are we sure that people here are really opposed to it?" Supposedly, "many respectable citizens buy it, some do not deny it." He does admit that there are no confirmed drunkards in town except an occasional transient individual. Who makes whiskey sale prosperous in Westfield? It is the merchant who before and after and between business hours privately takes his glass, it is the mechanic who daily drinks his quart and sweats it out at his bench or anvil, the farmer who buys his jug for ague medicine, into which he puts 10 percent quinine or a little dogwood bark. A preacher buys six bottles of Hostetter's bitters at one time for his wife and finds that he has been greatly revived and strengthened by it also. The doctor not only uses it himself but also recommends it for all manner of diseases.

"We are a whiskey drinking people," this correspondent claims. "The man who does not drink is an exception to the general rule." The local respectable druggist has said that "there was but one preacher in Westfield or vicinity that does not buy whiskey. The man has left us so now have no preachers that do not use whisky. Imagine an intelligent audience listening to a preacher who gets his inspiration from a bottle of Hostetter."

The writer tells of temperance campaigning organized and "flourished for a season without any diminution in the amount of whisky sold or drank, but with this difference in the object of its use: before taking the pledge it was used as a beverage, afterward as a medicine. The chairman of the temperance group's tongue is thick with use of head-ache medicine" as he presides over "members present at the same time being half drunk on ague medicine. They are very harsh in denunciations of the whisky traffic and talk loudly of resorting to mob violence to suppress it." Townspeople "must have whisky to mix their medicine in and there is no place to get it but the whisky shop. A few whisky sellers have quit for conscience sake; the opposition to the whisky selling is terrible indeed. There are hundreds of men in Westfield and its vicinity that are strenuously opposed to the sale of intoxicating liquors but you come to search for the man who does not use it, he is nowhere to be found."

Of course, a rebuttal follows. Another hobbyist correspondent seems to award sainthood to every person in the towns and township who can lift a glass but won't. Neither letter writer can be entirely believed or be completely dismissed.

That answer in kind is printed in the September 27 issue and signed "Vindicator," stating that "Darius" is "all wrong about merchants, mechanics, doctors, the whole shebang accused of imbibing in Westfield, and out in the entire township who he accuses of drinking on the sly, and claiming medicinal necessity." Vindicator "has lived in Westfield for twenty years." With one exception, "there is not a merchant in town but is a temperance man." And there are "no drinking farmers; just ask the value of farms near Westfield, $100 an acre if sold. Take a ride with me to the farms, the homes, etc." and see how many empty bottles can be found. "None," Vindicator says.

In late September, the mill and factory appear to be doing much better. And "a hack will be run daily from Westfield to Indianapolis commencing on

Monday next and continuing the trips until after the state fair and doubtless longer if the patronage will justify. We do not see why the patronage of the town would not keep up the hack line. In that way they might have a daily mail." (A maintained gravel turnpike was opened from Westfield to Indianapolis in 1865.)

Many obituaries are informative of early times. In the September 27, 1869 *Hamilton County Register*, there are good words about Elijah Talbert, an "early settler." He supported "all moral and political reforms in which this township was prominent." He "worked in the anti-slavery cause; his house was ever open to the poor fugitive from human bondage." There were "heavy drafts upon his income to support the poor and destitute." Mr. Talbert died after an honest day's work in the field thrashing wheat.

In the fall of 1869, "Mrs. Melinda Campbell is prepared to furnish photographs, ambrotypes and gems and melainotypes in all the best styles. Photographs per dozen, $2, large pictures in frame each $2.25." She adds the romantic and poetic maxim, "Secure the shadows ere the substance fades. Satisfaction guaranteed." Westfield has perhaps its first "photograph gallery."

The doctors in town have all they can do with "prevailing diseases: chills, fever, fevers of a bilious nature." One who apparently does not need their attending, "Jerry Lynch of the 75th [Regiment] known here as 'iron head,' was struck by twelve pound canon ball" but survived and "is living here and waiting for the next war."

Another medical man sets up in town: "Dr. Garner will open an infirmary or hospital to treat all chronic diseases. He has had the waters of the springs about town thoroughly analyzed by one of the first chemists of the country and they are pronounced equal to any in the country. If the doctor is a success, Westfield may become a miniature Saratoga."

Many announcements serve the public. The Presbyterian church in town hosts a "business men's prayer meeting every Wednesday morning at eight o'clock." The town board meets the last Saturday of each month "at the furniture store of R. Ballard."

Again, about the mill: "Samuel Johns, Jr. has rented the grist mill and is purchasing new machinery. He will have it thoroughly repaired." But before long, it is reported that John Kerr had purchased the Westfield Mill and "proposes to change the manner of doing business."

And a local jest: "The Westfield Mills [flour and wool] have changed hand so often and have been tangled up so in litigation that no one knows

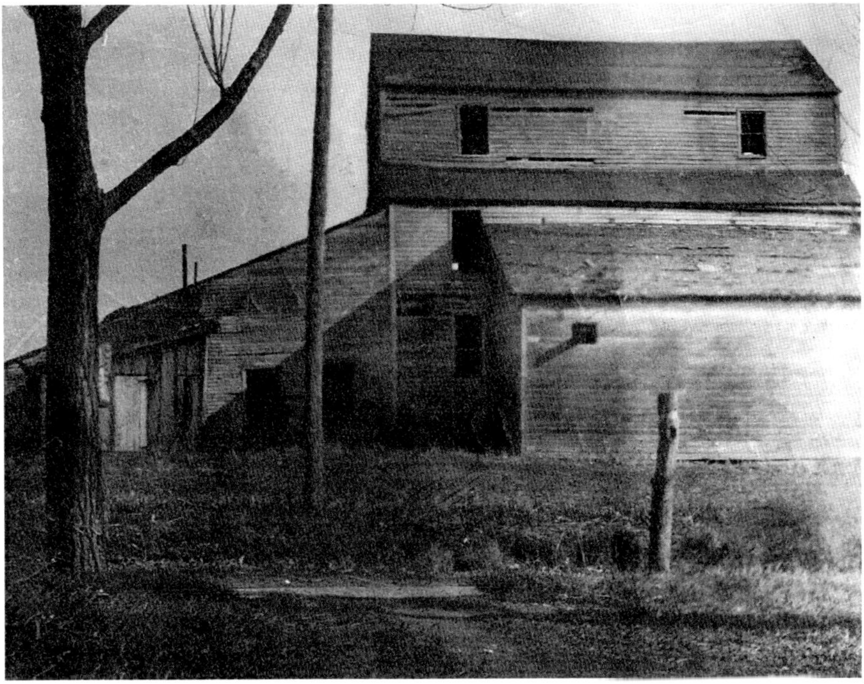

Former Westfield flour and woolen mill.

just exactly who owns it. And the present owner says he has nothing but possession and he believes in the right of possession."

Westfield's first flour mill of 1848 was called Isaac Williams and Co. and located on a lot southeast of the east end of Penn Street. Williams had worked for Asa Bales in the first store in town. Williams sold out in 1854 to J.L. Seamans and Peter Rich. In 1855, Rich sold to Jonathon E. Pike and Micajah C. White and Company in 1857. White sold to Joshua Wilson in 1858 and then in 1862 back to Seamans, who added an addition and machinery and sold half interest to Jabez Neal in 1864. Three years later, Neal sold half interest to Abner Atkinson. Thomas Stout purchased Neal's remaining half interest in 1868 and added a boiler and engine to the woolen mill. That same year, Atkinson sold his interest to Stephen Harvey. One wonders how the hired hands knew who to ask for their pay.

By 1870, J.L. Seamans held an unpaid mortgage against the mill, brought suit and purchased the mill back at the sheriff's sale in May 1871.

6

The 1870s: It Comes With the Promise

What the New County Directory Shows

Directories mostly answer only their own questions. But the varieties of the answers given in the new county directory of 1874 are helpful now and will continue to be in the future for those pondering a forgotten fact or two. *The People's Guide: A Business, Political and Religious Directory of Hamilton Co., Ind., together with a Collection of Very Important Documents and Statistics Connected with Our Moral, Political and Scientific History; also a Historical Sketch of Hamilton County and a Brief History of Each Township* has been published by the Cline & McHaffie Printing and Publishing House of Indianapolis. This directory lists individuals' names ("heads of households"), addresses, dates arrived in the county, places of birth, religious affiliations and political leanings.

And the editors of this compendium do not begrudge the occasional additional few words requested by the individual listed to be appended to their personal entry. One resident wants it known that he is "the only Democrat in Hamilton County." W.D. Vestal describes himself as "Liberal" but still a Friend. He is a carriage and wagon maker in Westfield. He was born in 1827, and he arrived in 1860 from North Carolina, just before the war broke out. Martin Vestal, born in 1841, and Alfred Vestal, born 1804, were both born in North Carolina. They are Wesleyan Methodists. Each entry gives more information about those listed than might be acquired on first meeting the person.

Farmers, of course, outnumber any other category of workers. For Washington Township, there are 533 farmers listed (18 retired) among the 678 entries in the township—78 percent of all names included. Those living in the farthest reaches to the west in the township get their mail in Zionsville in Boone County, closer to them than Westfield.

In April 1870, farmers of Washington Township "living in district 17," two miles north of Westfield, have formed a farmers' club to elevate the standards of agriculture, horticulture, etc. There are "some thirty members." They think they will get "paid" for attending once a week." (Folks say "paid" to mean to benefit from, rather than receive money.) The directory editors write that there should be "such a farmer's club in every schoolhouse in the county."

Farm Friends could be members of a Friends meeting at Eagletown, Jolietville, Pleasant Grove, Hinkle's Creek, Oak Ridge, Poplar Ridge, Chester or Greenwood. Of the farmers not stating religious affiliation, 26 percent are from North Carolina; so they, too, could be Friends or perhaps came with Friends families. There is a total church membership count of 1,011 Friends (70 percent of total), 152 Methodists (10 percent), 128 Wesleyan Methodists (9 percent), 120 Christians (8 percent) and 40 United Brethren (3 percent).

Those who make or repair products in town or out in the township include a cabinetmaker/undertaker, carriage maker/wagon painter, eight wagon makers, tailor, "tailoress"/dressmaker, sawmill worker, pump maker, gunsmith, nine boot and shoemakers, six mechanics and two harness makers. Those with special skills include teacher, teacher of penmanship, painter, sawyer, stonemason, eight blacksmiths, butcher, eight engineers, potter, tinner, eight carpenters, bricklayer, nurseryman, steam thrasher and gardener. Others work as laborer, stock trader, three sales clerks, tollgate keeper, fruit agent, "logman" and eleven "hireling laborers." Those working in stores or other businesses in town or elsewhere deal with dry goods and notions, groceries and notions or "fancy goods and notions" or serve as "druggist and drug clerk," two "sewing machine agents," "boarding house owner" and "huckster wagon driver." With this information, one can form a visual impression of the daily work activity in and outside of town.

Women are listed if they operate a business, such as Miss H.O. Brown, a milliner, "Give her a call"; Mrs. Hannah H. Cox, born in North Carolina in 1832 and arrived here just this year, is "tailoress" and dressmaker, "all work done to order." Mrs. Jane Hiatt is listed with the other farmers, born in Virginia in 1817 and settled here in 1844. She is a Friend and a Republican. Mary John is another Friend farmer, born in Tennessee in 1826, moved here in 1850.

A few women are listed without occupation, but in the case of Friend Elizabeth B. Lindley, her home is four miles northeast of Westfield, so she apparently is of a farm family. She was born in 1817 in Ohio and came here in 1841. Mrs. Mary J. Manlove, out on the west edge of the township, was born in Indiana in 1823 and came here in 1843. She is a Methodist. Mrs. Sarah Pruitt is from North Carolina, born in 1829, arrived in 1852; she is a Wesleyan Methodist. Mrs. Charles W. Phipps and her husband are also on the far west side—she a milliner, he a carpenter. He came here in 1869, born 1839; she came the next year, born in 1841. He is a Methodist; she is of the Christian denomination. Sarah E. Ramsey is a farmer four miles north of Eagletown. Born here in 1842, she is a Methodist. Mrs. S.A. Smith is another resident of the far west side of the township and a Methodist. She lives seven and a half miles northeast of Zionsville. She was born in 1836. And finally, Mrs. Wheeler, no first name given, a Methodist, was born in Indiana in 1831 and moved here as a fourteen-year-old. Now she runs a boardinghouse in town.

Some additional information for a few entries adds comic relief when reading several hundred personal names. Elam Hiatt, born in North Carolina in 1821, who settled here in 1839, wants it known that he is "the only Democratic Quaker in Washington Township." Charles Hunt is a "literary student"; J.W. Hoskins is a carriage apprentice; Thomas Hinshaw is a student; A. Hiatt, born 1794 in North Carolina, arrived here in 1839, is "at leisure" now in his eightieth year; and Enos Smith, up for "everything" as an occupation, was born in Virginia in 1830, came here in 1872. Zachariah Rees is still here; he bought his claim in 1832.

There are eighteen schools in the township with a total of 1,120 students enrolled, taught by 24 teachers (men paid $2.16 per day, women $1.87). Businesses listed include Williams & Hinshaw, dealers in dry good and groceries; Wm. A. Seamons & Bro., woolen factory, manufacturers of flour and stocking yarn; Parr & Lane, dealer in dry goods and groceries; Chappell & Bros., sawmill and tile factory; Hess & Bro., manufacturers and dealers in boots and shoes; the Mesdames Lovell and Brown, milliners; and W.H. Conklin, drugs, grocery and notions. Drs. Benson and Kane have offices in town; seven other resident doctors have offices in other towns in the county.

The Washington Township portion of the directory includes the proviso, "Some claim this as the banner township of the county." There are five granges in the township organized two years ago and indicating cooperative efforts of farmers for fair market prices and so forth.

Those named above are but a portion of the residents of the town and township, of course. All wives, mothers, grandmothers, sisters and those unmarried are present and active, even if not acknowledged in the listings. The children are represented only in the total number of them in school. But their constant motion and chatter can be assumed. But still, an official name list with personal information attached for the town and township is at least a printed introduction to many people who give the place its character.

WATER, WATER EVERYWHERE

A particularly creative act of kindness helps open the year 1875. Two medical students, Tom Chappell and Eliau Mendenhall—both of Westfield and of founding families—and a few others took a seasonal break from their studies and cadavers to contribute to a worthy cause. They bought a "Durham bull" from "Bunk" Funderburg to fatten and slaughter, the meat to be distributed "to the poor" now in midwinter, a particularly trying time for those in need. References are made in the *Noblesville Ledger* about the poor being a considerable population of their own. The county has a "poor" house, actually a farm in its own right, with gardens in season and other means of producing food and other basic needs. If young Chappell and Mendenhall intend to aid those people, it is not so stated. Perhaps the good deed is meant for those needing the help right here in Westfield.

But in general, the year begins like any other, with a few respites between "cold snaps" and worse. Someone wonders at the unusual number of weddings of late, and then supposes it was just young people trying to stay warm.

For several weeks the low temperatures are the subject of many column inches in the *Noblesville Ledger*. The ones who write about Westfield report on town news, about who visited whom in town or out of the county and once even about someone getting a new hat. At present, the local "correspondent" signs his columns "What Next," and readers know to apply a grain or two of salt. Another occasional correspondent in town, signs "Charlemagne" (a classics literature student at Union High School, a teacher even?).

To show the effects of the low temperatures, "What Next" tells his own story of going to Noblesville during one of the worst onslaughts of life-threatening cold, "nineteen below" as he tells it, for a meeting of a committee he felt obliged to attend. He took food, he said, "for the hour of high twelve," actually a pumpkin pie that he placed on top of this head to keep his hands deep in this pockets, the pie covered with his hat. Arriving in Noblesville, he thawed his frozen feet in a horse bucket at Jack Cook's livery. When time to eat, he reached for the pie, which, to the amusement of all present, had frozen to his head.

"What Next" refers once or twice to "these panicky times." This observation, at least, can be taken as the truth. A general depression, an official "panic," begins in 1873, the result of yet another of the cyclical speculative bubbles that shock the economy every few years. Some banks in the state have actually closed, and others have cut the amount of individual withdrawals allowed. Such financial train wrecks occur when wild speculation is brought on by a robust national economy and debt is run up assuming huge profits that do not actually materialize. This time it came on the heels of a real estate boom when the Civil War ceased and better times ensued, for a while. Towns like Westfield do not have the financial cushioning of larger cities, but then residents of small towns grow garden vegetables, many have hogs for annual butchering at the back of the lots and those on farms can produce an appreciable amount of their own food.

Times like these can cause some to ask for help from on high. There is usually a revival going on at some church as advertised in the paper. It is the same all across the Midwest. Churches are packed with those who are urged to "get right with God" through emotional preaching and lengthy calls to the altar to ask forgiveness and "be washed in the blood of the Lamb." In December just passed, "about 600 or 700 people sought pardon at the mourner's bench" at one of the churches in town during one of the "protracted meetings." (Friends are conflicted in this regard, so much so that a split is occurring between those who wish to participate in the revivals and those holding to the silent worship orthodoxy who avoid worship in a high emotional state of mind, where one individual, the evangelist, is the center of enticing attention instead of each worshiper communicating with God on her or his own behalf and quietly, so as to hear the "still small voice" of heavenly inspiration.)

The cold weather is confining folk at home, and when overwhelmed by that and desiring more spacious surroundings, they can go, as one suggested, to the general store and gaze on the variety of products or watch the grocer wrap five pounds of loose coffee beans in a large sheet of paper and then tie it all up with string, the common way to package such a purchase but amusing to watch all the same.

The local correspondent reports many colds and breathing-related difficulties common to the winter season. With the first signs of spring, illnesses are still being reported: "lung complaint, typhoid fever, lung ailment, liver complaint, sore throat, effects of congestive chill, fever and bronchitis" and "an attack of dry wither."

By the end of April, spring farm work is in full gait, oats are all sown and most farmers are "fitting" fields for the king of crops: corn. The very exhalation of the township as a whole can almost be heard like the thrum of a mighty heart in full exercise. The founders imagined it, even in their limited scope of the future. What they came to establish is now two generations the stronger and remarkably productive. In early May, Union High School reopens with plans for a summer "short term." Again, popular educators of the resident Estes family will instruct classes.

June, bringer of the summer solstice, follows the sprouting and cultivating of new field plants. "The wheat never looked better," they say where people convene for socializing. Surely, this staff of life crop will strain the capacity to store it. It is widely believed that all the crops will exceed in quality and quantity anything that has come before.

Then an article titled "The Flood" states that "the storm of last week caused quite an amount of damage in this county, particularly to bridges and fills on the pikes. Damage on the Westfield pike can be repaired for $400 or less, and the company will go to work this week to make all necessary repairs. Much damage to wheat blown down; a thousand dollars damage to Lafayette pike" angling through the northeast corner of the county.

Even with this damage from a heavy rain, there does not seem to be a sense of alarm. A group of the good people of Westfield has approached the county commissioners with their interest in building an orphanage here in town. They are asking for the kind of assistance the county officials can give. The town has already donated a lot as a building site where a temporary structure is headquarters to prove serious intent. Other unspecified aid is "being rendered," they say.

But the commissioners are quick to point out that the people of Westfield did not present a "specific" plan (it was not their intention at this introductory inquiry). Also it is questionable, they say, with the county's present "organization of charitable work," that the county can "render much aid." The commissioners say the county is already "maintaining the poor house, contributing very largely to indigent persons outside the poor house." And all that "renders our charities very expensive and even burdensome"—charities, they do not add, that are required by state law. But the presenters do not leave without accomplishing something. They did impress on the commissioners that there should be better communication between these officials and "their people." And they stated for the record that the county should "make better preparation that is not provided for taking care of women and children upon the county farm," site of the "poor house."

Actually, the subject of widows and orphans has been mentioned in the hearty exchange among readers of the *Ledger* in debating railroad building. A resident out in the township "wrote in" that instead of "grubbing" for the new courthouse to be built in Westfield, there are, in the town and township, "at least fifty widow women who are struggling to give their families the necessities of life, many of them living in locations where a railroad will not benefit them [an] article." He also reminded readers supportively that women "have no voice in the matter," an aside regarding woman's rights, a cause with a full head of steam already in Westfield, now a center of organizing activity strengthened by well-known speakers invited to address local advocates.

The advocates for an orphanage in Westfield, already mobilized in some respects, carried the discussion to the township government itself. And while it isn't the specified duty of the township to fund such a concept, "it should be considered the duty of township trustees to interest themselves in the welfare of orphan children. There are homes for all the healthy children of the township." Yet the matter is put to rest, for the time being.

In general, all nature is behaving most cooperatively. No hint here of threat to the annual verdant saunter into fall being anything but a banner experience. Perhaps a farmer somewhere in the township is repeating a couple of maxims he's heard from his parents and grandparents, advice regarding farming and the weather. First, be thankful for timely rains in needed proportions. And second, a cardinal rule, remove standing water from the land as soon as possible. Dependable advice, when all is going well.

But the harbingers of trouble began on Thursday, June 3, with a heavy rain in such a force seen at first only as an overabundance. But soon the ground's absorption capacity was overwhelmed, and before long this impressive deluge was becoming a concern that soon turned to outright fear for personal safety. A sure enough flood was building before their eyes.

Soon, amateur correspondents from all around the county begin describing the magnitude of the destruction in their immediate area. Former bridges are now flotsam somewhere downstream, whole sturdy structures gone and out of sight.

Bridges on the Westfield and Indianapolis Pike between here and neighboring Carmel are simply gone. The creeks, or where they used to be, show only slightly discernible current, a mere, unassertive directional movement on the surface of the standing water. There is a crazy system of cross currents, competing currents, currents for seemingly no reason at all and much motionless standing water where water had never been imagined. Fascinating in its strange, otherworldly impact, these are scenes of wide and costly destruction. Any hint of fascination is soon lost, and the awareness of widespread destruction assaults the senses.

Whole field lengths of fence are gone. Cattle are free to roam at will—those that do not balk with water up to their bellies. They are confused and dazed. It is impossible to graze or even be fed effectively. And there is also the sickening sight of drowned cattle afloat, already bloated, someone's prize heifer, a horse with a first name, sodden sheep resting dumbly atop the water and drowned hogs bloated and afloat.

James Kellum has lost twenty-seven head of sheep along with a total of half a mile of fencing. Lightning has struck several barns, killing what cattle remained inside and starting fires unreachable to fight despite the presence of too much water.

The bridge over Cool or Cold Creek in town, two blocks south of the cross streets, simply is no more, no sign of the structural timbers. The town is now divided in two, without any effective, helpful communication between the two portions, except for hallooing across the expanse of water. It is unsafe to try crossing; a cross current threatens, and there is little above the water to hold on to for doubtful rescue. A ferry is needed, and someone creates a hastened version, taking some across for a small fee for his time and efforts.

Wells are inundated with dirty, gritty, undrinkable effluvia—wells that before were the only sources of drinkable water for many homes. Someone jokes weakly that at least the high water will drown the hoards of cinch bugs and other insatiable insects, hoards of which ruin crops, which are now in standing water.

Then the Westfield correspondent, his supply of gloomy adjectives depleted, states simply, "The flood has subsided." The writer had been out far enough to see that farmers were rebuilding washed away fences and a bridge or two was being rebuilt. It is said that half the corn crop in the county has been destroyed, either by scalding, washing out or being ruined by the standing water.

The oldest residents have never seen anything like it. At the tollhouse south of town on the pike, keeper Jeff Armstrong was dead center in the way of the force created by the flooded creek that turned the road into an immediate stream, and he reportedly "declared plainly to the family that they might do as they pleased, but he was not going to 'stay thar' any longer." Others abandoned homes with what they could carry and, soaked to the skin, sought refuge with those not so helpless on higher ground. Some went to neighbors with a second story and huddled with the residents all night and into the next day. No official rescue effort was mounted; people just helped one another as they could. The few boats around could not meet the need.

Where roads had been under water, and few were not, the runoff into the side ditches was not the end of it. The grading has been washed away, mostly into the ditches, leaving long stretches of road needing scraping and leveling all over again. There are miles of this to be repaired.

The crop damage includes corn, oats and also the wheat just put into shocks. Cornfields were blown and rain-pummeled flat as if an immense roller had done the deed. The "jointing" of the corn stalks just begun is broken and will be entirely lost, and that which may partially rise again will be so twisted and tangled that further cultivation will be impossible. Oats that promised such an abundant yield, never better anticipated in this county, will be almost an entire loss. What stock was left to many can forage as best they can in ruined fields of oats. Many farmers had commenced cutting hay, now ruined by the heavy rain that followed in the wake of the devastating winds. Fortunately, there is quite a large amount of grass yet to cut, and the generally good quality of it will make hay of excellent nutrition, perhaps just enough to satisfy the local demand.

Beginning with the fierceness of the storm, which in its one hour of heaviest rampage did the serious damage, much not blown down was ruined by the ensuing downpour. The winds were so severe that the ancient oaks still standing since long before the founders arrived were uprooted and twisted and reduced to splinters "so as to render them unfit for lumber or rails." Houses lost chimneys and windows. Some roofs dislodged and flew away. The larger the barn, the more the damage—if not struck by lightning and burned to the ground.

Less than two weeks after record heights of floodwaters had been marked, it happened all over again. Some said it was worse this time for damage to crops, timber, orchards, fencing and buildings and lost livestock, all of which "will be far more serious than the flood of a few weeks ago. And if the wheat crop should be ruined, a calamity will be upon us," the local correspondent writes.

On Sunday, June 25, the rains come again, and already rattled nerves are further frazzled. The unusually hard rain lasted until Wednesday evening.

The rise of the White River was nearing the high mark of two weeks ago. Come Saturday night, more rain, and until next Sunday, the rain falls in torrents. Stoney and Cicero Creeks have risen astonishingly, reaching levels not seen during the first onslaught. The White River at Noblesville laps near the top of the banks on Monday morning. Listing the names of farms hit again is like reading the new county directory. Once again, the local correspondent was considerably shy of a vocabulary that met the circumstances, managing only lamely, "These vast fields of splendid corn are doubtless ruined."

By Wednesday, rising water was still carrying away acre upon acre of shocked wheat that had been spared earlier. Another ferryman went into business; Bud Lowther poled an odd craft from side to side between the wagon bridge and Stone's Hill on the Westfield Pike.

But with all this, there is something of an unlikely positive nature in seeing people cope, then build back with the same everyday effort expended to make a go of it in less troubled times.

Union High School, now fifteen years in operation and still an exceptional example of teaching at its best, advertises the school's tuition rates and class offerings at the beginning of new terms. Occasionally, teachers or students are acknowledged in the paper for an achievement. Many public gatherings for holidays and other special events take place in the sun-dappled grove that is the familiar grounds of the school. Graduates have been distinguishing themselves in a variety of professional occupations, many as teachers, each contributing to the school's wide reputation for educational excellence.

7

An Informative Entry into the 1880s

It is a most impressive book, an odd, oversized shape and the more inviting for it. People here knew it was coming: the artists and compilers canvassed the county a few months ago. It is titled *History of Hamilton County, Indiana, with Illustrations and Biographical Sketches of the Prominent Men and Pioneers to which are Appended Maps of Its Several Townships*. It has been published by Kingman Brothers of Chicago in this year 1880.

T.B. Helm, author and editor of the *Hamilton County Atlas*, acknowledges help he received from many local sources, a "superabundance" of information, he states, much of it "in a crude shape, undigested, and unarranged." He mentions his obvious reliance on the "reminiscences" of a local authority on county history, August Finch Shirt.

Those who paid extra to have illustrations of homes and autobiographical sketches have also contributed to the history of this place by putting forth the illustrations that will be treasured in the future. In nearly all the farm scenes the original rail fences remain but at a far back field as with the original log cabin, now a functional enough farm outbuilding. But this full page of the farm of John and Lucinda Edwards shows a rail fence in the foreground, perhaps to commemorate their pioneer heritage.

The illustration of William Wheeler's farm also shows a rail fence in the foreground bordering a close neighbor's field across the road from the house. The single-story house has two chimneys, one at each end of the house. Perhaps that is William driving a properly stacked wagon of hay into the

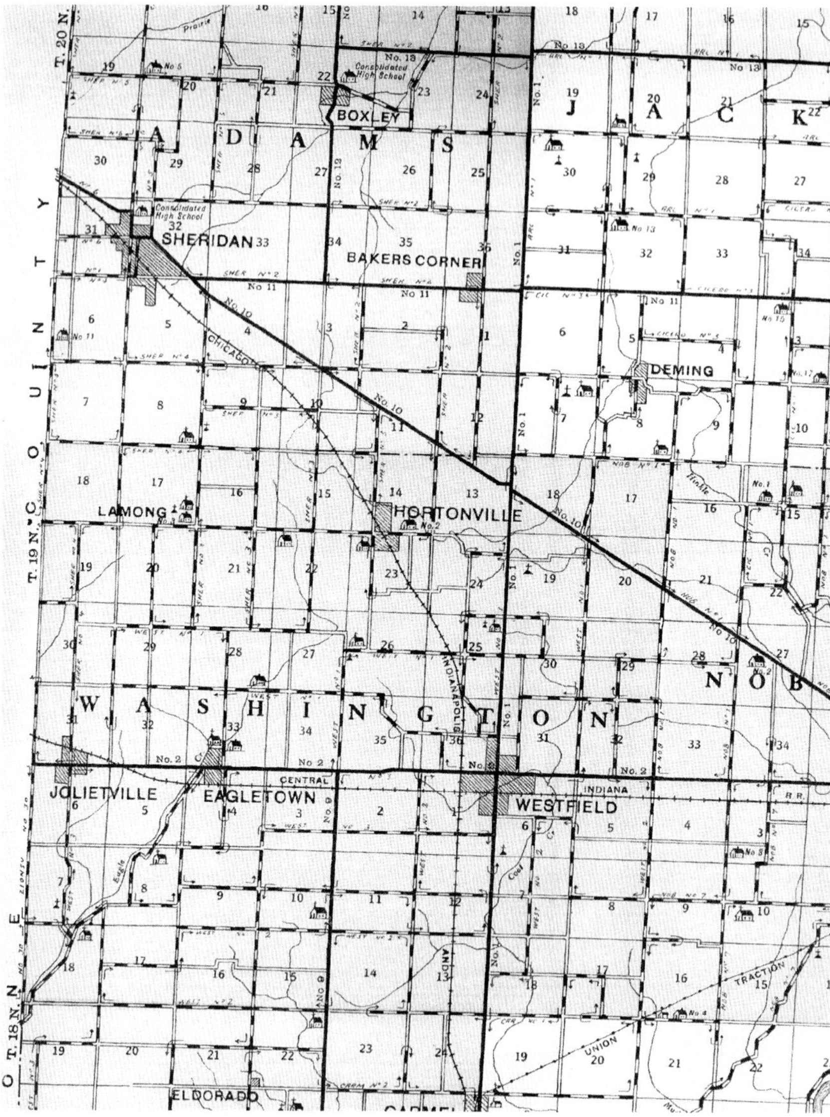

Plat map of Washington Township in *Hamilton County Atlas of 1880*. The county seat of Noblesville is to the east (right) in Noblesville Township.

Oppposite, top: The farm of John and Lucinda Edwards, Washington Township, from the 1880 atlas of Hamilton County, Indiana. Atlas patrons paid extra to have their farms, homes or portraits illustrated in the atlas, the county's first.

Opposite, bottom: The William V. Wheeler farm, Washington Township, in the 1880 atlas of Hamilton County. Many such illustrations show the pioneer-era fences along with contemporary fences, a sign of progress. Note rail fences in back fields also. Some illustrations also show the original log cabin home of the farm family, usually in the distant background.

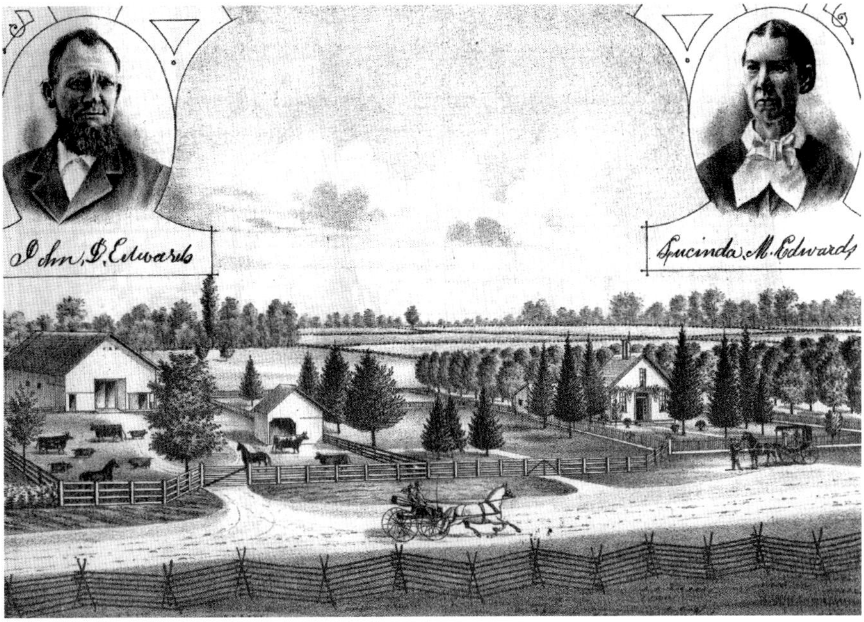
John D. Edwards
Lucinda M. Edwards

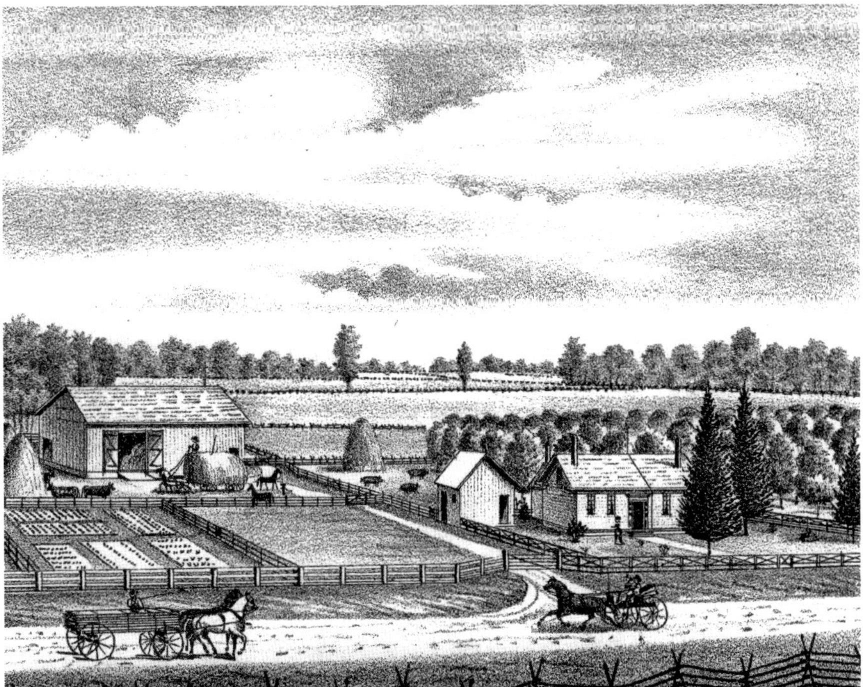

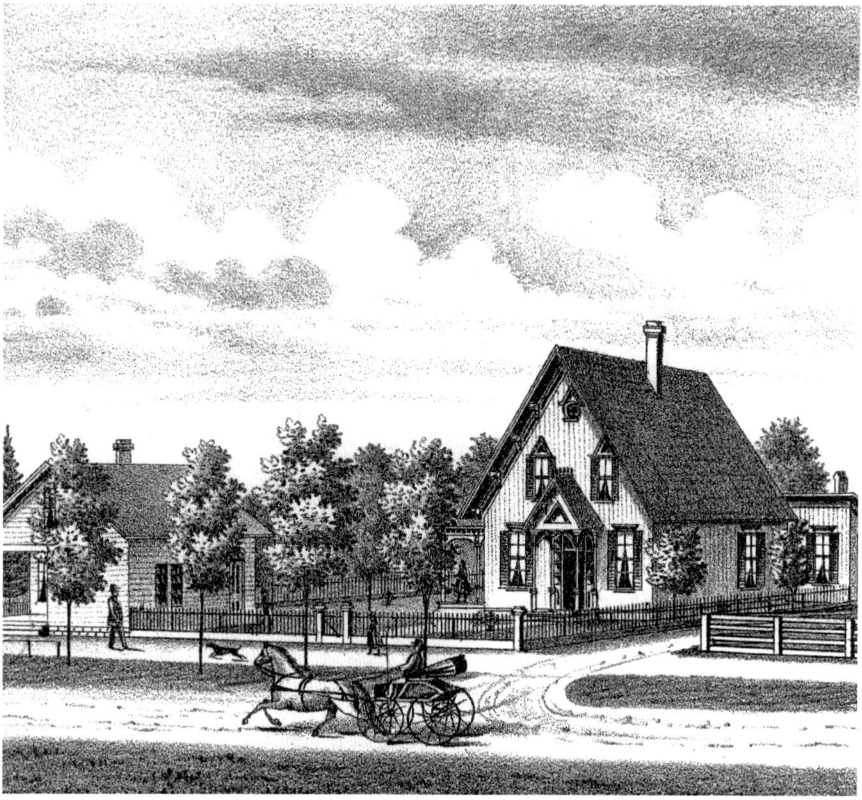

The home of Dr. Silas Charles Dove in Westfield, from the 1880 atlas of Hamilton County, Indiana.

barn. Like that of the Edwardses, this farm also shows broad, level fields. Those who labored for years at it remember that all that acreage had to be "improved," the term for where thick stands of trees stood and from which stumps had to be pulled with considerable muscle strain. The large fenced garden plots near the road indicate not only good order but also much food to be put by for the winter.

Dr. S.C. Dove's house in town is shown on the other half of the page with the Wheeler farm. The doctor's house is two storied and steep roofed with shutters at all windows, a common architectural style. The small steep-roofed overhang at the front door is artfully done, its roof the same angles as that of the larger roof. A gentleman is passing the house on the walkway in front, along the proper iron fence, perhaps the doctor himself.

Near the back of the atlas is the 1880 business directory for the township, listing fifty names: ten originally from the Carolinas, four more from other southern states, thirty-two of the total farmers and sixteen with added careers in a wide variety of endeavors such as blacksmithing, raising stock, teaching, dealing in lumber, carpentry, hog breeding, township trustee, thrashing, insurance agent, county commissioner and justice of the peace. Dr. Benson came here in 1851, graduated from Indiana Medical College and Butler University and served as a surgeon in the war.

The county atlas of 1880 shows Westfield as the third and fourth generations of founding families know it. The big flat book will have its special place in the home.

In 1885, the *Index* newspaper begins publication in town. As proclaimed on the masthead, it is "a Progressive and Reform Journal." Daniel Bond is editor, and the price is one dollar per year. This paper is "devoted to Prohibition, Woman Suffrage and other Reforms, Political and Social, A weekly paper devoted to the best interests of the family and home."

The format is typical of this time: a front page of two columns headed "Business Interests of Westfield" and then a column of news from some distance, mostly reprinted from some eastern newspapers of the same social philosophy. There is also an Indiana column offering news from around the state and an "Industrial" column head or a similar title having to do with forward thinking about new products, labor practices or the like.

The Saturday, August 13, 1887 issue of the *Index* is number forty-two of the second volume. The ads of this late summer issue include Abel Doan, dealer in Jersey cattle; D.J. Mendenhall & Co., druggists; and paints, oils, varnishes, wall paper and perfumeries. J.A. Williams is a dealer in groceries and provisions. T.W. Coffin meat market offers fresh and smoked meat, fish and the ever-popular oysters (a staple of gatherings of young people). Davis & Beals just opened a new hardware and implement store featuring the Deering Harvesting Machinery. W.H. Conklin, in the post office building, has drugs, medicines, books and stationery, "all the leading school books at very low prices" (the local public school has some difficulty managing parents' choices for textbooks; no standard texts have yet been chosen). Binford, Talbert & Co.'s saw and planing mills produce "all kinds of building materials, inside finish, scroll and lathe work." When the railroad came through not long ago, more architectural building treatments, fancy filigreed additions to front porches and so on are available from the large catalogue merchandisers. But Binford & Talbert can make some impressive decorative features for

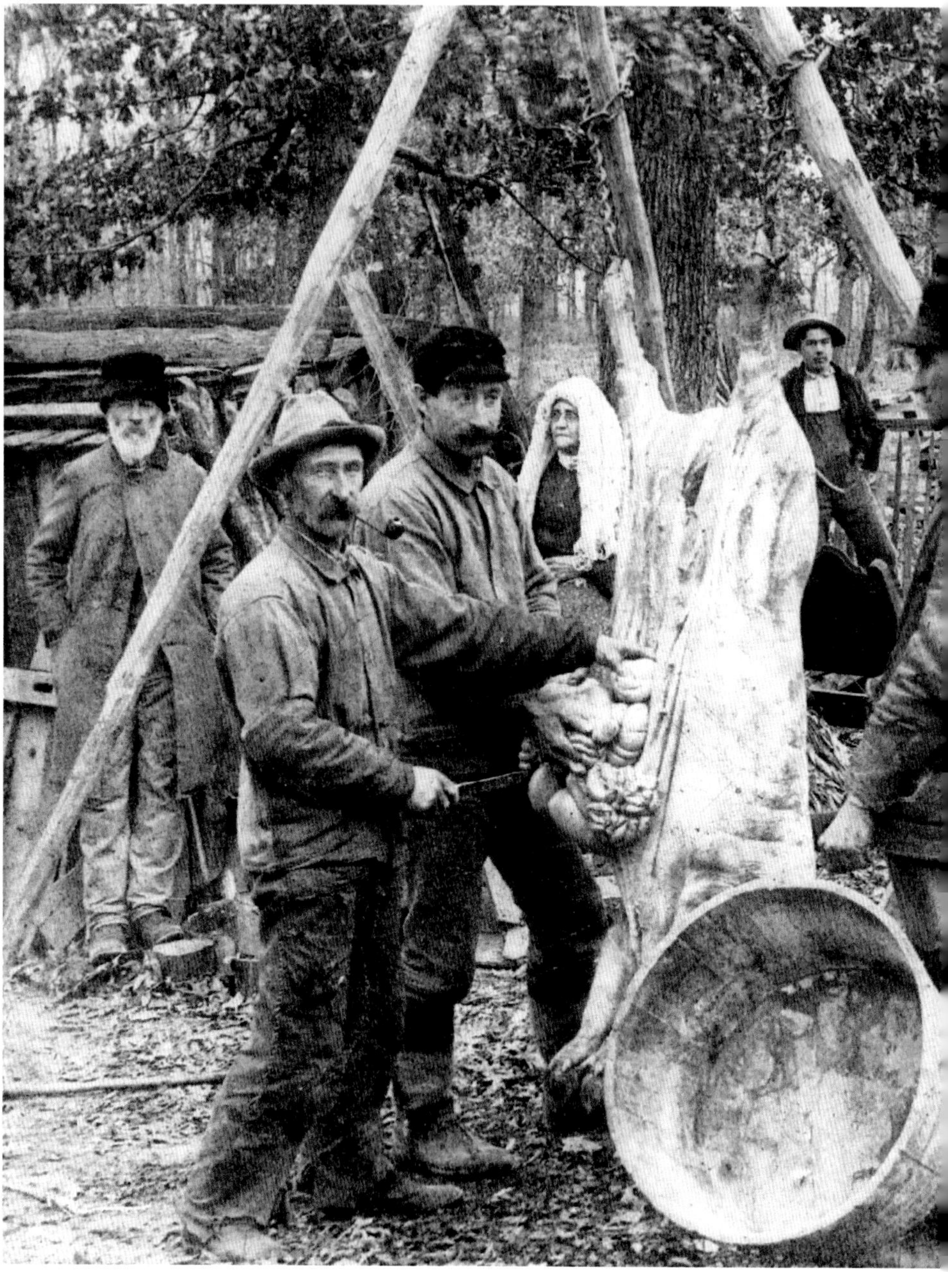

Typical hog-butchering scene, north of Westfield at the turn of the twentieth century.

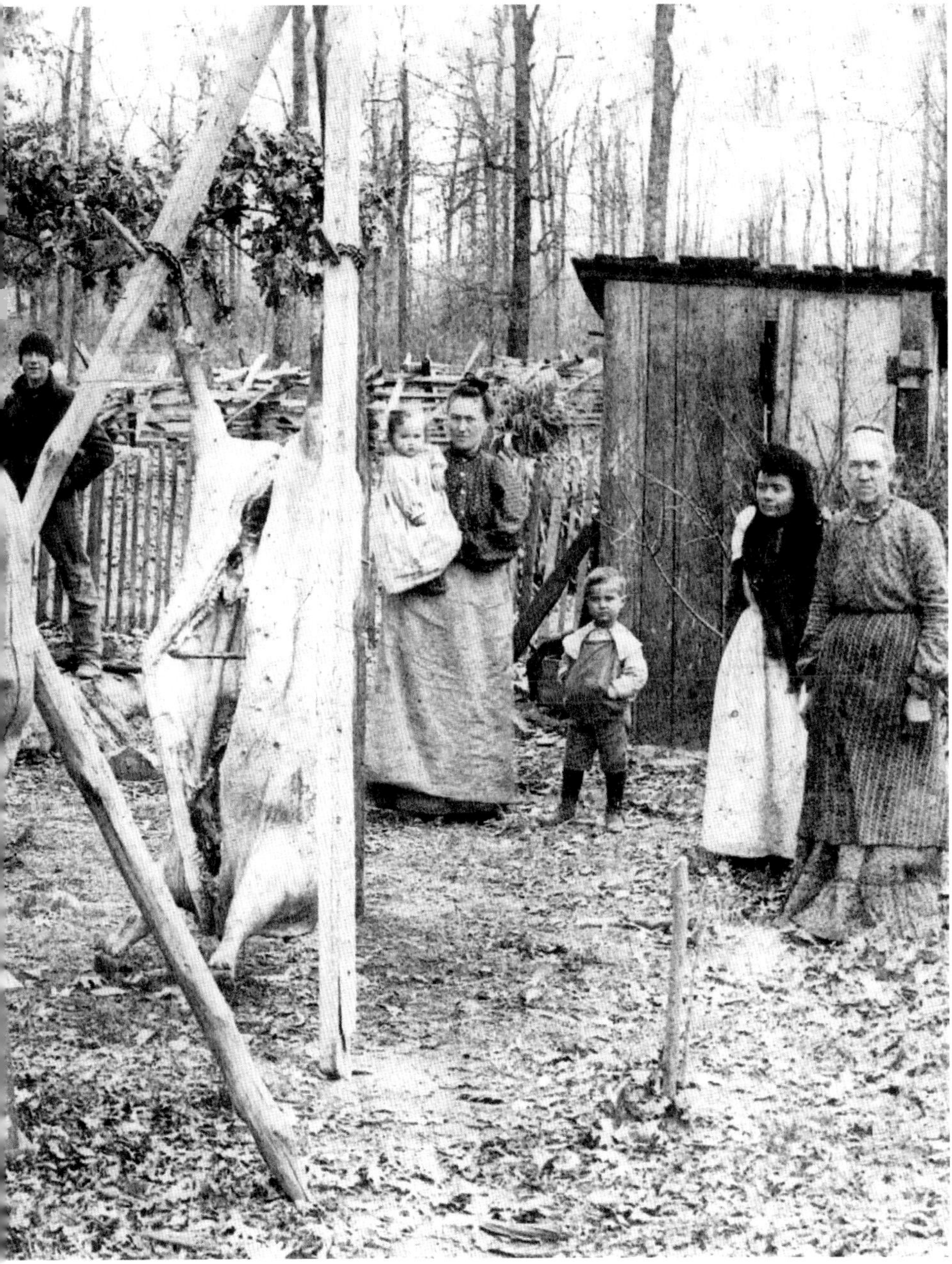

buildings themselves. W.E. Pfaff Groceries also stocks choice tobacco and cigars, pays "high" prices for country produce and has "the best coffee" at twenty cents per pound. "Resident" dentist W.R Wolf is equipped to make "artificial plates of all styles, gold and silver fillings" and all other superior work desired or needed. T.T. Bray is another grocer and provisionary, with added Queensware, glassware, schoolbooks, stationery, notions, anthracite and Pittsburg and block coal. The print of the closely spaced columns, seven to the page, is rather small, and no "glasses doctor" has come to town yet, but those who need "specs" have their magnifying glasses alongside their hearing horns. From the publisher's viewpoint, the smaller the print, the more content he can provide.

The train schedule is printed in great detail for the Monon Railroad, officially the Chicago, Lafayette, Indianapolis, Cincinnati and Louisville Railroad. The Monon, an all-Indiana trunk line with excellent connections, was built at the west edge of town in 1883, and the system's map shows the schedule for the entire state, with, in tiny print, all the possible regular stops of the original line from Jeffersonville, across the Ohio River from Louisville, to Chicago and for the new "Air Line" that passes through here from Indianapolis to Chicago. The possibilities are impressive; the map of all the railroads in the region looks like the arterial and veining systems of the human body. The map makes an important point visually—the fairly new implication that now Westfield, too, has its connections as part of the many railroad systems in the state and even the choice of many more destinations ticketed out of Louisville, Cincinnati and Chicago at the edges of Indiana and each with its own larger distribution of connections.

The *Index*'s chief theme, temperance, is given prominent placement and length, with much about liquor laws being passed making the stuff more available than ever. The temperance mood in Westfield has always been feistier than in many other places. Temperance is in constant repertoire at the churches; the large local temperance society includes almost as many men as women. The men have signed a never-use pledge, for a woman to sign is rather an insult, implying that she needs to quit usage to begin sobriety.

The three departments of Union High School will be opened for students September 13, "with new rooms, increased library, and good teachers. This school will be more worthy of patronage than ever before." The same motto as before applies: "Character and scholarship one and inseparable." Further, "Location good, tuition low." A catalogue is available from Erastus Test, MD, Westfield.

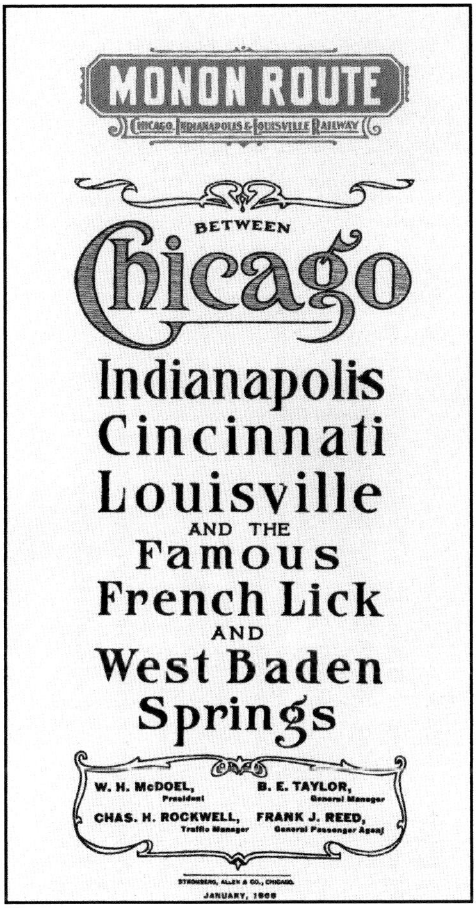

Above: Monon Railroad excursion ad for travel to the hot springs of southern Indiana.

Right: Late nineteenth-century ad for the all-Indiana Monon Railroad. The "Air Line" was built through Westfield in the mid-1880s, giving residents access to the many transfer options at Union Terminal in Indianapolis (one of the nation's first) and to major railroads in Chicago. The original route was from the Ohio River at Louisville to Michigan City on Lake Michigan (and access to Chicago) to link Ohio River shipping to the oceangoing ships of the Great Lakes.

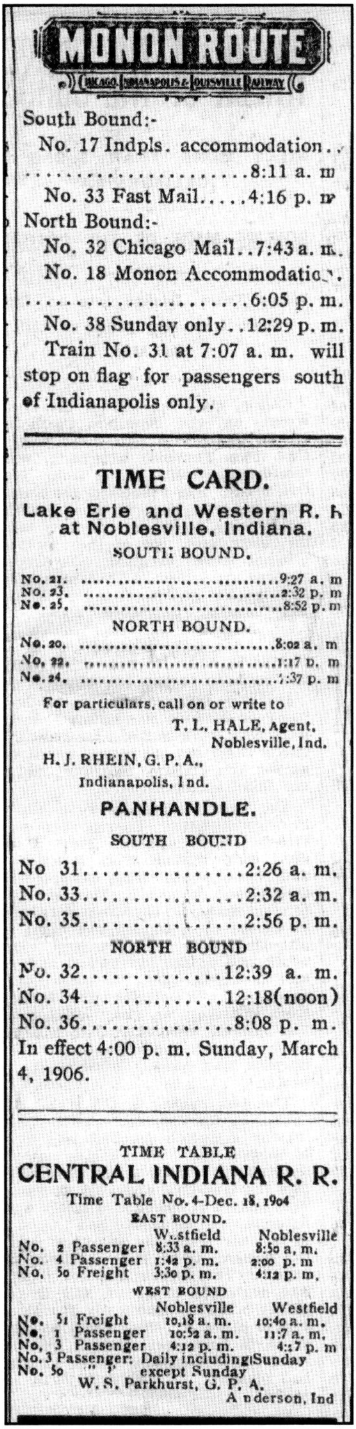

MONON ROUTE
CHICAGO, INDIANAPOLIS & LOUISVILLE RAILWAY

South Bound:-
No. 17 Indpls. accommodation.. ...8:11 a. m
No. 33 Fast Mail.....4:16 p. m
North Bound:-
No. 32 Chicago Mail..7:43 a. m.
No. 18 Monon Accommodation. ...6:05 p. m.
No. 38 Sunday only..12:29 p. m.
Train No. 31 at 7:07 a. m. will stop on flag for passengers south of Indianapolis only.

TIME CARD.
Lake Erie and Western R. R.
at Noblesville, Indiana.

SOUTH BOUND.
No. 21. ....9:27 a. m
No. 23. ....2:32 p. m
No. 25. ....8:52 p. m

NORTH BOUND.
No. 20. ....8:02 a. m
No. 22. ....1:17 p. m
No. 24. ....?:37 p. m

For particulars, call on or write to
T. L. HALE, Agent,
Noblesville, Ind.
H. J. RHEIN, G. P. A.,
Indianapolis, Ind.

PANHANDLE.

SOUTH BOUND
No 31.........2:26 a. m.
No. 33.........2:32 a. m.
No. 35.........2:56 p. m.

NORTH BOUND
No. 32.........12:39 a. m.
No. 34.........12:18(noon)
No. 36.........8:08 p. m.
In effect 4:00 p. m. Sunday, March 4, 1906.

TIME TABLE
CENTRAL INDIANA R. R.
Time Table No. 4-Dec. 18, 1904

EAST BOUND.

	Westfield	Noblesville
No. 2 Passenger	8:33 a. m.	8:50 a. m.
No. 4 Passenger	1:42 p. m.	2:00 p. m
No. 50 Freight	3:30 p. m.	4:12 p. m.

WEST BOUND

	Noblesville	Westfield
No. 51 Freight	10,18 a. m.	10:40 a. m.
No. 1 Passenger	10:52 a. m.	11:7 a. m.
No. 3 Passenger	4:12 p. m.	4::7 p. m

No. 3 Passenger: Daily including Sunday
No. 50 " " except Sunday
W. S. Parkhurst, G. P. A.
Anderson, Ind

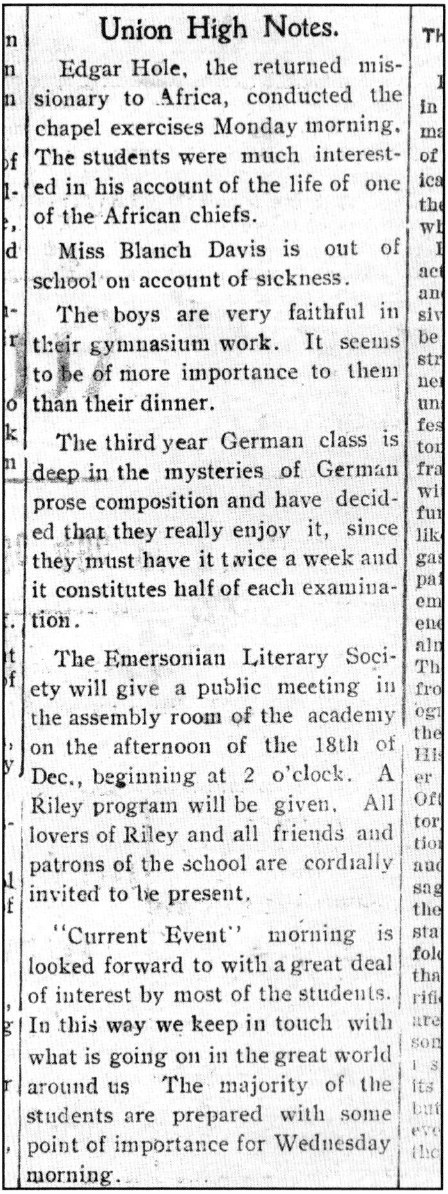

Union High Notes.

Edgar Hole, the returned missionary to Africa, conducted the chapel exercises Monday morning. The students were much interested in his account of the life of one of the African chiefs.

Miss Blanch Davis is out of school on account of sickness.

The boys are very faithful in their gymnasium work. It seems to be of more importance to them than their dinner.

The third year German class is deep in the mysteries of German prose composition and have decided that they really enjoy it, since they must have it twice a week and it constitutes half of each examination.

The Emersonian Literary Society will give a public meeting in the assembly room of the academy on the afternoon of the 18th of Dec., beginning at 2 o'clock. A Riley program will be given. All lovers of Riley and all friends and patrons of the school are cordially invited to be present.

"Current Event" morning is looked forward to with a great deal of interest by most of the students. In this way we keep in touch with what is going on in the great world around us The majority of the students are prepared with some point of importance for Wednesday morning.

Opposite: News clipping of activities and events at Friends Union High School, 1880s.

The paper points out with pride, "This school has grown in efficiency and favor until it stands second to no institution of its kind in the state. Let our young people avail themselves of its advantages. To those more distant we say that Westfield is a good place for your children. A clean, moral atmosphere, and boarding as cheap as can be obtained elsewhere."

The Midland (Central Indiana) Railroad will begin carrying mail on August 22 from Noblesville to Lebanon; still under construction, the railroad will reach Ladoga in Montgomery County in two weeks from Sunday. "Then look out for business." One case of typhoid fever is in town. Rain on Thursday helped the drought, and "all our industries are prospering" in spite of the serious lack of rain. Dwiggins & Hinshaw are "so crowded with work that they are obliged to increase their force," and the business done at McClary's new carriage shop is "enough to astonish the natives." Lee McClary makes carriages, buggies and farm wagons and is especially good at making "eastern buggies." A.W. Six's store has tomatoes, apricots, corn, strawberries, blackberries and lobsters. A.W. Six is also the agent for the Midland Railroad and has tickets, timetables and freight rates. H.O. Johnson's ice cream parlor is the boss. Burroughs has the "boss" lemonade and soda water in town.

A letter to the editor asks how the liquor traffic can be stopped in any four-year term of political office if the church has not accomplished it in two thousand years. "We have had murder and mob law preached in the public press at Westfield on diverse occasions. Is it not time for the citizens to call a halt?" The *Index* editor takes him to task; if one does not hold to the *possibility* of prohibition, indeed, all is lost, he argues.

"Old and Young Settlers meeting will be held August 30, 1887, in Bowman's Grove, Westfield, Ind. Presents of chairs, silver, knives and forks, canes, toilet sets, lamps, cradles, etc. will be given to old and young settlers. Excursion rates on railroad." In the matter of longtime residents passing from the scene in death, that of Mrs. Sarah Porter is "a well known and respected colored woman of this town."

Westfield flouring mill, bought by Samuel A. Vare, wants the patronage of farmers and citizens of Westfield. N.B. Lewis and J.R. Green work there and "will give thirty six pounds of flour and twelve pounds of bran for wheat that tests sixty pounds a bushel."

Some growth in the town has occurred of late, particularly in new businesses of the inventive sort. "Foster & Barker manufacture the best carpet stretcher." Mr. Dwiggins the blacksmith has invented a wagon-lifting jack. Professor Sanders at Union High School has invented a superior school desk and is preparing to have it manufactured in Westfield. "Prospects are bright for our quiet town." Vacant lots are sold "almost every day," and a number of new dwellings are going up. "Business men and those with capital should come to Westfield. They will come and realize the benefits of natural gas."

There is a new restaurant at "Stanford's old stand." The McMillan Brothers' baked goods are "fresh from the oven." The Floral Hill Green House is operated by N. Stout & J. Conklin. McClary & Mills now offer secondhand buggies and manufacture wagons, buggies, surries and carriages, all of which they can repaint and repair. Someone found an 1811 silver dollar where an old house had been.

"Those interested in starting a building and loan and savings association meet at Vare's Hall." Cutworms and little ants are destroying the young corn. Get "baseball goods at The Big Three" and croquet sets. There will be fireworks for the Fourth of July. Ice is for sale at the Children's Home.

If possible, the name of the place in Westfield where orphans and children without a guardian are sent is a fairly inviting name: the Indiana Receiving Home. One of the many duties of the person in charge is the occasional report of periodic activity. A small sheaf of papers reveals much about the very nature of the place beyond the questions answered quickly with otherwise static numbers.

A State Board of Charities annual report form for November 30, 1889, counts eleven "whole orphans," twenty-one "half orphans" and twelve having both parents living. Eight have been taken in during the past twelve months. Thirteen have been returned to their parents in the past year. The rescue and care of orphans has been a county endeavor since at least 1881.

On March 26, 1890, Mrs. E.E. Ellis, matron, reported forty-four children at the "Hamilton County Orphans' Home." She notes that the water supply is defective. From the 180-feet-deep well, a "large wind pump…pumps from quicksand more sand than water." There is a small garden and some "small fruit." Some additions to the original structure, a large house at the north end of town, have been "built at different times" that "do very well for the purpose." This is "a nice lot of children, really pleasant, several choice examples."

All seems well, as far as such a setting with its silent stories of human suffering can be so judged. But notes penned on a small piece of paper, undated and unsigned, residing in the scattered records bear heavy messages of disappointment and worse. The notes were made by an aide to an official visitor to the home. And what that person wrote quickly for an official report is quite troubling:

> *A dinner at the Hamilton Co. Orphans' Home noted by Hagaman, Supt. of Boone Co.: one half bowl of bean soup, one slice of bread, a small piece of cheese. Mr. Hagaman says children are miserably fed in order that* [the Home's] *Supt. may profit. Boone Co. sends its children there; eight or nine were present during the visit. Supt.* [Hagaman] *will oppose continuance of the arrangement.*

What is written on this small scrap of paper casts a pall over the entire existence of the Home. Thankfully, other reports on official forms indicate much better treatment of the defenseless and abandoned children who, for a hopeless period of their young lives, must depend on the pleasant or otherwise personalities of their elders.

A report dated September 10, 1890, is more forthcoming with essential information. Here "Matron" Mrs. Elizabeth E. Ellis reports to the county commissioners under whose authority the home is sustained, such as it is, about the children and the property (four and a half acres owned by the county, as well as the furniture and one cow). The commissioners pay twenty-five cents a day for each child and provide schoolbooks. This is all the funding the home receives.

This funding does not include new clothes; the children often come with "just a change" of clothing. An assigned committee for the commissioners and the sitting grand jury has already inspected the home, but Mrs. Ellis says that while those visits were thorough and positive, there are many matters that cannot be observed or understood in a single visit. For example, in the "taking in and putting out" of children, time is needed to know the background of each child who comes, as well as inspecting the homes and persons who wish to adopt. The matron is concerned in particular about how discouraging it is to see children returned "to those who cannot give them the care and training they need."

Twenty-five "new" children have come in during the previous year—eighteen under age ten and "several quite young." Of these newcomers, there are fourteen girls and eleven boys. Seventeen children have been placed with families, of whom three are "on trial." Three others have been removed from trial homes and sent to different homes, some at a considerable distance, which adds to the time the matron must give to follow-up inspections.

In total, there are forty-six children in the home, twenty-seven boys and nineteen girls. The home conducts a school, and all but the three youngest have had daily instruction in the previous four-and-a-half-month term taught by Miss Lottie Garrison and later by "the Misses Doan." Miss Susie Teter has just arrived from Boxley to take charge of the teaching. She has attended "Mrs. Baker's training school for kindergarten teachers." The matron plans a kindergarten for the youngest ones, but without space at the home, she is waiting for the public school to open to use space there. The matron pays the tuition of the students; their books are supplied by the county. Each child is given specific training "in the industrial departments" so they can learn to do something well before being assigned to another task, so they can become "competent in general work." There is also a "governess" present, Miss Cora Osborn. A Miss Wink has given the children weekly music lessons. Mrs. Ellis does ask the commissioners for fire extinguishers for the home.

Local physician Dr. S.C. Dove makes quarterly visits officially and treats children as needed during the year. He reports also that on September 5, 1890, the children are in remarkably good health, considering "this is the sickliest part of the year," and there is "a great deal of sickness in this part of the neighborhood." In this regard, he compliments the sanitary condition of the home and credits that for the children's good health, along with the "good nutritious and very appropriate food" served the children. Indeed, the children all appear "healthy and happy."

There are a few apple, cherry and pear trees on the grounds. A crop of strawberries has been raised. But they report there is "water to prime the

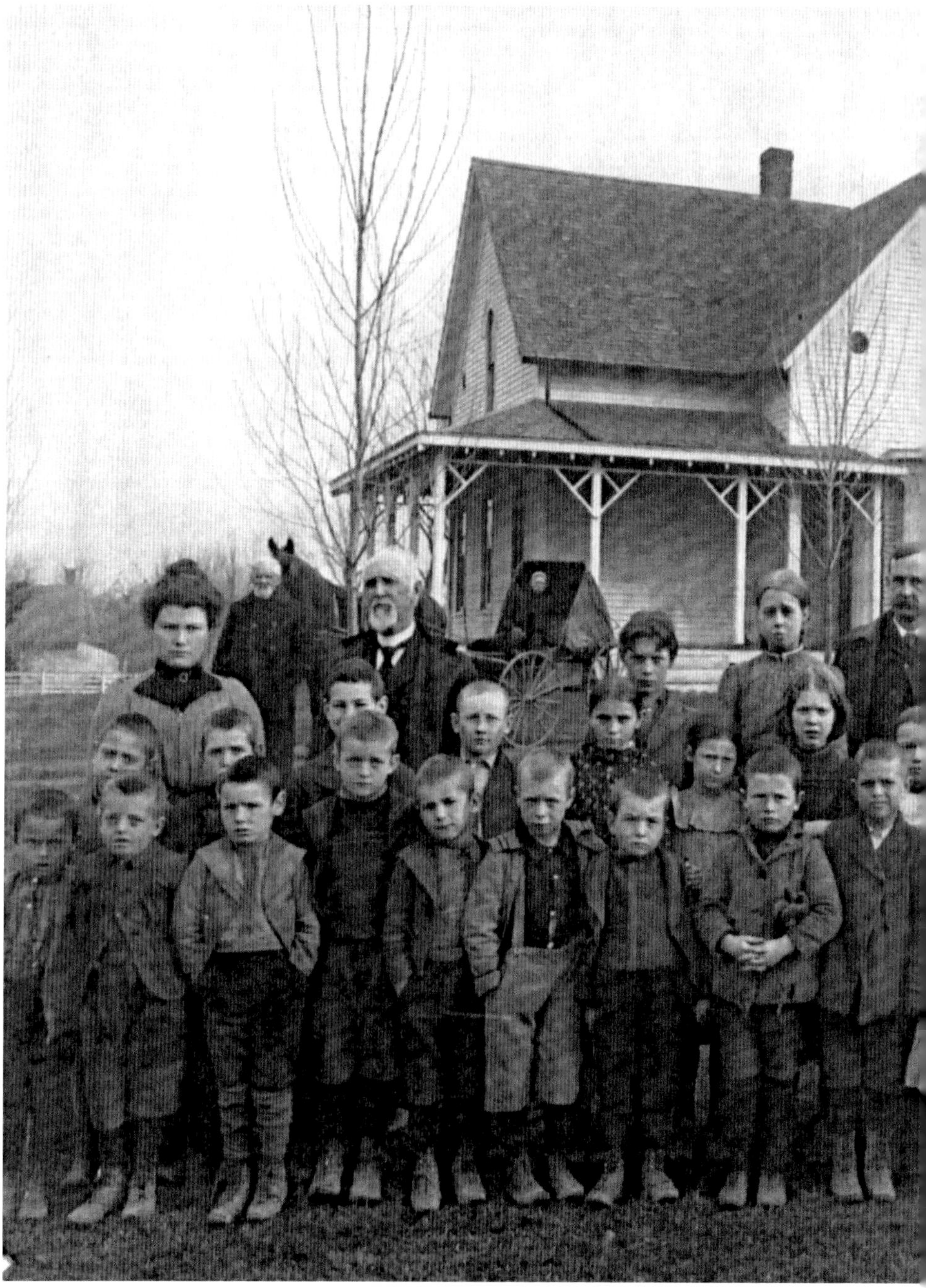

Westfield Children's Receiving Home, opened by Mrs. Rose Carey and administered locally; the home sheltered children from thirty-five counties in Indiana, the second-largest orphanage in Indiana for several years. The home opened in 1881 and closed in the early 1910s.

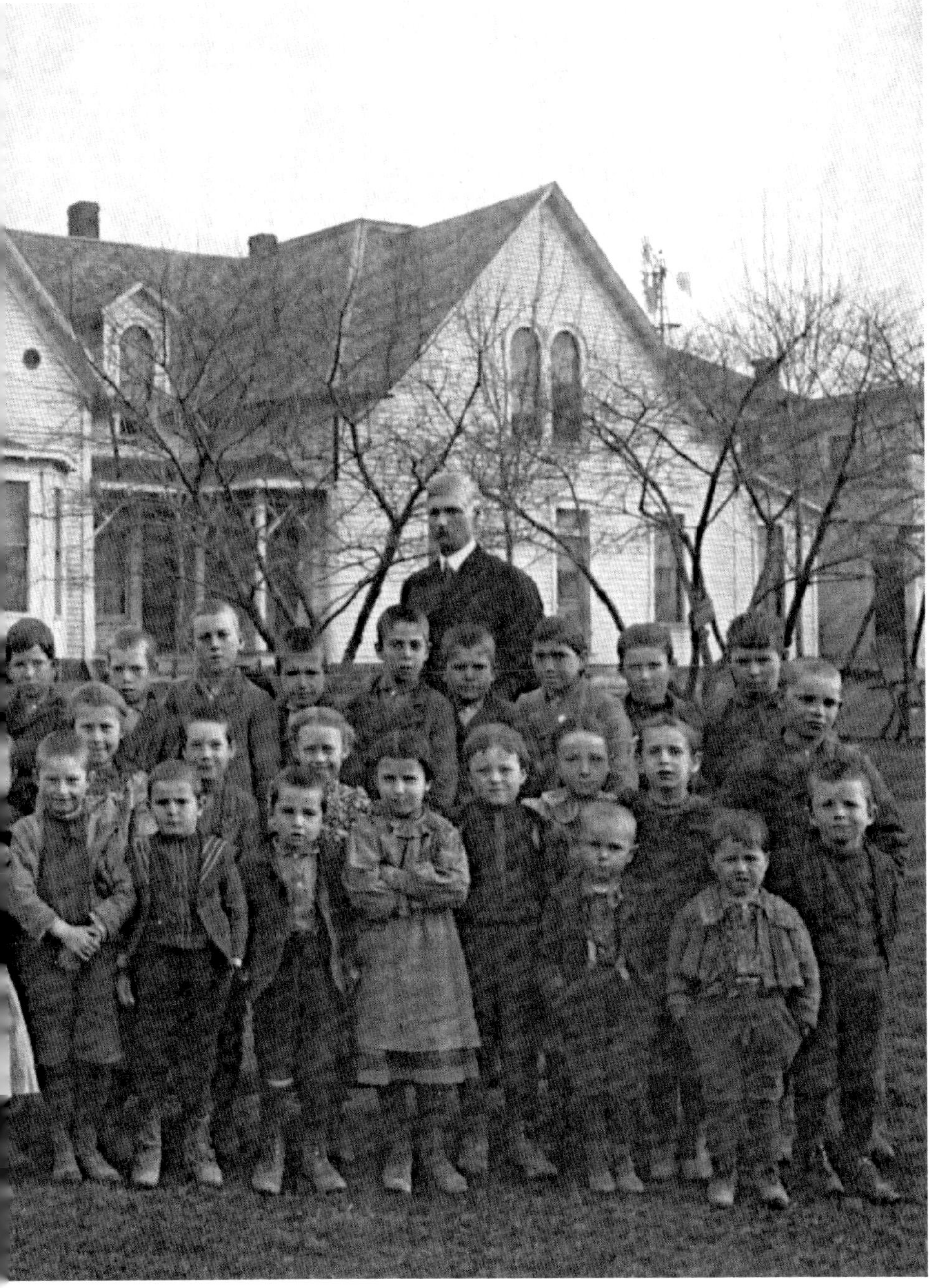

pump only when the wind blows" the windmill, and the supply of shirts and shoes has "ran down."

Another note of observation, dated October 28, 1892, counts six children from the Board of County Charities of Marion County, fifteen from Boone County and twenty-four from Hamilton County. The home has had as many as sixty-one from Hamilton County. One boy from Indianapolis, left in the care of a grandmother in Hamilton County, was returned to his father who is "quite likely to hurt him."

In late 1893, the state report form, redesigned, lists sixty-seven "inmates": forty-six boys and twenty-one girls. "Whole orphans" number thirteen; "half orphans," forty-two; twelve have both parents living; and twenty-three have been "indentured" in the past year. The matron now is S. Ella Young, who adds, "We are caring for children from Boone County, and some that are controlled by the Board of Children's Guardians." On March 11, 1893, the Indiana Children's Home Society came into being as another welcome official oversight function.

As of November 1, 1894, J.E.G. Young and S. Ella Young complete the state report form, now under the title "Hamilton County Orphan's Home." During the past year, there have been thirty-nine "inmates" (twenty-three boys and sixteen girls), of whom five (three boys and two girls) are "whole" orphans, twenty-nine (eighteen boys and eleven girls) "half" orphans and seven (three boys and four girls) have both parents living. Eight (six boys and two girls) have been "placed out." None has been returned to relatives. Again, there are children from Boone County here.

Another example states, "The number of children discharged from the Hamilton Co. Home in the year 1895, transferred to other institutions, ten, returned to parents or relatives, twenty-four, placed in new homes, nine, died, two, total forty-five. Signed S. Ella Young, Westfield." An additional note states that five babies have been boarded out.

Another notation, undated, says that three children are out on trial in Hamilton County: "They usually stay about 30 to 60 days on trial." A brief note about food: "Milk once a day, give the milk one half skim and one half whole milk."

Each year, the State Board of Charities and Correction sends a small form with suggestions for completing report forms (conditions to report). One is addressed to "Westfield, Childrens' Home Society, date visited, Aug. 23, 1900."

In a small pad with undated printed questions are a few pages of succinct notations:

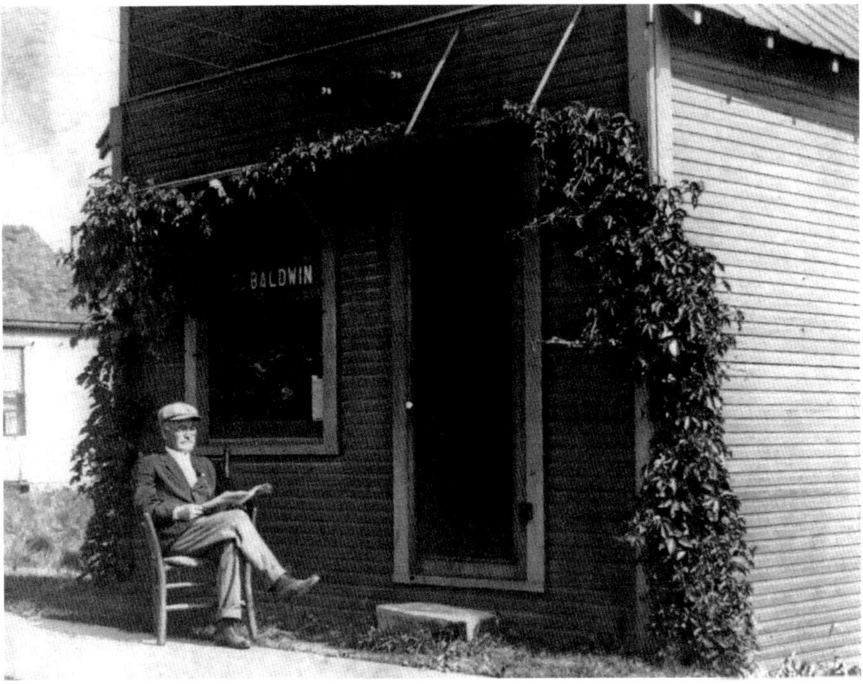

Dr. Lincoln J. Baldwin, MD, in front of his office in Westfield.

[Page one] *Furniture,* wooden cots; *how lighted,* gas; *how heated,* stoves, gas fuel; *how ventilated,* windows; *food,* beans and potatoes; *health,* good; *is physician employed?,* yes.
[Page two] *Reading matter,* yes; *religious services,* go to church and SS or at home; *number going to school,* last year had 30 to public school; *what employment have children,* work about bldg. and grounds; *construction of main buildings,* wood with additions.
[Page three] *Visited by,* P.N. Hiser/Hisen; *Superintendent,* R.J. Reagin, salary $1,500; *farm acres,* 10 acres tillable; *cows,* 1; *swine,* 3; *garden,* 5 acres, about 3 acres in corn; *orchard,* one acre; *small fruits,* one fourth acre; *estimated net annual expenses besides products,* about $600.
[Page four] *Visited by* AW; *Superintendant,* S.E. Elliott; *farm acres,* 12 acres; *cows* one; *garden,* seven acres; *orchard,* 20 trees; *small fruit,* raspberries, black berries, strawberries, grapes.
[Page five] *Population,* 61; [another], *population,* 40, boys, 34, girls 6.

The last documentary item is a typed message on the letterhead of the "Board of State Charities, State House, April 19, 1901," addressed to the auditor of Hamilton County, Noblesville: "Inform when orphan's home at Westfield was first established, and when it was abandoned by your county." The answers, unsigned, are handwritten at the bottom of the letter: "Established Sept. 9th, 1881, Abandoned Oct. 18th, 1898. Reply, Isaac Powell, aud[itor]."

Finally, a small two-page list shows children placed in private homes, giving their birthdates and the names of those under whose care they had been given, under the handwritten heading "State Board of Charities, Indiana Children's Home Society." The home addresses of the foster parents are Arcadia, Carmel, Hortonville, Noblesville, Sheridan, Tipton or Westfield (for seven children). One child had the advantage of being taken in by Dr. Baldwin in Westfield, a prominent Friend and well-educated professional. Seven of the children went to rural route addresses, to new lives on family farms. There are seventeen boys, ages two to seventeen, and four girls (three named Mary and one Marie), ages four to fifteen. These could represent all of those who over the years have been "put out" from the home; not as grim as it might seem, the "putting" refers to finding suitable homes for each child leaving the home. In this fashion, the home under its different names functioned as a temporary respite for children robbed of a stable and safe home life.

The September 24 *Westfield News* (published since 1872) informs about the status of the local consumption of natural gas, the new wonder fuel said to be in inexhaustible supply, although "the supply during the past few years has not met the demand." The paper assumes that most in town agree that the price has been fair. Cicero has a superior supply apparently and will sell gas to Westfield. With winter approaching, the consumption in Westfield "must be stabilized and sufficient." People seem willing to pay a higher price for a secure supply. Mr. Thistlethwaite, the nonresident owner of the gas company in town, "was here yesterday trying to get a better supply for the coming cold months."

A short "contributed" article on Sabbath breaking gives good reason for obeying: "Last Sunday several persons brought hogs to Westfield for the purpose of shipping them. This seems to be a violation of the Indiana Statute concerning Sabbath breaking, which reads: 'Whoever being over fourteen years of age if found on the first day of the week commonly called Sunday rioting, hunting, fishing, quarreling, at common labor or engaged in his usual avocation, shall be fined in any sum not more than ten dollars nor less than one dollar.' We should regret to hear of further Sabbath desecrations, and wish all citizens of Westfield and vicinity may 'remember the Sabbath to keep it holy' and thus avoid liability or prosecution."

The twenty-seventh-annual reunion of the old settlers of Hamilton and adjoining counties gathered in Mr. Jones's grove near Eagletown on Saturday, August 14. By ten o'clock in the morning, there were "thousands" there already. Thirty-six pioneers over the age of fifty had died the previous year. Dr. William Niles Wishard Sr. of Indianapolis, a former Union High School student, spoke. There has been mention of a "colored" speaker who saw his mother sold away from her family. It is said that more than two thousand soldiers from Hamilton County went to the war to preserve the Union, "knocking the shackles from the hands and feet of four million slaves." One veteran was thankful for "the honor of carrying a musket under Abraham Lincoln."

8
The Turn into the Twentieth Century

The View From the Wagon Shop

Around the turn of the new century, a good place to watch the street activity in Westfield is from the Beals & Hinshaw Wagon Shop. Amos S. Hinshaw is the primary owner. J. Frank Beals has sold his quarter ownership to Amos as of early August 1891.

There are 340 individual and business customers from 1896 to 1909 whose accounts are tabulated in book "A" with the list of customers, and book "B" contains carryover from book "A." Just about anyone who owns a wagon or buggy comes by at one time or another. Some, like Amos Doan, are repeat customers many times over with a variety of repair work done and items purchased to repair farm machinery himself and some items handmade by a shop blacksmith.

Truly, inside the shop is like the "carriage hardware and supplies" departments of the Sears & Roebuck and Montgomery Ward catalogues come to town. And what isn't on a shelf somewhere in the shop is ordered from the Vancamp Hardware Company in Indianapolis.

The list of shop customers shows what vehicles could be on the few streets of Westfield during any workday and, in fact, the number of horses in town and the township needed for that local traffic. The 1888 state agriculture department report claims that Indiana is now even with Kentucky in quality horse breeding.

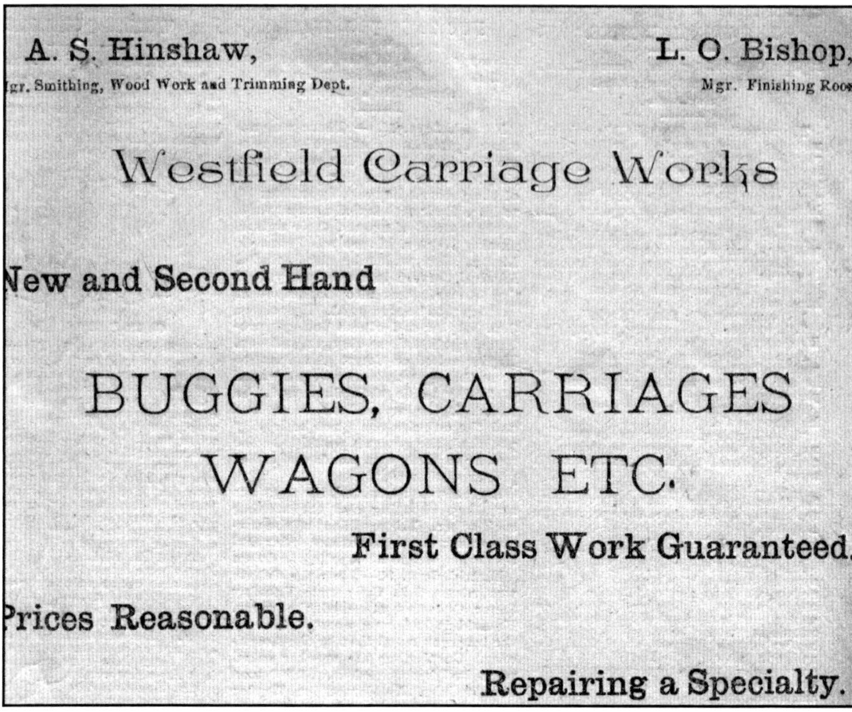

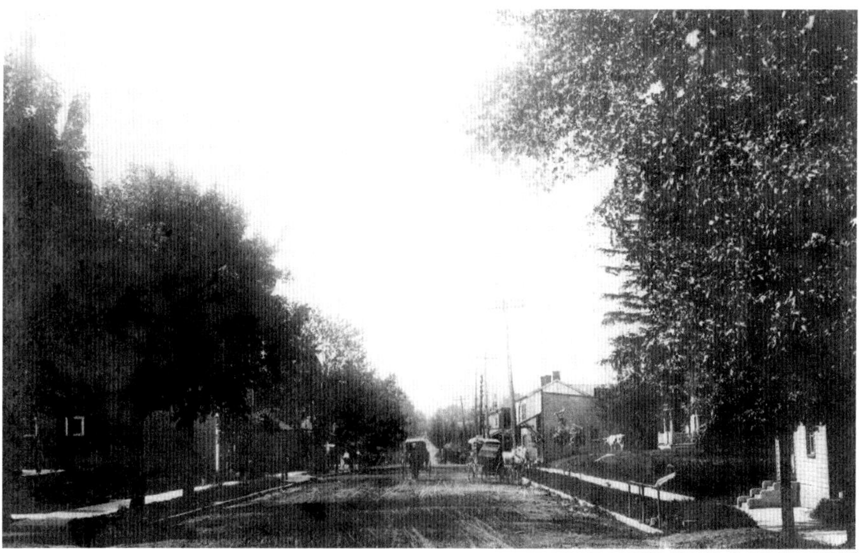

Top: Ad for A.S. Hinshaw's wagon shop, a good vantage point from which to observe the town's horse-drawn traffic from the late nineteenth century until automobiles came to dominate the roadways.

Bottom: Union Street in Westfield, looking south. Note the cow in the front yard at right (circa 1890s).

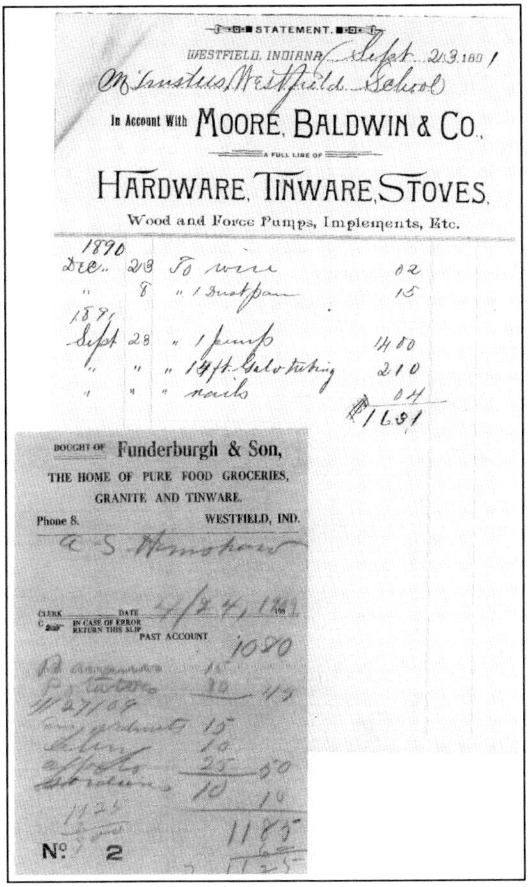

Sales receipts from two long-standing Westfield businesses: groceries from the Funderburh & Son store bought by wagon shop owner Amos S. Hinshaw, April 24, 1909, and Moore, Baldwin & Co. items bought by the trustees of the Westfield School, September 23, 1891.

The rigs of many local businesses need to be in good repair. There are the milk wagons of Holiday Milk and of the Westfield Creamery Co. Those of the Westfield Milling Co., Westfield Roller Mills say "Flour, Cornmeal. Feed. We Buy Grain, Thomas Thompson Proprietor" on the sides of the wagons.

Other businesses in town and the surrounding countryside that need the occasional replacement item or some repair include the White Star Telephone Co., Standard Oil, the Valley Oil Co., the Westfield Gas Co., Williams Grocery and J.E.C. Young. Dr. J.H. Baker uses a wagon at his farm. The town itself ("Westfield Corporation") has a wagon; as do the Binford & Talbot and the Westfield lumber companies; the Gravel Road Co.; the Westfield School Corporation; the Goodrich Bros., Noah, Early and Spanneth; Sanfesty Bros.; Funderberg & Son; the justice of the peace; Williams and Dwiggins, Mantle Factory Co.; Westfield Import Co.; Petigo & Hinshaw; Rose & Whitmore; and the Westfield Packing Co. Even the Building and Loan has a wagon.

The shop advertises to make completely new wagons, do "fancy painting" of buggies and surreys (can attach the silk fringe on top) and repair pony to full-size carts and spring wagons. The shop's blacksmiths can hand make

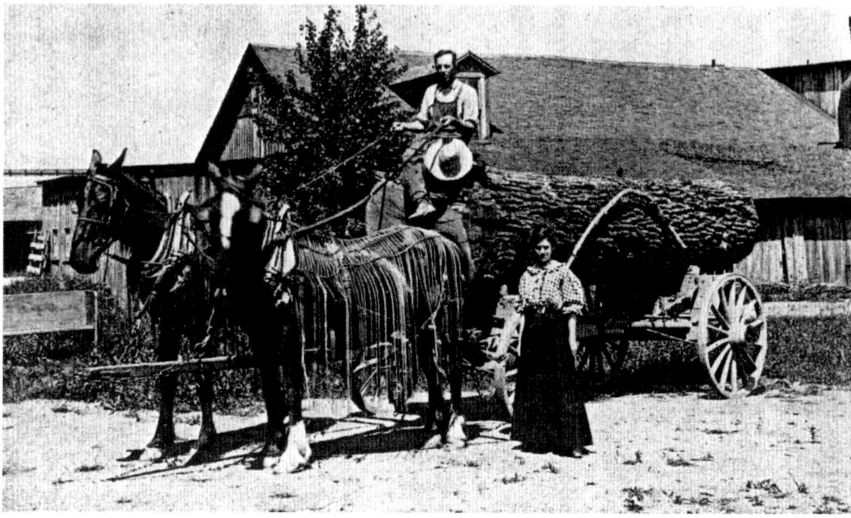

A log cut in Washington Township and delivered to Talbert's sawmill and lumberyard. Farmers in the county sold virgin timber for ready cash with the coming of sawmills and the increasing market for lumber, fences, etc.

many other parts as needed. Many are the charges listed that begin "for making" a corn planter scraper, a hay ladder, bolts, wood brace for a plow, a mud boat, buggy tops and many more items.

The shop also does "mending" of buggy seats and tops, fifth wheels, shaft rails, old fenders, cart springs, reaper reels and hack doors and some "remodeling" of vehicle paraphernalia, "repairing" a sleigh, a buckboard, a pump and farm machinery. Some items need sharpening, such as plow shears, harrow teeth, corn drills and repairs to cultivators. Welding is done, and threads are cut in pipe as for natural gas lines. The most common job, of course, is "setting tires" and horseshoeing. Boys who dream of driving their own wagons one day try to learn these part names; it helps if they loaf some at the shop, if allowed.

Work has also been noted on a "bicicle" and a "tricle" and even some surprisingly small items such as a shoe stretcher, a shoe-button fastener and a shoe last. F.M. Elliott at the Children's Receiving Home on the north edge of town has had work done on their carriage, a washing machine "mended" and some of the home's garden rakes and hoes have been repaired. (A report about the home in late 1890 stated, "The larger boys do good work on the little farm.")

Customers pay cash mostly, but many accumulate a tab, and some even barter occasionally, such as by trading potatoes, flour, beans, hay and so

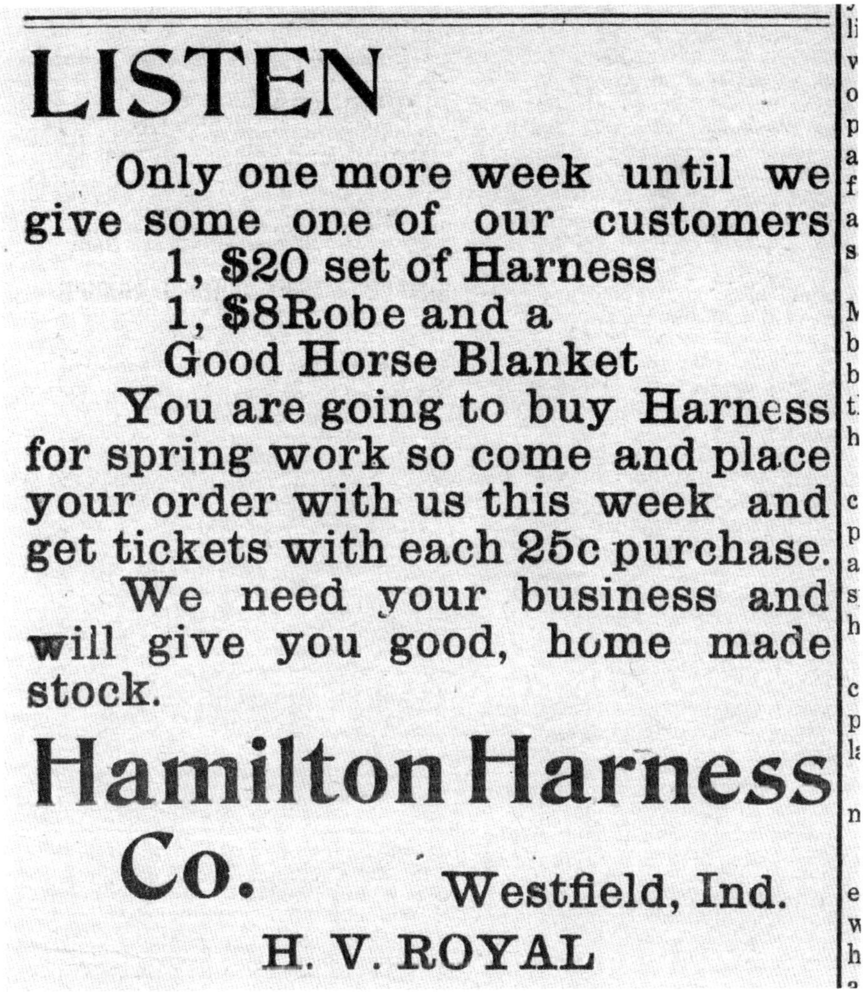

An ad for a harness shop in Westfield, from the *Westfield News*, February 24, 1911.

forth for work done. Use of the shop "telefone," as they spell it, is twenty-five cents a call, not a piddling amount, but some calls are that important.

All this makes for a nearly continual flow of horse-drawn vehicles to the shop during a typical workweek, a parade of the town's commercial life. (Others in town and the township who work on wagons have their own customer lists.)

Public Health, a Brief Accounting

If there is to be pride in one's place of residence, the physical health of the people must be considered. For a few years now, eight doctors have practiced in town, and all of them made entries in three record books. The doctors have included J.J. Baker, Hinshaw, S.C. Dove, J.B. Pettyjohn, Fodrea, H.S. Hess, John W. Dansforth and Cyrus W. Johnson. The most informative volume is titled "Record of Returns of Diseases, Dangerous to Public Health in the Town of Westfield." The other record books document births and deaths and cover the period from March 21, 1882, to February 17, 1896. The "Diseases" volume begins with a case of variola or smallpox noted by Dr. S.C. Dove. Actually, two facing pages are filled with cases of this illness. Two deaths are noted here, though Dr. J.B. Pettyjohn's notations from April 17, 1882, to May 31 report recovery in three to thirty-one days. (There is both variola major and minor.)

The next year, eight patients succumb to scarlet fever. Drs. Baker and Pettyjohn treat mainly cases of measles in February 1883. In the same month the next year, Dr. Hess notes thirteen cases of measles along with one case of scarletina.

The illnesses are typical. There have been many, many cases of measles—one resulting in death, that of eight-year-old Maudie Baldwin, who died of "complications." Other illnesses have also resulted in death: typhoid fever (two deaths), scarletina (a few) and diphtheria. A few wounds and other injuries have been recorded, one a "gunshot through the right lung."

Death "called," in the grim lines of the book, from consumption/tuberculosis, "anasarea" tuberculosis, pneumonia, smallpox, diphtheria, typhoid fever, prolonged fever, Bright's disease of kidney, cholera, blood poisoning, scarlet fever, malarial fever, grippe, paralysis, "old age," asphyxia and even rheumatism. One succumbed "by taking poison, carbolic acid."

Other deaths are caused by less common medical terms, including membrane croup, "glutial" abscess, "entero" colitis, strangulation by goiter constriction, lung trouble, chronic gastric catarrh, disease of the testicles, blood passing, "plathisic" and gunshot to the neck resulting in deformity.

In the record of births, most mothers are noted as "housewife," of course, in the "occupation" column. Men's occupations include "laborer," a railroad telegrapher and a "section boss," as well as one who "runs livery stable." A reference to a glassblower living locally is not surprising considering the many glass factories in this locale due to the cheap and abundant natural gas from wells drilled in several counties from Allen County across the Ohio state line from Toledo (a center for gas and oil production) to Grant, Blackford and even some in Hamilton County. It is not surprising that in the "born where" column, "North Carolina" is a common notation.

EDUCATION, AN OBLIQUE VIEW

More positive and hopeful are a few random records from 1884 to 1893 that show school scenes, most in the town graded school, views from angles not seen in grade and attendance books. Some school expenses are: wood at $1.35 a cord ($12.50 total, reimbursed by the township trustee) and burned for heat in 1884, '85, '87 and '88, with coal used also in '88, and gas in '89 and '90. Purchases also include blackboards, chalk, window shutters for the first-floor classrooms (made in town by William Talbert at the lumber company), paint, an organ (Pearson & Co.), $35 for maps and a horse feed bin ($1.25). A Westfield Gas Company bill in 1891 has found its way among this sheaf of papers, as well as a receipt for $2 as toll on the gravel pike. The schoolhouse grounds have been rented out as pasture for $10.

Another record book contains file copies of teacher contracts with salary figures ranging from $40 to $80 per month. Teachers named include Katie Coffin, Ella Pickett, Regina Mills, Lissie Ellis, all as of July 7, 1891.

Two school principals have held the job during this time: A.P. Howe, "elected" as of July 2, 1886, and Amos Sander, June 24, 1889. This "graded school," the term still used for schools that divide students into grades by student age, is composed of "primary," "grammar" and "intermediate" grade, "first through fourth" and "fifth and sixth" grades. Schools out in the township are listed geodetically at Range 18, Township 3E, 19-4E, and at 19-3E, 18-4E, 19-4E and 18-4E.

The minutes of school board meetings between June 9, 1884, and June 10, 1893, are brief, varying little one meeting to the next, consisting mostly of listings of and motions to pay bills for the school in town.

The relationship between the town and the township schools is detailed. An agreement was made between the township trustee and the school trustees of "Westfield Corporation" for "a joint graded school" referencing Section 4446 of "the state school law" of Indiana, to be taught in the Westfield school on Penn Street and "in such other buildings as may be provided by the trustees of the two corporations." There is also an agreement giving the township trustee "entire management of

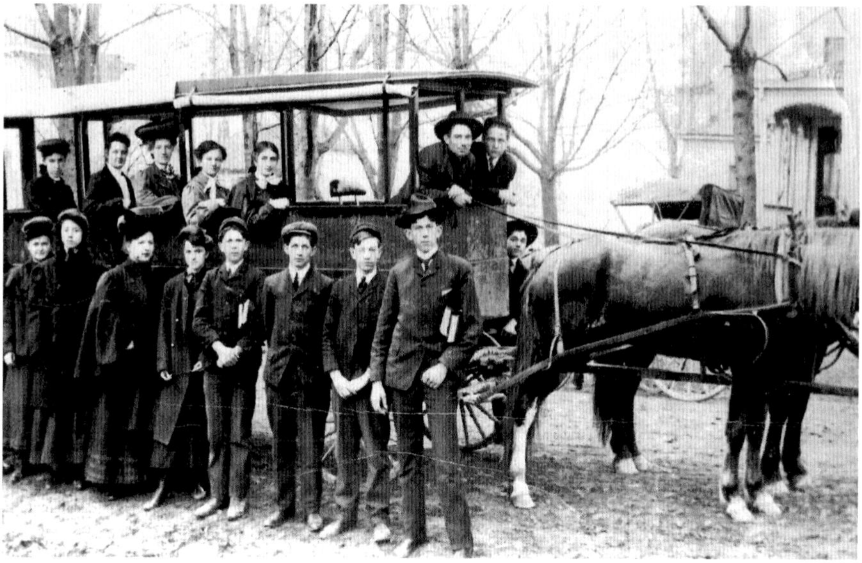

School hack, Washington Township to Westfield High School, early 1900s.

the 'joint' school." Fifty girls and thirty boys are named to be transferred to the joint school "to be better accommodated by the change."

In another agreement signed on July 5, 1892, the township trustee agrees to "furnish the town of Westfield good and efficient schools." At the same time, an amendment to the agreement will allow for tuitions paid out of the "School Fund of Westfield Corporation" to be reimbursed to the township trustee by the county treasurer.

Not mentioned in these random records is the matter to eventually require all students in each grade to use the same textbook instead of parents choosing books from an assortment at a store in town.

9

Growing Up from the Early 1900s

Lives as Bridges

Two longtime residents of Westfield personify both small-town beginnings and the expansiveness some can know in their lives with achieving significant success well away from their hometowns. Both are children of the first decade of the twentieth century. Both were graduates of Westfield High School. Mary Stalker Bray and Malcolm Bray can well represent their generation, born, raised, educated and residing here for the major portions of their lives. Mary was born in 1918 not far outside town, Malcolm two years earlier in 1916 out in the township. Both were born at home ("You only went to the hospital to die," they laugh). She is the daughter of Herman and Esther Baker Stalker, her pioneer-era last name dating to the 1840s, and he was born to Porter and Gail Banen Bray.

Mary attended several schools in her twelve years of public education. Her father was a teacher and principal. She attended Earlham College. Malcolm graduated two years before Mary and, with a fellowship to Massachusetts Institute of Technology, received his doctorate in chemistry. He would find important work in oils and fuels during World War II, eventually becoming a chemist at Eli Lilly Pharmaceutical Company in Indianapolis, where he achieved several patents with the native Indiana company with the familiar logo. Both were brought up

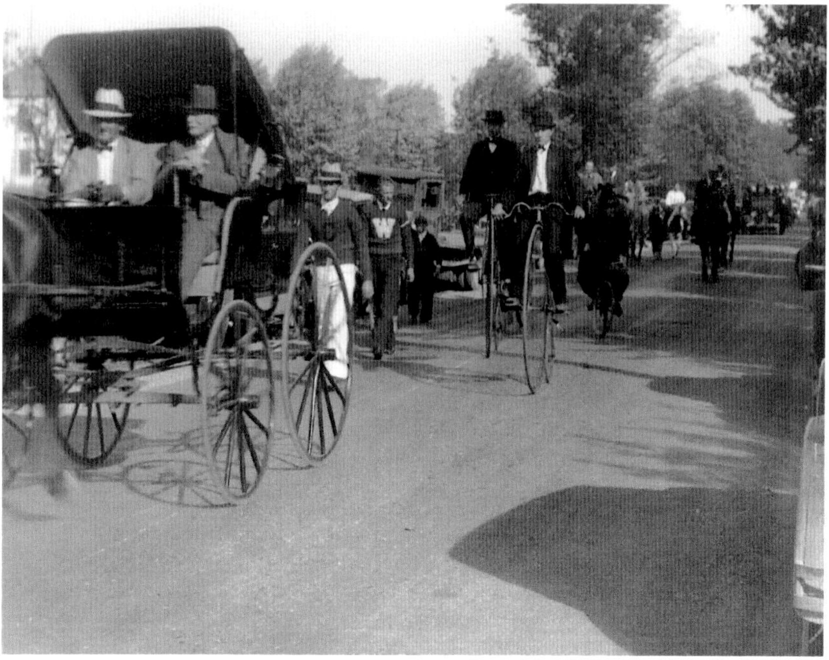

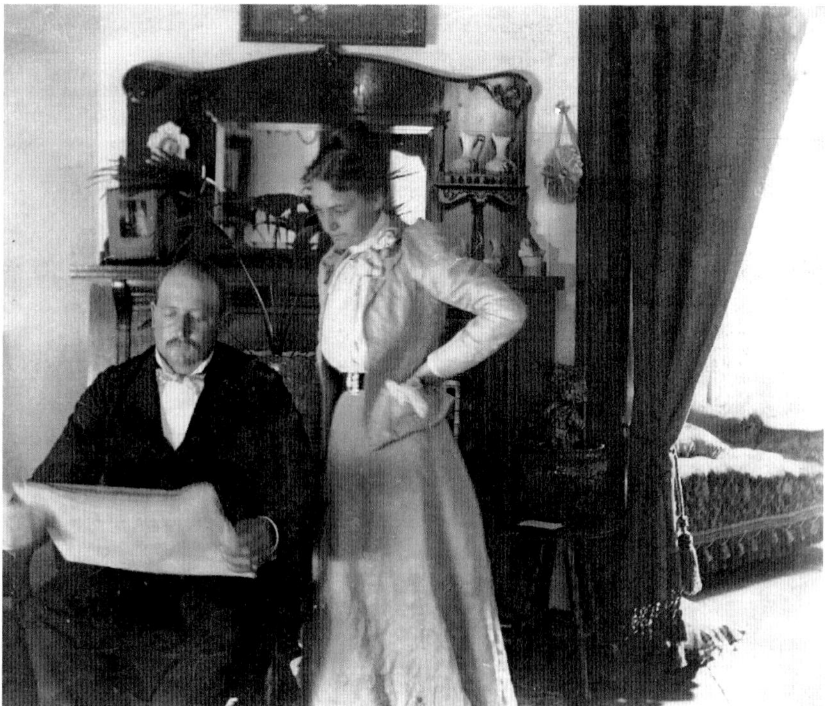

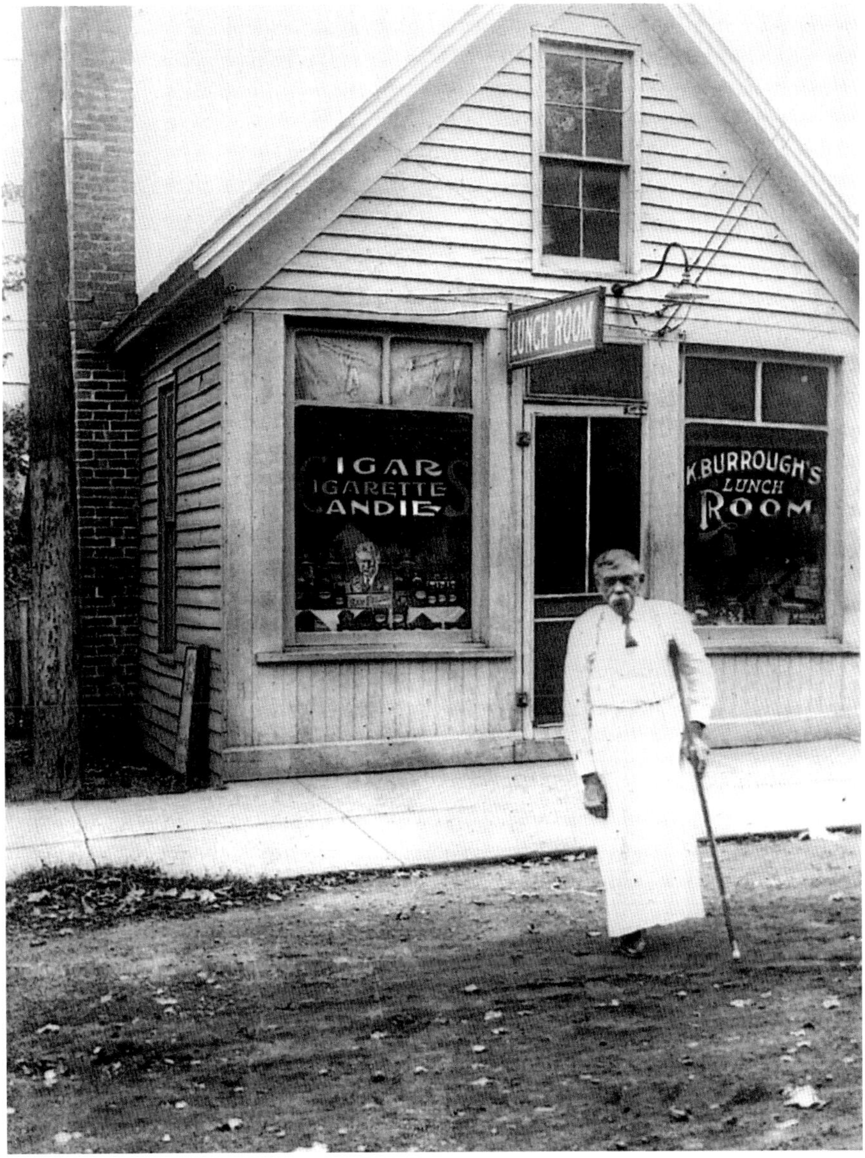

Burrough's Lunch Room, Westfield, early 1900s.

Opposite, top: Parade during the 1934 Centennial in Westfield.

Opposite, bottom: Home interior in Westfield, 1898.

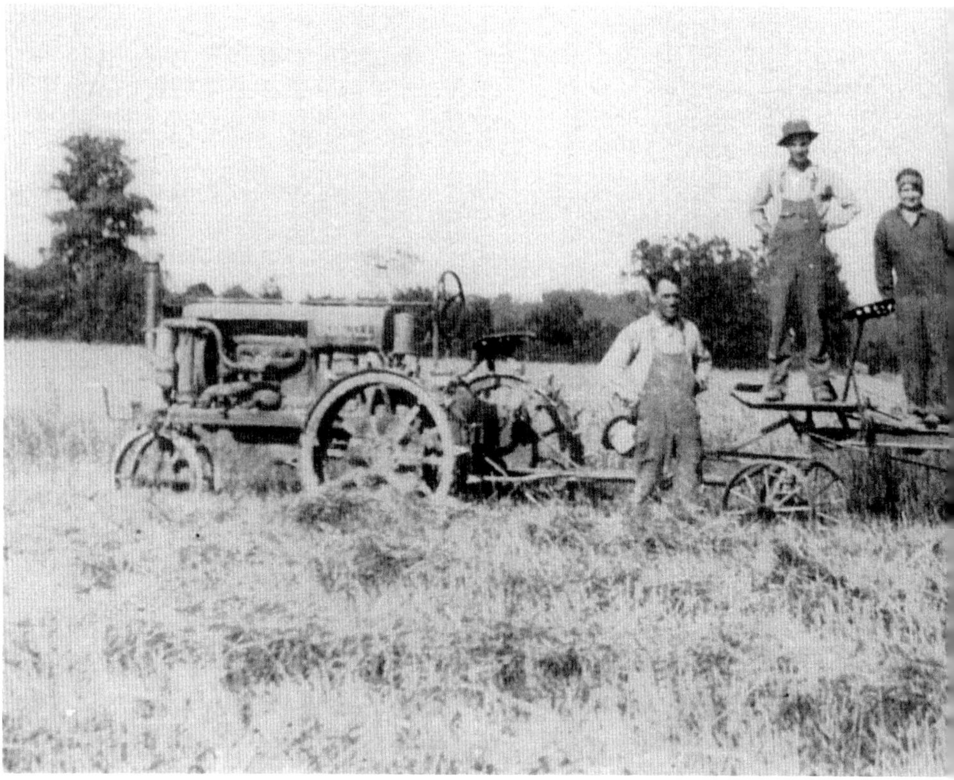

Threshing on a Washington Township farm.

well aware of the distinct religious heritage of their Quaker faith. Their elders had distinct ethical and moral codes. They both were instilled with an appreciation and an appetite for continuing education. Mary's father and Malcolm's sister both graduated from the widely respected Union High School in 1908 and 1909, respectively.

Malcolm enjoys recalling the former farm scenes, like the iconic threshing of wheat. "Along about the Fourth of July, when the wheat, sewn the previous fall, was ready to cut but not quite ripe, it was cut using the old cradle scythes and put in shocks." Then the shocks were brought to the threshing engine, and the stalks would be run up a conveyor and tied automatically and run off into a bundle carrier that had to be dumped every so often. Sheaves caught up in the bundle carrier, and the operator had to dump that every so often. "The wheat had a milky content and had to dry. The whole neighborhood would come out, and we'd thresh."

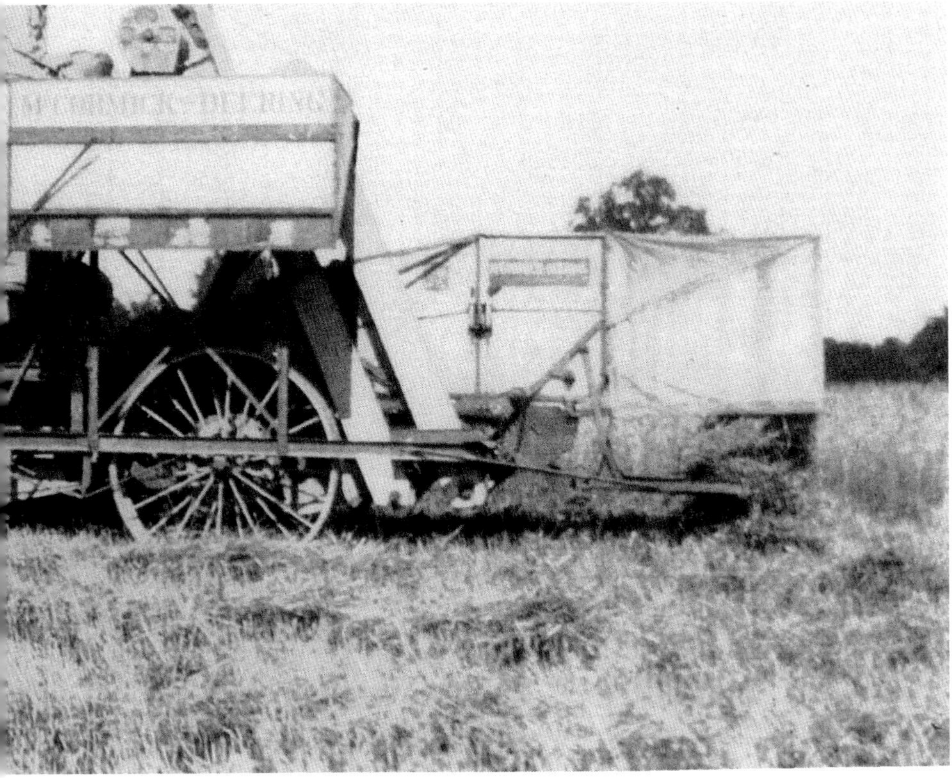

"The threshing engine would start north of Hinkle Church and go east a mile or so, and from there we'd start threshing and work our way down through the farms almost to Route 32. Everyone in that area would come out and help." The steam-driven threshing engines of his childhood were replaced with kerosene or gasoline-burning stationary tractors with a belt running the threshing machine and the bundle wagon beside it.

They remember when the two railroads crossing at Westfield helped define the town's location. When Malcolm's dad was a boy working on a threshing crew and something broke and a part was needed, he would ride his bicycle to town, hop the Monon to Indianapolis, get the part and return with it, and the threshing would continue. He remembers before electrically lighted train signals that there was "a big pole with signal arms on it at the top at the crossing and if the train was 'in the block' a signal arm would move to show it was coming." Mary made train connections to Muncie to visit relatives. "As late as 1949 I took the train from Sheridan—it didn't stop at Westfield by then—and rode to Chicago and then to Santa Fe and to the west coast."

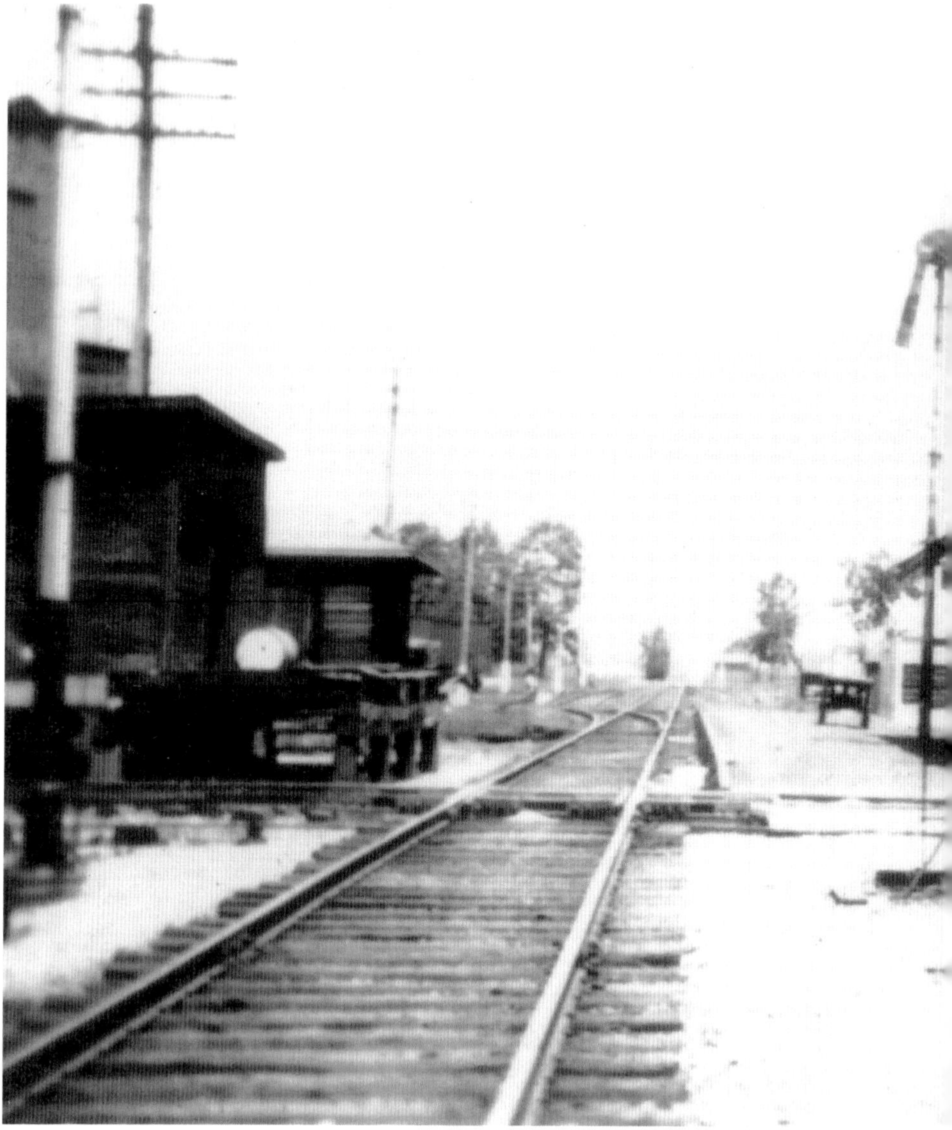

The Monon Railroad depot in Westfield, 1929.

Mary's family had "an open Maxwell with side curtains for bad weather, and a luggage rack on the running board." For a trip to Peru, "we had to start early in the morning. We stopped about halfway at Hopewell Church for a packed lunch. The fifty-mile adventure took at least four hours. And if it

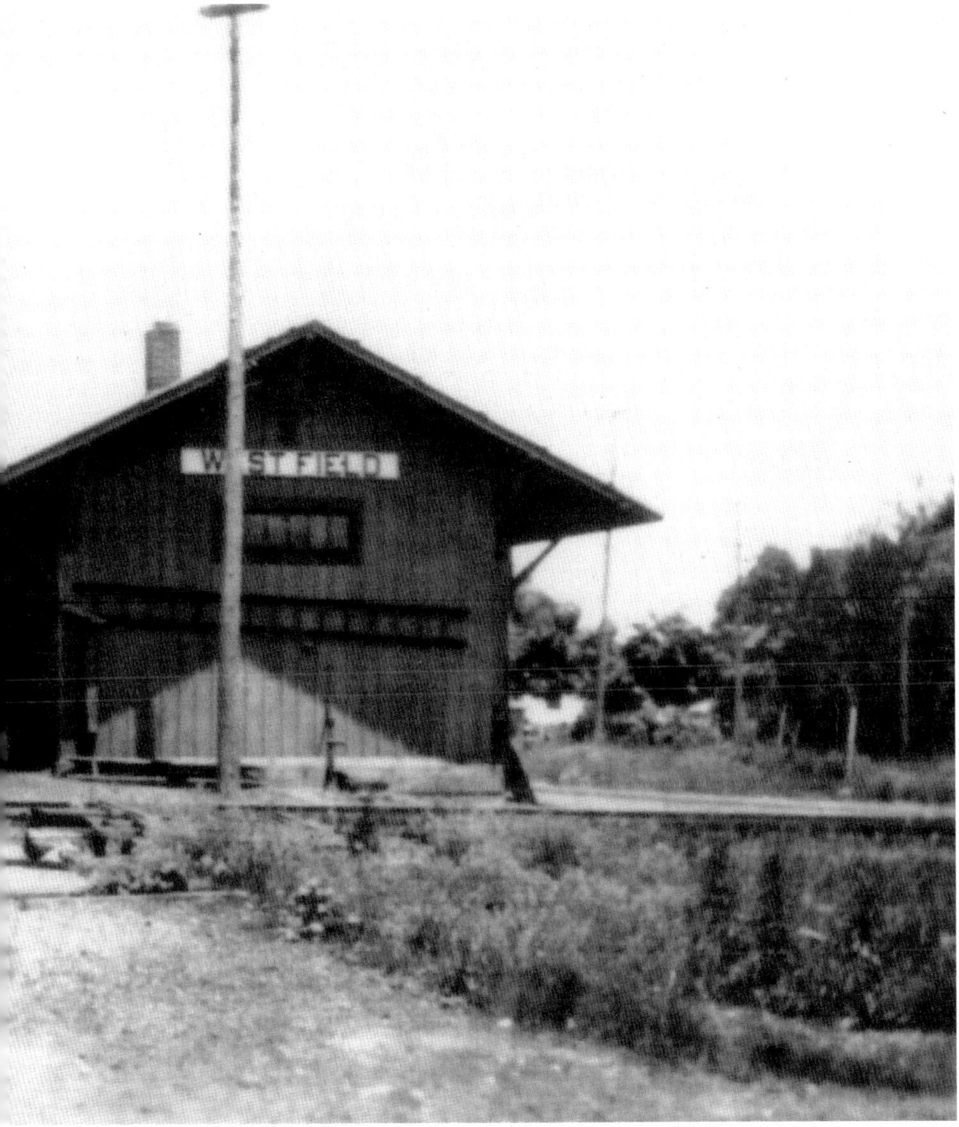

had rained it got muddy so much so that the trip was wisely canceled." Her grandfather Baker had one of the first cars in Westfield. "You could drive if your legs could reach the pedals." To get up the hill on 31, "we backed the car up the hill." Malcolm explains: "The gear ratio in reverse was so much lower than going forward," hence the extra boost for climbing hills. He also remembers the dust on the old roads being "kicked up" by the horses. "It could be stifling," he says.

Malcolm learned to drive in a Model T, but he went to school with a horse and buggy, before a school hack was available. The hack was a "little wood body on a Model T Ford chassis," a convenience of sorts but without heat in winter. "When we came to a snow drift, the neighbors living on the road came to help dig out."

Mary's great-grandfather was "old Doc Hunt," who sometimes took his son along to play with the children of the patients he treated. The doctor who delivered her was "old Doc Fodrea." She still has the twenty-five-cent check her father wrote for her delivery. (Even later in the 1950s, local doctors still made house calls.)

Malcolm, the chemist, describes the patent medicines of their times, like castor oil and "syrup of pepsin," which he explains was a kind of "neutralizing cordial." And the age-old purgative calomel "was mercury chloride. If it had been a soluble it would have killed you, but it was insoluble so it went right through you." If the patient insisted on a pill, the doctor might use calomel as an obliging sugar pill. And there was always the "Lydia Pinkham" bottle handy, used mostly by women, popular, in part, for its alcohol content. "Many doctors mixed their own Lydia Pinkham–like stuff with their handy mortar and pestle."

"The first penicillin used had to be injected every four hours. The dosages would decompose by gastric acid so it could not be given by mouth. With pneumonia, you'd fill out the death certificate and leave the date off," to be filled in when the fully expected happened. "Now, to really jolt the immune system, you give them pneumonia" to start the recovery reaction.

Mary mentions in particular the washing of clothes in a large copper pot on the stove to boil the clothes, then wringing each piece out by hand or between crank rollers and then hanging each piece on the backyard clothesline. "Then came the cradle-like thing that the woman rocked back and forth" to agitate the washing process. Though it was hard work, "some women didn't want the first electric washing machines; they said you have to scrub by hand to really get the dirt out. Then better soaps and detergents came along. Mothers filled the round galvanized metal tub for the family's baths, and the hot water added came from the hot water reservoir on the cookstove or from a teakettle. But then that was only a Saturday job," she laughs. The housewife also tended the essential vegetable garden, picked the "small fruit" grown, fed the chickens (fried for the Sunday meal or kept to produce eggs) and washed the dishes without running water, or they might have a small hand pump in the sink. She canned fruits and vegetables to preserve a large stock of food for the winter. She remembers the later arrival of "the 'Conservo cooker,'" a tall container that steamed the vegetables already in the canning jars and then sealed the capped jars with "red waxy stuff."

The many milling operations were as necessary as they were in pioneer days. Malcolm often hauled grain to the mill when in high school. "There were mills around, one at Horton, three at Noblesville. We'd sell some wheat and get the rest ground into flour." The trip to the mill was about four miles from the farm of Malcolm's youth. There was usually a wait until each customer's turn for the grinding. In winter, he faced the brisk north wind when returning from the mill. If the day was especially cold, he got off the wagon and walked to keep warm. Grain was also ground up for animal feed. Corn, oats and wheat were the common crops, as well as some rye.

Both the Brays laugh at their hesitance still to sign contracts; in their youth, business deals were done on a Quaker handshake. Such dealings were, when renting farm fields or buying a field, agree on the price, shake hands, pay and start to work. If buying hay, for example, the price was agreed on with a handshake, and when the hay was harvested, it was delivered and paid for in cash, no receipt involved. "The IRS didn't understand that," Malcolm laughs.

Mary says she read in the *Indiana Magazine of History* in about 1992 that many of the temperance people joined the Klan. "Not here," she insists. Malcolm describes the Klan parades in Noblesville and the cross burnings, the white robes and masks in the 1920s but, again, "not here."

The Brays have been involved in local schools, he as a school board member for twenty-four years with a special interest in teacher training. He remembers, "You could teach school after one semester of college." Mary mentions the "normals," the teacher conferences with emphases on teaching methods, held regularly in the school off-season, a continuing sign of interest in quality education. But Malcolm also remembers when, "sometime in the 1950s," some in the community would not support including a swimming pool in a new construction project "if boys and girls were going to swim together."

Malcolm remembers when a meeting was held in the old high school auditorium to discuss building a new school building, and even as "there were buckets in the halls, in the study hall and all around to catch water from the leaking roof, and this during a downpour," there was still opposition. And while this meeting took place, teachers allowed the kids to come and watch this tax board meeting. So much for observing firsthand local self-government in action. Maybe it all could have been avoided if new terminology had been used. Some years ago, in another public meeting about yet another building plan, the promoters called a planned swimming pool a natatorium instead, and as Malcolm tells it, "the idea went right through" with majority approval.

The Brays tell also of the natural gas phenomenon here playing out as it did elsewhere. It came in about 1900, he was told, and "there were gas wells all over this area. But they didn't take care of it all; they let the gas pressure drop." But for a while, his parents had "gas lines all through the house for light" but not for heat or cooking. "When the gas ran out, with the lines still running into the house, we went to an acetylene system, gas generated by dripping water on calcium carbide." This also produced lime that they put on the farm fields. "It was fairly common for people to have their own acetylene generators, though some went back to kerosene lamps." But before long, "the acetylene system rusted through the old pipes in the ground, and when that happened, we also went back to the lamps." Then the family installed "a Delco system" (for Dayton Engineering Laboratories Company). There were "quite a few in the country but were expensive." This was "a gasoline engine hooked to a 32-volt generator that charged batteries, direct

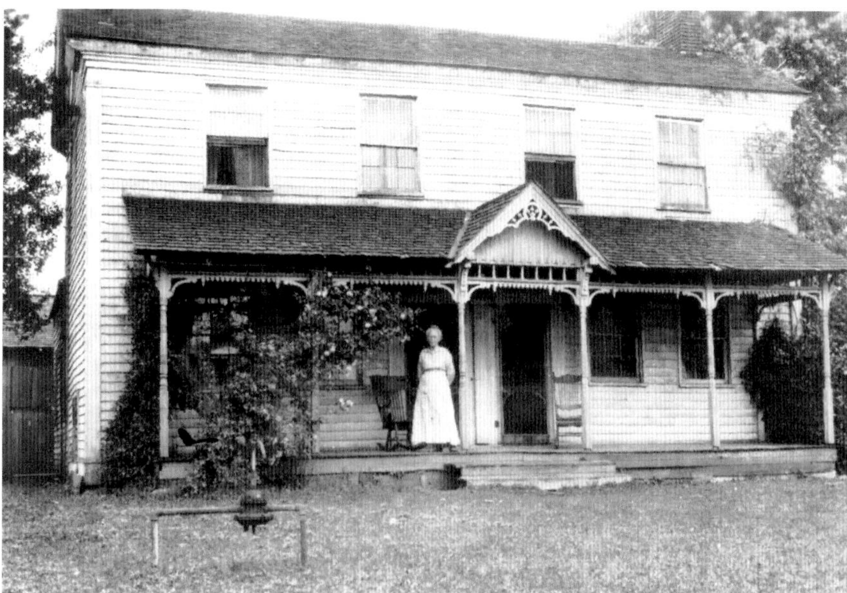

The home of Dr. Link Baldwin, North Union Street, Westfield, late nineteenth century. Note the natural gas pipes and meter in front yard. Many gas wells in the county supplied homes for several years before wasteful use depleted the well.

current. We used that for awhile." At the time, "there was a high-tension line going through here, but they wouldn't let us hook into it" for electricity. Eventually, "they got a 110-volt system" that they could access; he can't remember when exactly. Folks in town had electricity by about 1911, and many farmers moved to town when they retired.

Mary's grandparents Dolly and Aldin Stalker lived about a mile south of Horton and had a hot water system for heat. "The furnace heated a boiler that circulated hot water through radiators all through the house." And they had a Delco system for a while also. "It was noisy," she says. Her grandpa even put a bathroom in the house about 1917. It was one of the first country homes to have a bathroom, and it was a great improvement over the old outhouse used before. Before, during the night, and especially in winter, the family used a "slop jar" when nature called, and someone had the chore of emptying the contents each morning at the outhouse. Her family had a windmill that generated some electricity. And in that new indoor bathroom, they had a flush toilet that used an electric-powered pump: "Very unusual." That hot water system was in use until it was replaced by gas heating, some seventy or seventy-five years later, she says

They return to the time before the ever-busy Route 31 was moved from the center of town. Mary's grandmother had a sign in the yard, "Tourist Rooms," a fairly common thing in Westfield for a while. Mary thinks this was around 1927 or so. The tourists ate breakfast at the Westfield Cafeteria, handy across the street, owned by Lowell Carey, "where Mildred Stalker lives now" (Mary is recalling this in 1992). Mary doesn't remember the exact street address; "back then we just said 'four houses from the corner.'"

Before their time, when the "pikes" were financed by tolls charged, there was a tollbooth at the north end of town before the advent of federal Route 31. But there were also "shunpikes" to the west and east before traffic reached the tollgate, and people would use these bypasses to keep from paying the toll.

The two telephone operators Malcolm remembers were Lula Cox during days and Lola Cultrum at night. The system did not extend outside town for a while. The telephone was in a small cabinet-like thing that hung on the wall. "You turned a crank to create electricity to connect with the switch board," Malcolm says. There was the "general ring" on the old phones, a separate ring that alerted everyone of an emergency; "it rang as long as you cranked, and the operators could get help" for the one causing the ring. When Catherine Overman Casey's husband, Donald, had been overseas and had returned to the States, he called her from the East Coast late at night,

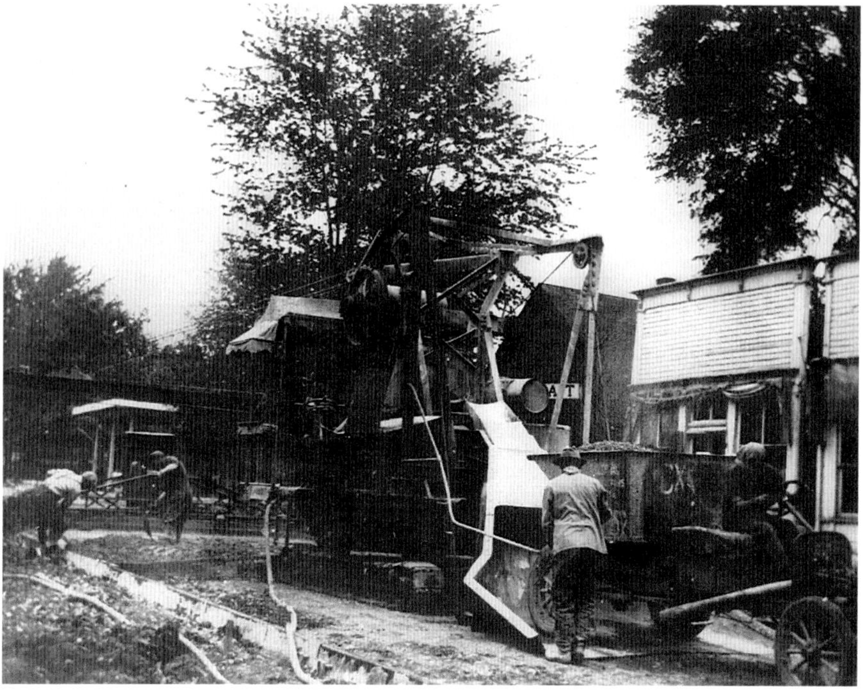

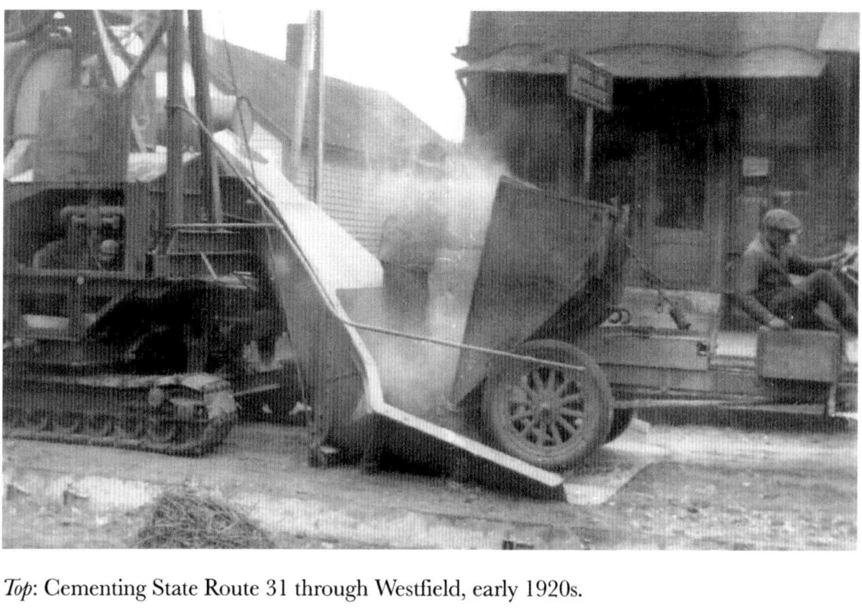

Top: Cementing State Route 31 through Westfield, early 1920s.

Bottom: Cementing State Route 31 through Westfield, early 1920s.

and Catherine was half asleep as they talked. In the morning, Catherine thought maybe it had been a dream, so she rang up Lola and asked if Don had called last night, and the operator said, "Yes, and here is what he said," and she repeated the entire conversation.

Even with doctors in town, people relied on some home remedies. To treat coughs, Mary's grandmother sliced an onion, put brown sugar on it, covered it with another saucer, put it all on the stove to melt the sugar and you had onion syrup. Mary laughs: "I don't remember if it worked or not, but I took a lot of it."

The Brays treated colds by rubbing goose grease on their chests and laid a hot flannel cloth on it, "to keep the cold from going into your chest" to avoid pneumonia, a potentially deadly illness. "Then mentholatum came along. It was a dilator for the mucus in your nose." In the spring, "you breathed the steam from sassafras tea to thin your blood," said to be necessary to energize you for the coming outdoor labor season.

10

The Late 1930s: The *Shamrock Times*

The weeklong spirited community activity during Westfield's 100th anniversary year of 1934 is hardly more intense than a typical school day with the entire student body under one roof. And all that energy and motion animates the Westfield High School (WHS) newspaper, the *Shamrock Times*.

The mid-1930s is the depth of the Great Depression. But no hint is given in the school paper of any local effects of the nation's economic crisis. To read the school paper is to live an active, enthused life with some minor irritations hinted at now and then, though the teacher is never named. For those with access to an automobile, cautions come from all sides, as in this little rhyme, a touch morbid, in an issue of the school paper: "Grandpa in a speedy car, pushed the throttle down too far, twinkle twinkle little star, music by the G.A.R." (In the 1930s, there were still a few Civil War soldiers around, in their eighties or nineties, members of their veterans' organization, the Grand Army of the Republic.) The *Shamrock* writers include comments of particular insight, some philosophizing and some maxims and truisms still meaningful if long familiar.

Occasionally, the paper will feature a faculty member or the principal and, once, even the township trustee. Among the teaching staff of ten shown at the front of the school annual for 1937–38, there are teachers with credentials from such renowned institutions of higher learning as Columbia and Cornell Universities. Several attended Indiana University, which under the leadership of Herman B Wells is taking its place among the

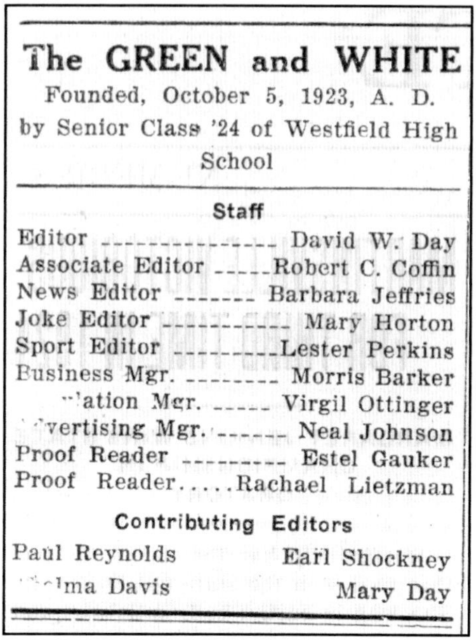

The GREEN and WHITE
Founded, October 5, 1923, A. D.
by Senior Class '24 of Westfield High School

Staff

Editor ---------------- David W. Day
Associate Editor -----Robert C. Coffin
News Editor ------- Barbara Jeffries
Joke Editor ----------- Mary Horton
Sport Editor ---------Lester Perkins
Business Mgr. -------- Morris Barker
...lation Mgr. ----- Virgil Ottinger
...vertising Mgr. ------ Neal Johnson
Proof Reader --------- Estel Gauker
Proof Reader.....Rachael Lietzman

Contributing Editors

Paul Reynolds — Earl Shockney
...lma Davis — Mary Day

Staff roster for Westfield High School newspaper, late 1930s.

top schools in the nation. Closer to home, several teachers have degrees from Ball State Teachers College and, of course, the Quakers' own Earlham College. Most have master's degrees or are completing them during the summers.

A few teachers featured in cursory sketches include Miss Myra Mendenhall, home economics teacher, of an ancient Quaker lineage, born and reared in Westfield, attended the nearly requisite Earlham College, as well as Bradley Polytechnic Institute in Peoria, Illinois, followed by an adventurous and courageous venture to Columbia University and then Aimes University in Iowa. The student writers for the paper ask each interviewee their most succinct advice. From Miss Mendenhall comes: "Use your vote and be informed." Concise but replete with meaning for this member of a prominent local family whose female members have been on the forefront of the everlasting temperance campaigns and among those calling for the vote for women. It has been but a couple of decades since the U.S. Constitution was amended so that women could take their rightful places at the voting booth along with men.

Helen Louise Lowe attended a Lutheran parochial school and Indiana University. Among her interests are piecing quilts and aviation. She prefers the *Firestone Hour* and *Kay Kyser's Kollege of Musical Knowledge* on the radio, favors Spencer Tracy and Bette Davis in the movies and relaxes by walking in the rain. And she has met Fritz Kreisler (Friedrich "Fritz" Kreisler, the world-famous violist, visiting this country this very year).

First-year history teacher Harold Blackburn attended Indiana University and Ball State. He is dean of boys and intones very seriously, "The results of the world war [World War I] are an underlying cause of the present world conflict [the agitation for war by Adolf Hitler]. Distrust…between nations and individuals has formed the attitude of war."

A couple of "downstairs" interviewees are Leonard Fisher, high school janitor, who advises, "Use some of your intelligence in tidiness of your desks and the surrounding floor." Janitor Mr. Woods at the grade school floor level "hopes the next generation will surpass the present one in fastidiousness."

In March 1936, Mrs. Francis Den Steightoll spoke in the high school auditorium on world peace "from the viewpoint of Quakers and youth." Like every serious speaker, she had her own superlative statistics to bolster her presentation. "The money spent on the world war," she said, "would have bought a $2,000 house for half the world's families, plus $1,000 of furniture, five acres of land at $100 an acre, a $5,000 library or hospital for every town of 20,000 or more and $10,000 for a college." Canada, she continued, spends $1.25 per person for armament; the United States, $5.60; and Italy, currently $8 per citizen. At the other end of the range of programs, a "convict" also spoke of the severity of discipline in reformatories and prisons.

The music department has created its own world of achievement, part of which is its many appearances in local venues. In April 1936, winners of solos and ensembles in district contests played at the Methodist church a trumpet trio; flute, bass and string trio; and violin solo. Some students played at their teacher's recital. WHS was represented at the piano festival at the Butler University field house for national music week. Lou Ellen Rouch, Francis Furnas, June Moore and Leona Ray were the WHS entries among a total of one thousand student pianists.

There are fifty-six members of the WHS band. They give concerts for students and the home crowd. The band plays at every football and basketball game, a total of thirty-one games. They have played for the National Mail Carriers' Convention in Indianapolis at the Hotel Severn and at Wild's Opera House in Noblesville.

The school orchestra of fifty members was begun in 1929 and has won four awards in first division, three in first division on the state level and one second division in a national competition. The orchestra includes fifteen violins, five cellos, an oboe, a bassoon, a piano and full-size harps.

A student writer listed several popular tunes arranged in one long sentence:

> *"Sugar Plum" was living in "The Great Way in London,"* [during?] *"The Rainy Night" because "Lulu's Back in Town" and "There's Nothing Like a College Education," but then "Boys Will Be Boys," when they're "Dancing Cheek to Cheek" with "Margie."*

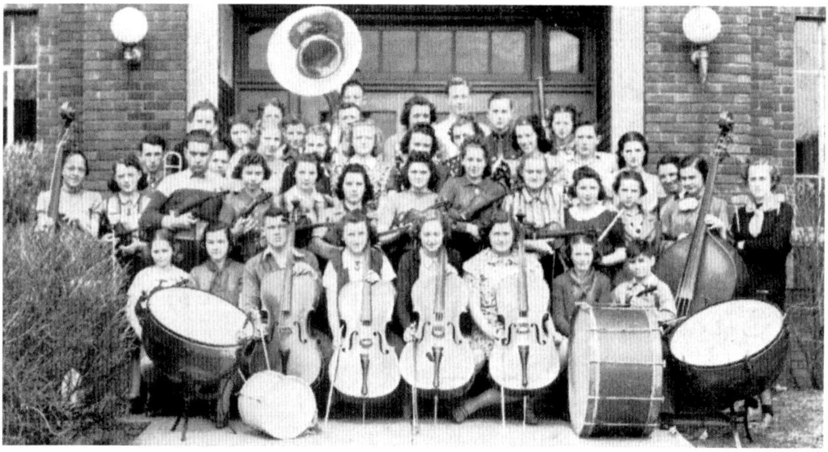

Westfield High School band, late 1930s.

The commercial students also travel to competitions, and they have popular contests at school, which bring them fan mail for the speediest typists. One contest counts words typed per minute as miles traveled on a car trip. Mistakes are detours. The champion typists in 1937 were Mary Morford, Alice Huffman, Mary Powers, Jean Harvey, Helen Davis, Helen Dary, Esther Wicker and Mary Alice Huffman. Mary Bower was the top achiever and won a desk set. At a state contest in 1939, the students saw their first electric typewriter.

Support from the business community is given as partial funding for the production of the school newspaper and as paying for ads for their businesses, all hand lettered and illustrated by art students. Many of the ads are for those establishments offering ice cream and candy.

There have been a variety of stores, shops and services over the decades, and new ones come often enough to quell the stagnating part of familiarity. At the Sandwich Shop, ice cream is five cents in a Dixie cup or a double cone, fifteen cents for a pint and twenty-five cents for a quart. All candy bars at Funderburgh's are five cents apiece, three for ten cents. Favorite stores sell beauty aids for the girls, and town barbers give the occasional cropping for hirsute boys. The paper features ads such as: "Get your permanent for commencement at Sunny Roberts" salon in town. The Westfield beauty salon of R.A. Dooley offers "today's modern coiffure, softly waved, curled and kept permanently beautiful with permanent waves." Boys were prodded

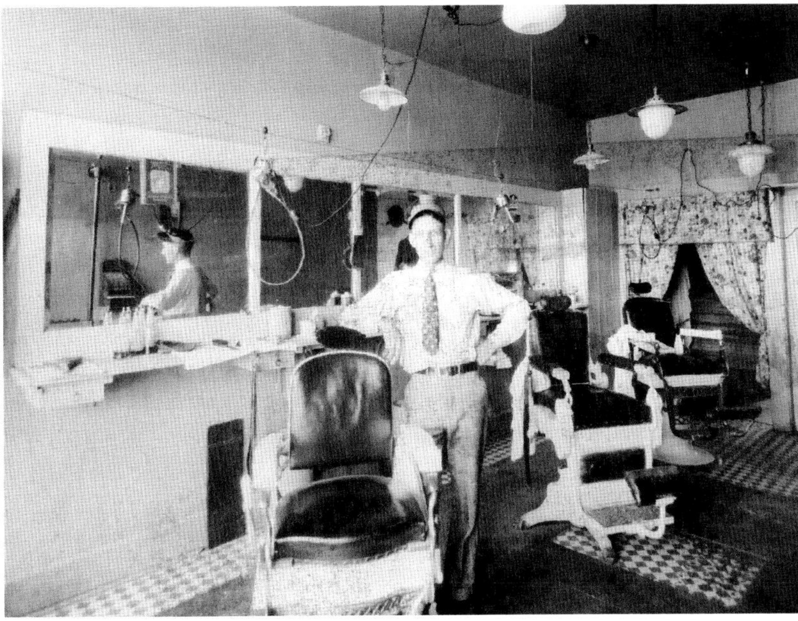

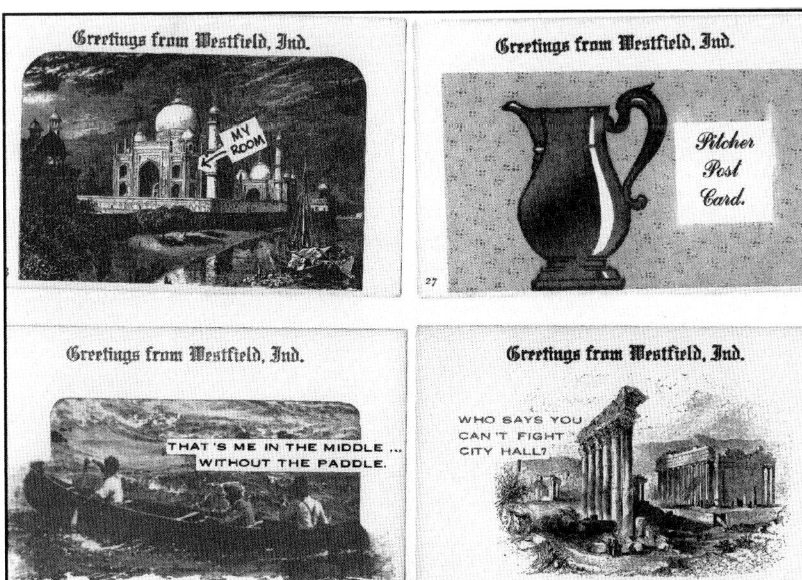

Top: "Doc" Ross barbershop, Westfield, 1930s.

Bottom: Humorous postcards sold in Westfield when State Route 31 was the primary highway north from Indianapolis to northern Indiana. Westfield restaurants and other stores were frequented for decades by travelers and tourists on the highway.

to "watch your hair, teeth, fingernails, neckties, shirt-tails. For unruly hair, use hair lotion or brilliantine."

With dating being perhaps the most nerve-rattling activity, students in the upper grades find occasional dating advice. Girls are advised to know how much money their dates have to spend before ordering their date night meals. They are also cautioned to learn the difference between "à la carte" and "table d'hôte" in pricing in the menu. And "Girls, be ready when your date arrives; trying for an hour to make conversation with strange parents is enough to daunt even the most valiant young man." Girls are reminded to "remember, make-up (rouge, powder, lipstick) is purely decorative, used to improve the face not hide it." And "don't reek of perfume." Also, "eyebrows plucked down to a mere thread are ruled out [and] don't paint your nails with heathen hues of red."

Nicknames appear in the issues, and most students know who is being referred to with monikers such as "Spud," "Dawsy," "Nonnie," "Chick," "Red," "June Bug," "Tank," "Tubby" and "Jitterbug." And then there is the girl called "Mae West."

School spirit "is more than vibrations derived from vocal chords at games." The paper reminds readers that school spirit extends to everyday activities as well. The February 14, 1936 issue included this student comment:

> *Our high school has a reputation for taking more razzing and still remaining on friendly terms than is possible in most schools. Visitors and teachers who have come from schools where good feelings did not exist have remarked on* [our] *good naturedly taking the razzing that was given in the right spirit. If we wish to maintain this spirit of friendliness we must be careful not to allow a censoring attitude. Our attitude along this line is very good.*

A major prompt for school spirit has long been "Glory to Old Westfield," written in 1912 by student Byford Inman, who won a five-dollar prize for his lyrics, which were arranged by WHS music teacher Harry Bowman. Other long-standing school rhymes appear now and then in the school paper, such as "Eastfield, Westfield, all around the town, Northfield, Southfield, nothing keeps us down, Original home of the Dove of Peace, Where slavery found release, City of Friends that shall never cease, We're bound to gain renown."

Students look forward to field trips. A senior class outing at a skating party at Pendleton had "practically no casualties," but a repeat on April

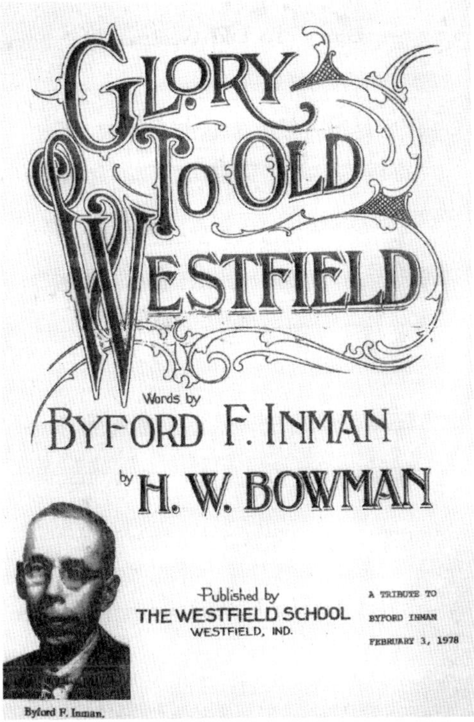

Westfield High School song, written by Byford Inman in 1912 and arranged by school music teacher Harry Bowman.

Fools' Day was completely safe: the place was closed. The proximity to the state capital city offers ready destinations. A field trip in the fall of 1937 visited the Children's Museum in Indianapolis to see "birds and animals from all over the world, the first automobile and bicycle." Then the students were conducted to both the W.T. Grant and the Woolworth "five and ten [cents] store" wonder worlds. They were also taken to the famous L.S. Ayers department store, to the eleventh-floor bakery, the tenth floor hospital and telephone departments, the ninth-floor art gallery and the eighth-floor beauty salon "and baggage department."

Each issue of the school paper would be considerably shorter but for the constant flow of school sports news. According to the 1935 school annual, the *Shamrocket*, Westfield High School was "the smallest school in the state to play football."

The 1936 football season was successful, with six wins and two losses, one of which was to Noblesville with its much larger population from which to recruit the particular athletic capabilities for football, and Manual High School, one with an even larger talent pool. One Westfield player was selected by the *Indianapolis Times* for a spot on the All State High School Football Team.

And there was basketball, of course, played against Arcadia, Walnut Grove, Sheridan, Carmel, Atlanta, Broad Ripple, Fishers, Noblesville, Cicero and New Augusta and, in the county tournament, Zionsville, Fortville and Kirklin. And the school track team, the "thins," occasionally got its due acknowledgements as well.

At the end of the 1939–40 school year, a few seniors named their choice of colleges to attend; the list included Indiana University, DePauw, Chicago Art School (two students), Earlham, Purdue, Taylor and "business college" (two students).

Expressions of religious faith are made at school, as well as at many civic and other public events. People here are comfortable with expressions of religious faith and prayer at events not otherwise associated with any particular church. There has always been acknowledgement at school and

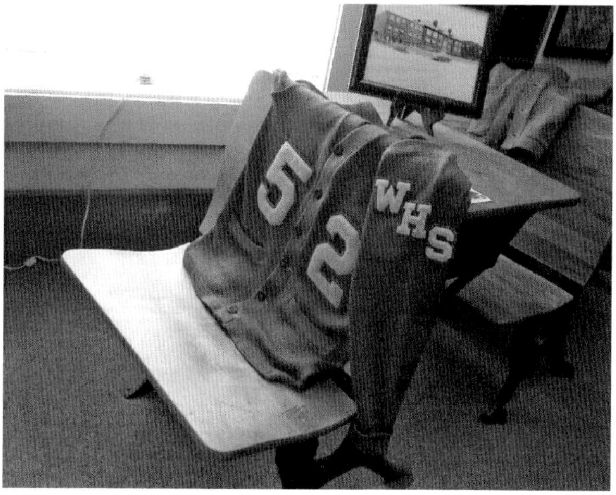

Westfield High School letter sweater, 1952, kelly green for the WHS "Shamrocks," the school mascot.

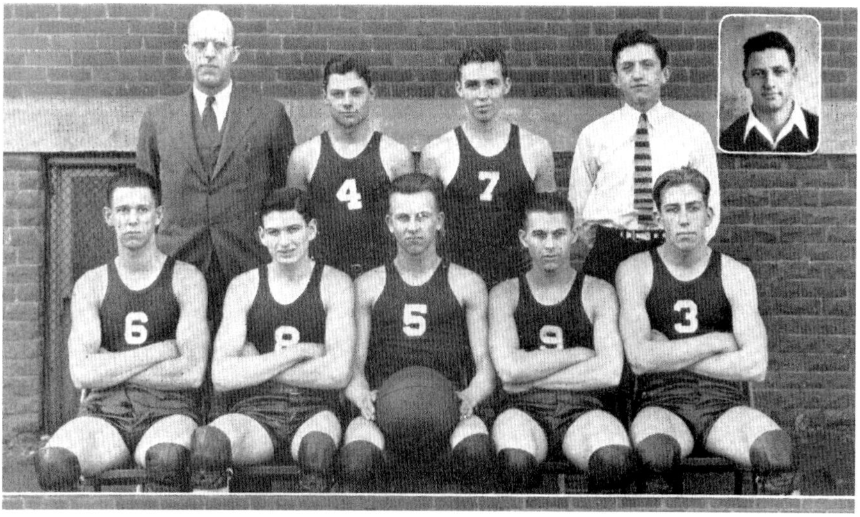

Westfield High School basketball team, 1930s. Note the leather knee guards.

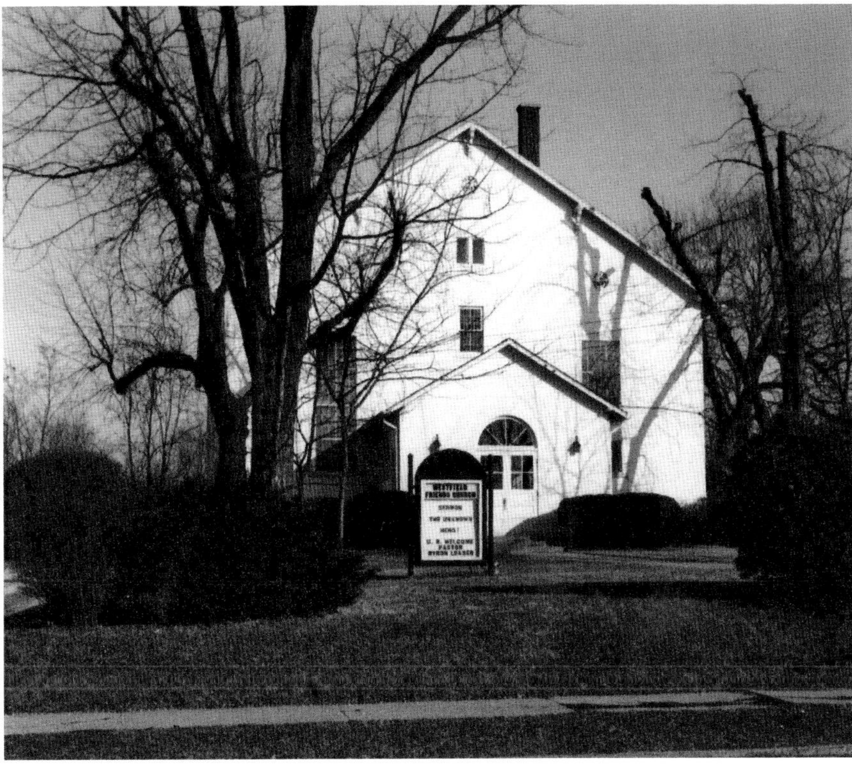

Westfield Friends Church (Meetinghouse), built in 1888 on the grounds of the original log meetinghouse of 1835.

public functions of religious faiths. Social club meetings begin with prayer. Many school activities that include the entire student body or events outside school begin with a prayer by a visiting pastor or others.

The second semester issue of the *Shamrock Times* in 1939 has additional pages to feature sketches of all the churches in town and gives the number of students attending: Westfield Friends (21), Methodists (11), Wesleyan Methodists (4) and the township churches at Hortonville Friends (8), Little Eagle Creek Friends (4), Eagletown Friends (6), Horton Methodist (2) and Hinkle Creek Friends (7). The adult editorial sponsor wrote, "The church is the crowning glory of all learning. Church helps us to apprehend the eternal verities of life." In tune with this acknowledgement of the familiarity of religion to nearly all in town and the surrounding countryside and its three villages, so the local PTA often begins meetings with prayer.

11

The 1940s: Close to Home

Upstaging the Great Depression

Shortly after New Year's Day 1940, Mrs. Mabel Hinshaw and sons James and Joseph of Westfield get word that their ship leaving New York City for Bolivia will not be sailing because, as stated in the *Noblesville Ledger*, "things are a little uncertain on account of war conditions." Their husband and father is presently in Bolivia maintaining the mission there of the Union Friends Church on South Union Street in Westfield, a long-standing supporter of the work there.

In early January 1941, another round of questionnaires from the county draft board were in the mail to young men, fifty of whom have already passed their physical exams and have been told to be ready for service when called. Another world war is imminent. America had been attacked at Pearl Harbor.

There is some disconcerting news on the local scene also. The *Ledger* calls it "an epidemic of robberies" in the Westfield community during recent weeks. The latest is a break-in at the schoolhouse. A door was pried open, and nearly every room was ransacked; in addition to the many pens and pencils missing, the thieves took "a compound microscope and a tripod microscope." No money was missing, and none of the typewriters "exposed to the search…were molested." The robberies have been puzzling the sheriff, who can find no clues on which he can begin to solve this serious annoyance. Last week, the house of Orval Cox, preacher at the Friends meeting, was robbed of fifty dollars. Sheriff Newby is asking that residents of Westfield and the township report anything they may know or see in this regard, reciting the essential law enforcement plea that "a thing that may seem of no importance might lead to something."

But life goes on apace. The annual banquet of the Hamilton County Dairy Herd Improvement Association met in January at Westfield on Monday. Local dairy products were second only to hogs in sales the previous year. The annual event brought together twenty-seven members owning a total of 457 cows.

During its ninety-fourth year, in 1944, the Methodist Church recognized seven individuals who had been members for fifty years: Mrs. Minnie Reeves Nordyke, Mrs. Gladys Funderburgh Benson, Mr. Paul D. Brown (church historian), Mrs. Emaline Fodrea, Mrs. Doris Fodrea Beals, Mrs. Margaret Fodrea Cardwell and Mr. Thomas O. Blair. Also the ladies of the long-standing Calendar Club were acknowledged for their direction of the church social life and fundraising. This early April Sunday service included a Bach fugue prelude and the appropriate hymn "The Church's One Foundation." The Methodists have been a religious influence in Westfield and the township just as the Friends and others have been over their long history here.

For fifteen years, beginning about 1850, Methodists here worshipped in private homes as part of a "class" awaiting organization while assembling with other religious "union" services, the most significant being Union Sabbath School. In 1865, they purchased the former Congregational church and organized. The Congregationalists, led by Reverend Jabez Neal, had built their church in 1855, the cost said to be $1,500 plus $300 for a bell. After a decade, they had diminished in number but had a lingering mortgage outstanding. A group of Baptists acquired the property for the $400 mortgage remaining, but they, too, failed to make a go of it. The church then stood unused for that purpose until the close of the Civil War (it is said the building was used as a recruiting station) when the Methodists acquired the building and grounds.

By the time the Methodists acquired the church, a sketch in the anniversary booklet shows two aisles aligning with the two front doors, wide pews in the middle with smaller ones on each side and a stove on each side about two-thirds of the way up from the back. At the front was the choir and organ on the left, the "mourners' bench" in the middle with the pulpit just beyond and the rousing "amen corner" on the right.

By then, the number of Methodist Episcopal worshipers was about twenty-five and included such prominent families as those of John Stephenson,

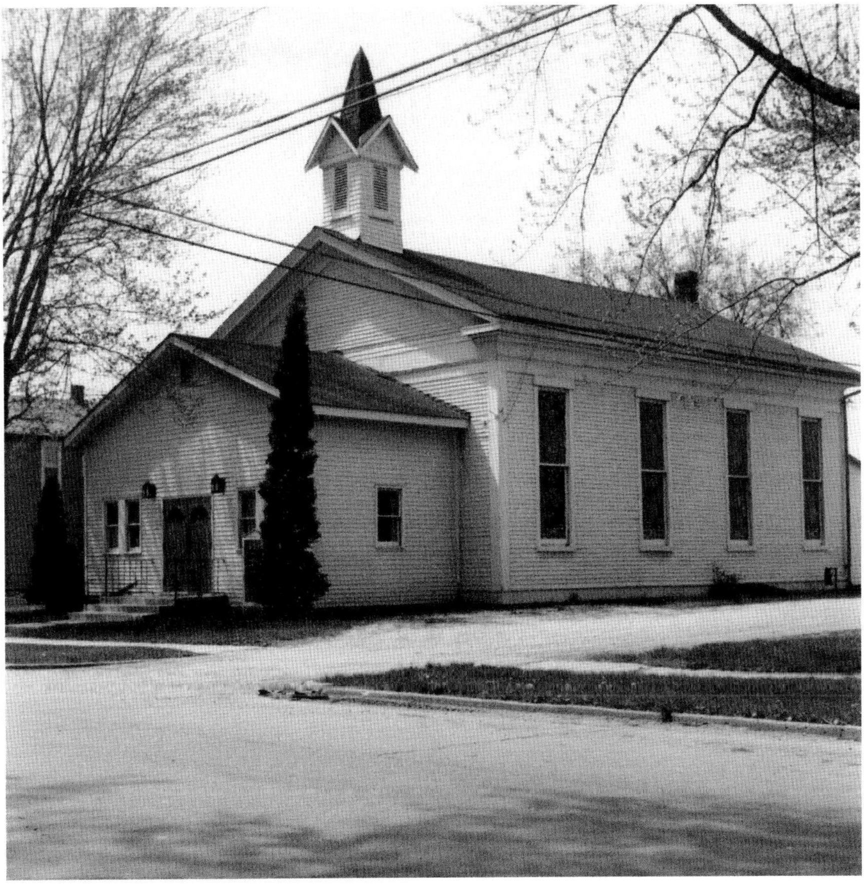

Westfield Methodist Church on Penn Street. The Methodists first built it in 1865 after meeting in homes for several years. The building is now Westfield City Hall.

Richard Hollis and John S. Conklin. (The few remaining Congregationalists had resumed the mortgage and offered it to any orthodox denomination that would assume the debt.) With this opportunity again open, the presiding elder of the district sent a young preacher, John Smay, to take charge. Smay began with a revival, which reportedly resulted in one hundred or more to be "gathered into the fold," one so enthusiastically that he borrowed the $400 needed to pay the mortgage then asked for subscriptions to pay off the loan. Westfield Methodist Episcopal Church then became a "Point" in the circuit centered around White Chapel church in Mattsville, south of Carmel.

Two years later, in 1867, under a second pastor, George Havens, the church gained circuit status with new congregations (Points) at Big Springs and Little Chicago, joined sometime later by those of Carmel, Jolietville, Sugar Grove, Deming and Hortonville. In these early years, paying the pastor was not a sure thing, but new arrivals were treated to a "pound party" of baskets of provisions and other useful items.

The Union Sabbath School had been attended by members of several churches, including the Presbyterians, United Brethren, Friends, Wesleyan Methodists, the remaining Congregationalists, the Newlights and the Campbellites. Then, in 1884, a determined Reverend S.V. Howard arrived from the East, where he had acquired a law degree, and insisted that the Methodists form their own Sabbath school, which he did regardless of the opposition of the organized union effort to break up a successful community religious service.

A parsonage was obtained for Reverend Howard. The Deming church was dropped from its affiliation for continual failure to pay their part of the pastor's salary. ("May God have mercy on their souls," Howard has been quoted as saying.) During his tenure, the bombastic pastor had two young men arrested for disturbing worship services, throwing one out bodily, for which he in turn was arrested, but with his law degree he beat the rap, and thereafter "we have had order all over the Circuit ever since." Howard introduced instrumental music to the church. (The church acquired an electric organ during World War II.)

Reverend Howard moved on in 1885, and by then, the church had thrived enough to pay the next pastor an annual salary of $750. And around 1905 or '06, the church's own parsonage was built. The church was remodeled in 1910. Over the years, memorial windows were added from the local GAR and the Women's Relief Corps (a GAR auxiliary) commemorating the military service of Civil War soldiers.

There is more talk about oil well drilling presently on land northwest of the county seat. This has been going on for a couple of years now; some fifteen wells so far in the county are producing oil, but none in great amounts. Several wells were drilled around Hortonville in the township in the past, but none of great production. Some local farmers have leased land for drilling, including Roy Woods's land and that of the Rogers, Foulke, Sumner, Stalker and Carey farms. Some of the wells on these farms have been linked with pipelines, the oil collected in metal "reservoirs" and then refined in Portland, Indiana. The two wells on Lowell Carey's farm have produced natural gas instead of oil, the gas useful in its own right. The Sperry-Cline Company of Indianapolis owns most of the wells around here. Front men from a couple of major oil companies have been seen lately.

In 1944, a major fire in town destroyed a longtime manufacturer with a world-famous brand for one product in particular: Van Camp Pork & Beans (there was even a "Westfield Pork & Beans" label). The business had actually begun

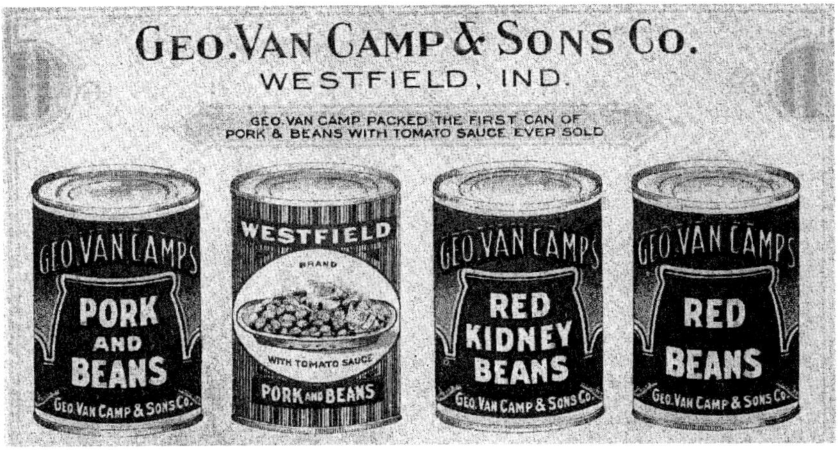

Sample products from the George Van Camp & Sons canning factory in Westfield. The town had its own pork and bean can label. A former employee, Irwin "Ike" Armstrong, of a prominent local black family, wrote home on a Van Camp bean can label while in France during World War I to say how good the beans from Westfield tasted in the trenches. Armstrong and his four brothers served simultaneously, and all returned home after the war. Irwin became a well-known educator and insurance company founder.

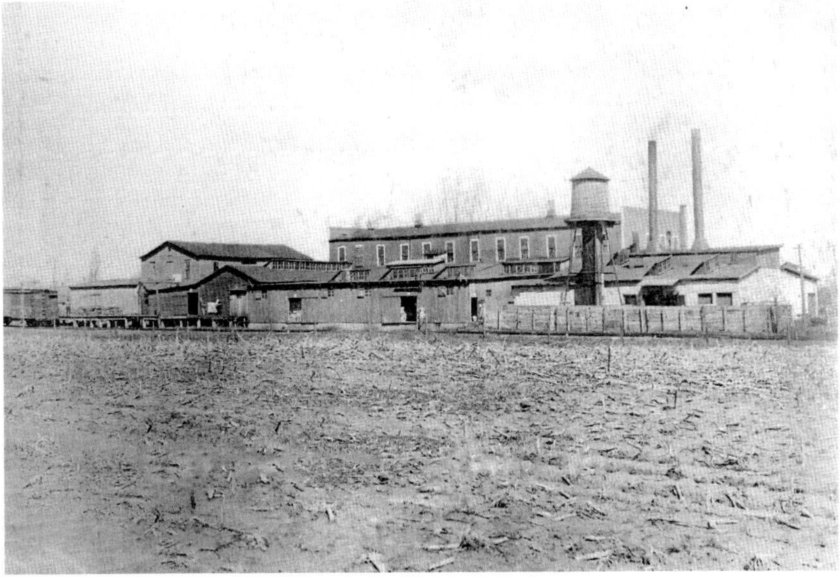

Van Camp & Sons canning factory, Westfield, Indiana.

in Indianapolis during the Civil War, but a third-generation son George Van Camp and his two sons, Elmer and Bert, opened a canning factory in Westfield in 1914 at the former Hamilton County Packing Company at the southwest corner of town near the crossing of the Midland and Monon Railroads. The operation here began with one hundred employees, but the company was compelled in 1928 to declare bankruptcy. Though family members were not associated thereafter with the brand name, the successors in Indianapolis wisely kept the name as a household favorite. The factory in Westfield was operated by others for some years after, but the fire in 1944 marked the end.

Westfield is in the news in a big way in early August 1947. "Annual [Agricultural] Fair Shatters All Former Marks" is just one of the extra bold and large-lettered headlines in the *Ledger* for the three days of the fair on the school athletic grounds in town. Temperatures have reached unheard of heights, but the show goes on proudly, including this year the addition of auctioning prize-winning stock during the afternoon following the judging in the forenoon. The seven bull calves (three Jersey, three Guernsey and one Holstein) sold were of top dairy bloodlines and were bought by local farmers and dairymen.

The youth exhibiting their animals are using any means available to keep their animals from overheating; some had to be taken home. Some are using electric fans to stir the stifling air. A few boys got the idea to put chunks of ice in their hog pens.

All the 4-H members work hard in showing their animals. Pigs have to be washed over and over, oiled and trained to move properly during judging. Sheep must be clipped and the remaining wool combed repeatedly. Calves and colts need brushing nearly continually. Horns and hoofs are cleaned and polished. The small animals and fowl require the same degree of fussing over for the duration of the fair. Vocational agriculture teachers are nearly overwhelmed with advising their students who are showing animals. The busiest and most consulted of all is probably Arnold Pahmeier, agriculture teacher at Westfield. Heading up what has turned out to be the largest gathering for a 4-H Fair in its history is no small task. A lot of pride is on the line here. The Westfield Lions Club is doing a land office business at their food and cold drinks stand. The fair closes on Thursday evening with a countywide horse show by the 4-H members. Frank Newby of Westfield, of the Circle W. Saddle Club, will direct the show of seven events. There is no entry fee, and the public is invited to watch for free.

In all, some eight hundred 4-H youth competed with show animals, displays and other entries for judging, and the entries define the farming community hereabouts. Non-animal entries were in clothing, food preservation and baking, gardening and many more categories. Westfield girls with entries of these kinds included Nancy Horney, Nancy Reed and Jane Seeright. The all-club historical sketches performed attracted a very large crowd.

On Thursday, August 21, 1947, Pastor Joseph White of the Evangelical United Brethren Church told the Kiwanis Club that the church must adapt to a new danger: world communism. "With an estimated 52 percent of the world's population engaged in some respect in religious faith, isn't that a significant force for good?" he asked. He sees a great danger in oppressive political movements such as communism, whose leaders are promising more than is possible and appealing to mass populations in the world, especially the most vulnerable—the hungry of the world—to embrace this new assembling of political and military power.

Later in September, townspeople and others assembled in the high school auditorium to hear *Indianapolis News* managing editor Wayne Guthrie tell of his "ringside seat at Bikini," as one of the newsmen aboard the press ship USS *Appalachian*, to see the air burst and the underwater blast of atomic bombs in July of the previous year. The Indianapolis paper was one of few invited for the tour of military facilities, the main event being the bomb blasts at Bikini Atoll in the mid-Pacific Ocean. His presentation was sponsored by the Westfield Women's Club and the Westfield Lions Club as a public service to inform the population about this monumental occurrence that demonstrated the destructive capacity of such weapons now sought by many nations but which very few have presently. Anyone who has heard Mr. Guthrie's popular and well-traveled observations and comments has new insights into this symbol of modernity, and at what price. Hearing the facts from an eyewitness to such an event has an impact. Information about this new age—and its fearsome symbol, the "mushroom cloud" of atomic bomb blasts—is sure to occupy much space in all newspapers to come.

Most of the talk about school sports of late is about the football team. Playing on a wet and muddy field at Sheridan, the Shamrocks won by a single touchdown in the third quarter, thereby winning the county conference title. The game began and ended in a downpour and was a hard-fought contest, both teams making good plays and suffering for some mistakes.

The students have tagged WHS teacher and all-around coach Victor Overman as "Victorious Vic," a natural for the alliteration but mainly for his winning teams. In October 1947, he and his champion football team were gathering the accolades due their string of successes on the field. Their victory over Sheridan gave them their second county conference championship in a row. Coach Overman seemingly has infused the players with his own high spirits and prowess as a standout player in high school and college. He has been in his present role for only two football seasons since graduating from Ball State just last year.

There is one more game to play, and so far the team has won five games, tied one and lost two to larger schools Kokomo (losing in the last two minutes) and undefeated Howe (again by a single touchdown). Known for a particularly hard-driving defensive line, the team simply out-powered other schools, whether playing on ideal fields or fields where traction is nearly impossible.

The coach has another advantage presently; he can start an all-senior team in the upcoming game with Kirklin. The number of injuries has been low, it is said, due to his training program and the players' following his instructions.

Now come the much-awaited county tournaments and a final win for Westfield. The county football champs were feted on October 29 at a banquet in their honor in the public library basement meeting room. The cuisine is rabbits and squirrels downed by local hunters; the front page of the school newspaper shows Santa Claus with a shotgun following rabbit tracks in the snow.

In November 1949, attention was shifted to the WHS basketball team. Said to have "height, weight, experience, spirit and a splendid attitude," the team is highly favored for a bright season. Coach Forest Stoops has been here one year and has had a fine coaching record subsequently. Last year, the team won half its total of eighteen games. By mid-December, the team was county conference champs, the ideal way to wrap up a season with memories that will live forever.

Parents of WHS music students will be attending the all-county band festival at the Armory in Noblesville on December 11. The guest conductor will be the director of bands at Indiana University. The schools attending are Westfield, Carmel, Jackson Township, Noblesville, Sheridan and Walnut Grove. The challenging program will include "The Star-Spangled Banner," of course, then the "Mandalay Overture,"

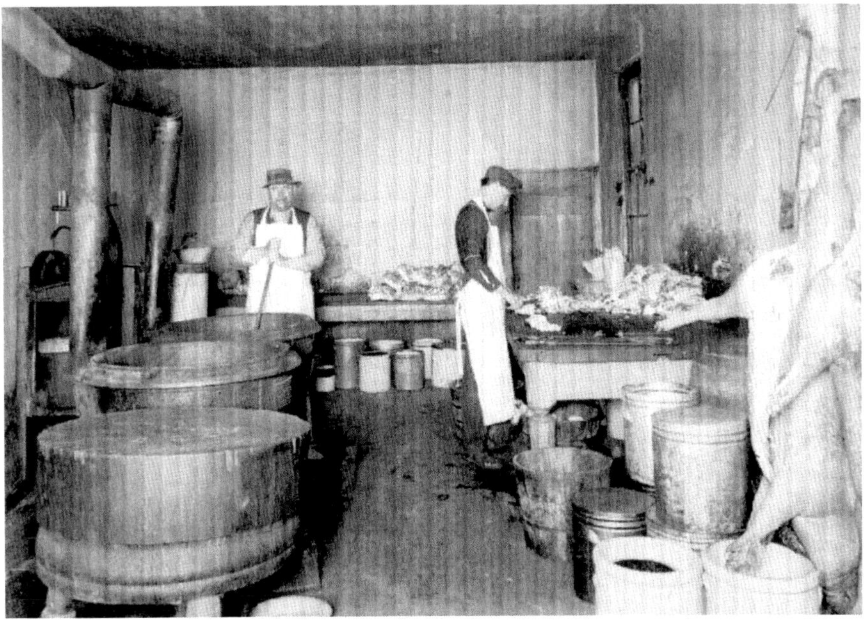

Marl Horton and Herman Stalker in Horton's meat shop, Westfield, circa 1904. The family patriarch, Hubert Horton, founded the town of Hortonville, Washington Township, in 1882.

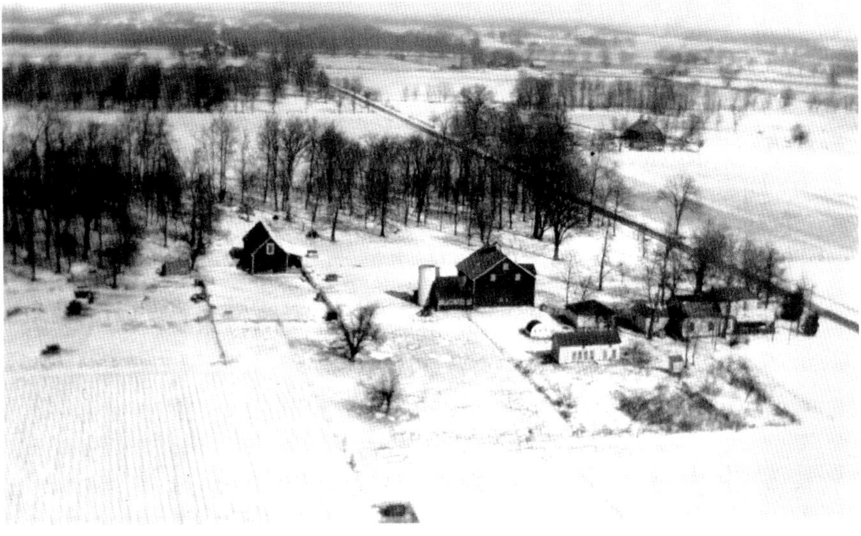

A typical Washington Township farm home, barn lot and fields in the winter. The farmland in Hamilton County is among the best in Indiana.

several military and funeral marches, some tone poems and will end with Beethoven's "Eroica."

In early December, the WHS agriculture students attended the International Livestock Exposition in Chicago. While there, they visited the huge meatpacking plant, where they learned that the average distance between livestock production and meat consumption is one thousand miles. They also learned that two-thirds of the meat produced comes from west of the Mississippi River, while two-thirds of that massive production is consumed east of the river. They likely knew already that, while their farm interests are centered on Westfield, the agriculture in any expansive region has links locally in some way.

The interest of some locally in the alluring gas well speculation has been increased by the capacity of two wells on the farm of Lowell Carey, former restaurateur in Westfield, producing two million cubic feet of gas a day, it is said, which is an impressive figure for those in the know. One of his wells has been rated as the best one drilled around here in forty years. Carey's wells are capped now; piping is scarce and very expensive. Some want the gas piped eventually into Westfield, but it all depends on the decision of the Cline-Sperry Company of Indianapolis when they begin marketing the gas. Carey says the gas in both wells resides in about six feet of sand, optimum conditions for a long supply. He has touted the potential for some industry to come to Westfield for such a supply of gas. The company is preparing to drill wells elsewhere in the township.

The world war has run its course, to great relief and great loss, so perhaps the echo of the train whistle on the old Midland (Central Indiana) Railroad is not so mournful now, and most are focused on the changes and goals of a postwar era. There is always time for reminiscing in a town the size of Westfield, and Paul Brown, retired Westfield pharmacist, has a particular interest in the history of the Midland Railroad. Paul rode in the first train to depart Westfield in the early 1880s and enjoyed talking with the Italian track-laying crews, though he understood little of what they said. He particularly liked to watch them prepare their meals. His father had some stock in the railroad but did not receive much return on his investment. Paul also rode the first Monon train at Westfield built through town in the early 1880s.

The old railroad is even featured in the October 18 issue of the *Indianapolis Star Magazine* with a two-page illustrated spread. The Midland has a single train a day now, hauling grain and returning with coal. By 1895, the line

Left: Unused tickets for passenger travel on the Monon Railroad.

Below: Midland Railroad depot and locomotive, Westfield.

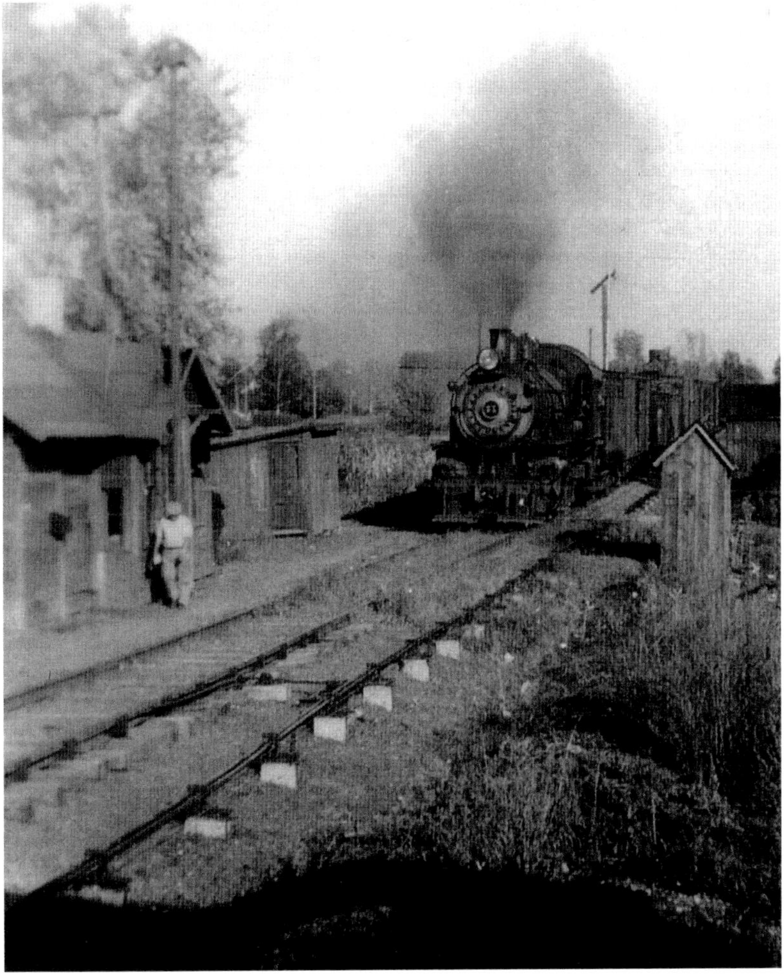

had reached the coal mining near Brazil in Clay County, just ahead of an injunction to halt operation for nonpayment of debts. At that time, the president of the line was the memorable Harry Crawford, he of the plug hat, spats and riding in his palatial private car, a thing of wonder, a true one-of-a-kind for all its opulence and beautiful woodworking.

Under Crawford, the railway made progress but lost as much if not more because of Crawford's irresponsible financial antics. The locomotives were occasionally chained by sheriffs for nonpayment of taxes and other nose thumbing of local laws. He even lost his contract with the U.S. postmaster general after failing to make mail deliveries for three days. It was not a refusal to deliver, he argued, but more like a prolonged delay for which he had a glib but surprisingly effective excuse.

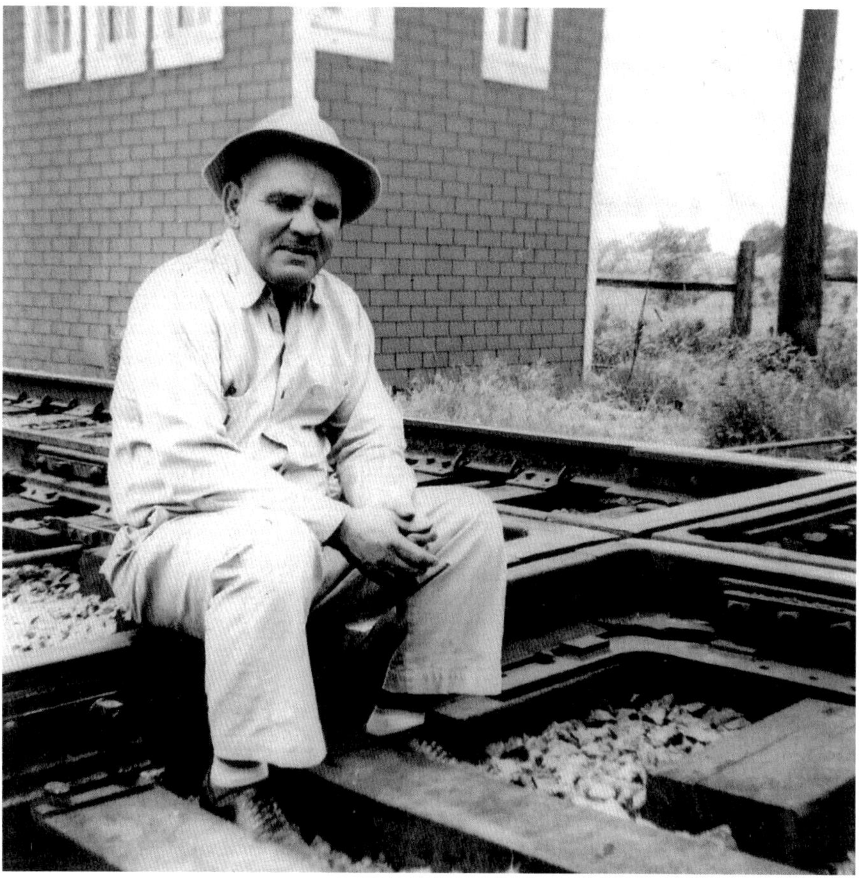

A railroad employee sits at the cross tracks of the Monon and Midland Railroads at the southwest corner of Westfield. In the background is the "tower" with large levers on the second floor for operating rail switches.

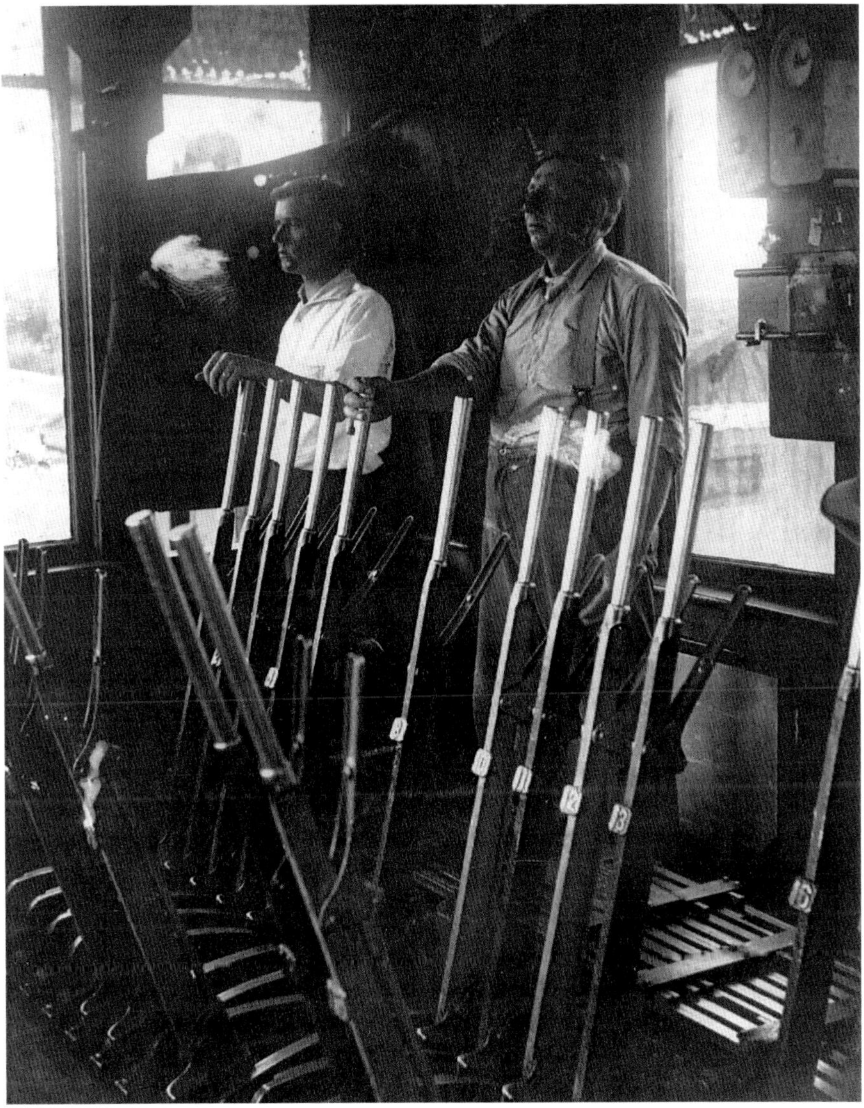

Switch levers in the two-story railroad "tower" in Westfield.

By 1922, the road had to suspend its popular passenger service; former passenger and freight customers were choosing the greatly improved roads and means of transportation instead of the Midland (high school students from Eagletown and Jolietville and the surrounding farms rode the train each day to school in Westfield). With the near demise of the coal mining around Brazil, the railway saw its bread-and-butter freight runs lose much money. With the implosion of the Wall Street stock market in the fall of 1929, the railway suffered further and was buoyed mainly because it was acquired by the huge Pennsylvania Railroad system as a useful trunk line.

During a general railroad strike in the spring a year ago, the Midland was the only railroad in Indiana in operation. But a few must think the old road is gaining some profit; one of those robberies that Sheriff Newby is investigating was at the Westfield Depot.

When the *Noblesville Ledger* went to press in the early morning on Sunday, November 2, 1947, the massive front page headline called it "the largest [area fire] in half a century."

Warren Elkins, who manages the lunchroom in town, was the first to see it. He thought it was a flue burning out in the corner drugstore. He called the telephone operator, who looked out the window and saw flames on the roof of Jack Statzer's Electric Shop. By the time she had roused the volunteer fire department, the entire block beyond the south wall of the corner drugstore was about to become one big blaze. Volunteer fireman Don Conner was one of the people roused and quickly knew he was suddenly involved in more than fighting a fire. Don is the manager of the Regal Grocery Store, and the roof was about to fall in on stock that was already nearly completely ruined. He did manage to drag the cash register outside, as well as a few cans of food. It was total destruction and the same for the electric shop. The Creson secondhand store and antique shop also went up in flames. Some massive presses and a linotype machine in the Community Press space are all beyond further use, but the publisher of the *Booster*, a "shopper" paper with a little local news, never missed an issue; the editor found other presses in his great need.

An entire block was being consumed. And what would be "saved" would be mostly water-soaked and useless. The water had been pumped by the town's equipment and by the fire departments of Carmel, Noblesville and Sheridan. The phone operator had made other calls when the huge size of the fire was quickly apparent. The firemen strung several hoses across South Union Street just south of the intersection with Highway 32. That street is also the ancient Range Line Road and now a highway in its own right, U.S. 31. Traffic was stopped, of course, until it was thought the danger on the street had passed. It is a major loss for a few familiar businessmen; the insurance is said to be woefully inadequate.

The Barker brothers said they had $1,500 worth of insurance on their structure, but it will take a total of many thousands of dollars to rebuild all that has been lost. What remains are sections of the outside walls of the stores, now hazards themselves. The extra-thick south wall of the Mendenhall drugstore saved it from the fire, but the off-putting odor of dense smoke will have to be expelled from that landmark building.

Some began hauling out the debris already on Sunday afternoon. The walls of the *Press* and the electric shop were pulled down on Monday. The front façade of the antique shop still stands, a useless survivor of the massive destruction. Jack Statzer had just taken delivery of some rather expensive products, and his tools of the trade were lost. Roger Irwin of the *Press* has suffered major loss, too. No dollar figure estimate of the losses has been made professionally. But anyone walking by that block can see that rebuilding must start from the ground up, and that can happen only after the rubble has been deconstructed, loaded and hauled away—a major task in itself.

12

The 1950s: Looking Ahead

The Atomic Age: Duck and Cover

The entry year to the decade of the 1950s has begun on a positive note. Shortly after New Year's celebrations, the Washington Township trustee announced the issuance of bonds for building a much-needed school addition on West Main Street in Westfield. When the announcement came, the excavating work had already been done, and the basic forms were in place for the next stage of early construction.

Later in the month, the Farm Extension School met at the original school auditorium to feature experts on the newest and best methods of raising swine and poultry. Last September, the Westfield High School basketball team had played in the thirty-third county tourney, and a new basketball coach had arrived. Walter A. Molinder followed Vic Overman, his friend and fellow teammate at Ball State Teachers College. Mr. Molinder has been given a busy teaching schedule, including introducing the industrial arts to the high school.

Westfield residents can see daily the strange ramifications of the national coal strikes. Along with the production of seasonal harvests as profitable freight for the two local railroads, coal is also major freightage, and the railroads are feeling the effects of the dwindling coal supply. Coal-burning steam locomotives are being sidetracked, and the Monon Railroad, said to be the first in the nation to "dieselize," is very proud of the foresight of its new president, who has made other impressive moves to keep that line profitable. It is called the "Hoosier Line," and some pride has been engendered in the public for the railroad's punctuality, its far-reaching connections in Indianapolis and Chicago and its color schemes—those of Indiana University, crimson and cream, for the new diesel locomotives pulling passenger cars, and of the yellow and black of Purdue University for diesels pulling freight trains. (Passenger depots and freight depots follow the same color scheme.) But now the Monon has petitioned to close its depot in Westfield. Insufficient passengers and now a drop in freight-hauled overall are the reasons given. Farmers are immediately concerned about the higher prices of trucking their grain to the local elevators. For its part, the Midland Railroad has purchased a single diesel engine to power its one train a day. For all its diminutive appearance and lackadaisical schedule, it is said to be the only profitable railroad in the state.

When the owner of a shop in town was closing up around midnight, he was accosted by two men who demanded money, taking $90.00 from him. He was not injured, but the money, he said, had been intended for a current tax payment the next day. The two thieves were described as "dirty, rough looking," and one "brandished a gun." An unnatural wariness resulted, made more acute when the Shamrock Inn, the only all-night restaurant in town, was also robbed about 3:00 p.m. Those two thieves were apprehended in less than an hour some distance east of the neighboring town of Fishers. They had kidnapped a restaurant customer and forced him to drive the car they stole in town to make their escape. The money these ruffians pocketed for a couple of hours was $31.50 from the restaurant and $4.00 from the hostage. A third customer was robbed of all his money: one single dime. The hostage was not hurt, but he was home on military furlough, precious time at home not to be interrupted by such a thing. A couple of months later, when Joe Parker came to open the Regal Grocery Store he managed, he found the front door open and an egg crate full of bacon and some butter just inside the door. No money had been taken (he seldom left any there overnight), but he missed seventy-five cartons of cigarettes and seven cured hams.

With spring comes an experiment by the Monon Railroad. The company introduced the "Budd Car," a single self-powered car similar to the old interurban cars to see if the public would patronize quick transportation in this form into Indianapolis from Westfield and points to the northwest.

It is spring 1950, and farm tractors park on town streets by stores where farmers shop while waiting for grain to be weighed and ground at the elevator. The Holstein dairy herd owned by the Field and Harvey farm has just won the monthly recognition of the Hamilton County Dairy Herd Improvement Association for a high mark in milk production, a butterfat content of 54.2 pounds per cow for the nineteen cows tested. These cows are the leaders among the twenty-five herds in the county entered in the testing. The local farm economy is still a major support of the wider community.

Parents of young children are greatly concerned about the health of their children, especially now. Public notices appear continually warning parents about exposure to the crippling diseases of polio, tuberculosis and infantile paralysis now feared across the nation. There are instructional sessions at schools, hospitals and other places in the county on the symptoms and other important information. Concessionaires at Forest Park in Noblesville have reported that there were fifty thousand fewer visitors the past season for the park's popular attractions and activities due to warnings from local health officials about the communicability of these dreaded maladies that affect children for a lifetime.

Yet the decade proceeds apace. The nation as a whole looks forward to increased production of consumer products after a deadly and costly war with its dreadful news of casualties and annoying rationing. But on the local scene, the common and cherished manner in which neighbors help neighbors, especially in times of tragedy and great need, is confirmed after the Wesleyan Methodist church catches fire on Sunday, January 9, between the morning and the evening worship services. The town "turns out" to help provide meeting space and as much volunteer work as needed for cleanup and preparation for rebuilding the portion most badly damaged. The fire that destroyed the grain elevator in 1952 was a loss of another kind, and the quick reconstruction of that vital local enterprise was proof of its importance to the local economy. Now also the town makes major improvements in 1955 to the local waterworks constructed in 1929 with a few dozen customers then, grown now to 450.

In 1958, an important anchoring industry has come to town. Curtis Automotive Devices, Inc. moved here in March and employs about one hundred people. The company makes industrial-size equipment for spraying and fogging of compounds such as insecticides, liquid fertilizers, disinfectants, fungicides and detergents used by many familiar food and other well-known industries. Smaller models are on the drawing board for home outdoor use. The company also makes a variety of sizes and types of valves for aircraft.

Curtis products are shipped all over the "free world," now a familiar term in the "Cold War" between the immense communist nations of the Soviet Union and China and "the West," the United States and its allies in Europe and elsewhere.

There is another residential addition to Westfield in 1958: Westfield Heights on the northwest side, one of twelve additions made since World War II.

Though the decade had its excitement and loss, overall it was just good to be free of the constant cloud of the threats and losses of the world war a decade and a half ago. But there had been more costly combat in Korea with more tragic American loss of life; many of those soldiers had just survived the previous war, only to be thrust again into harm's way, that overused term for more horror and death. And now there is the constant threat of communist powers bent on world dominance.

13

The 1960s and '70s: Still the Community

The census enumerators in early 1960 counted 4,868 residents in the entire township, including the 1,217 residents of Westfield. With those statistics in hand, Westfield enters the 1960s as a relatively quiet and secure place to live. Elsewhere, the 1960s will never be confused with the 1950s on the national scene.

But in Westfield, one public notice regarding death was but a nod to the past. On October 20, 1962, the *Ledger* printed a brief public notice from the town trustees of Westfield—Allen Stanley, Robert Armstrong and Roger Ervin—informing relatives of those buried in the Friends' ancient cemetery that they had "six months to remove the body" of their ancestors. The little graveyard had not been used, it was said, for half a century. Westfield civic clubs and women's groups had suggested that it be transformed into a small town park from its present

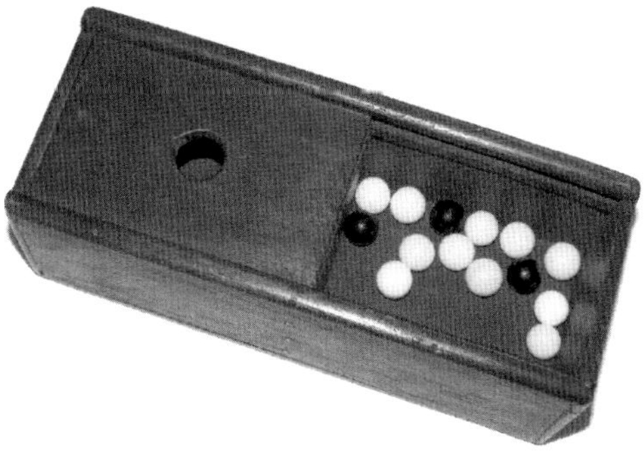

Voting box, Westfield (ladies) Outlook Club, early twentieth century. A black marble in the hole on the sliding lid was a vote against a prospective member, "blackballing" her.

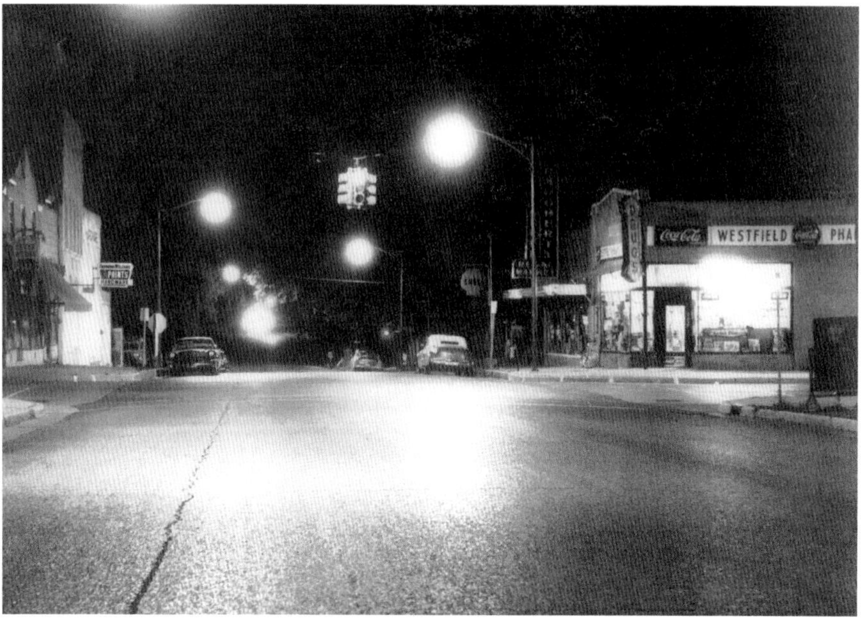

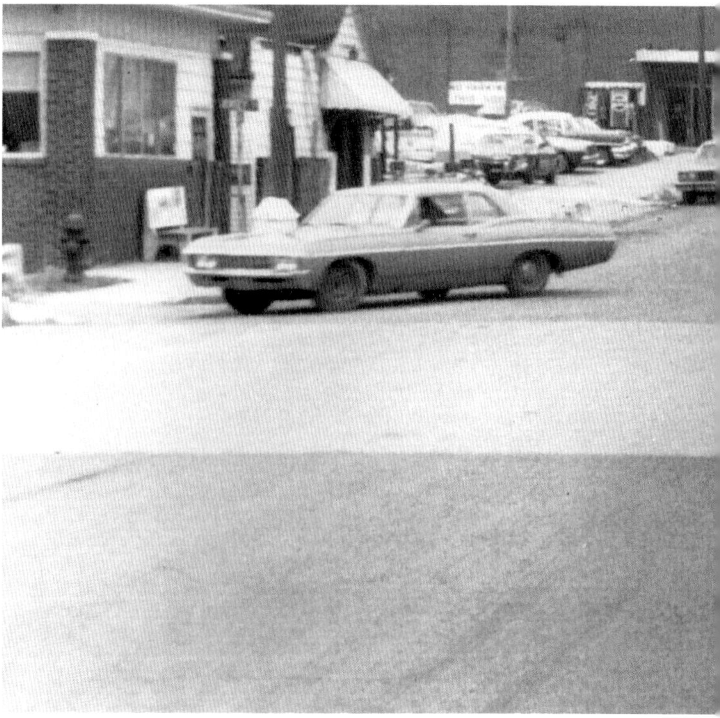

Above: Intersection of Union Street (looking south) and State Route 32, 1960s.

Right: Union Street, looking north from the bridge over Cool Creek to the intersection of State Route 32. The fire station office and truck garage are at left center, and the Sheridan–Indianapolis Bus garage is top right, circa 1970s.

Opposite, top: Intersection of State Route 32 (with lane lines, looking east) and Union Street, 1960s.

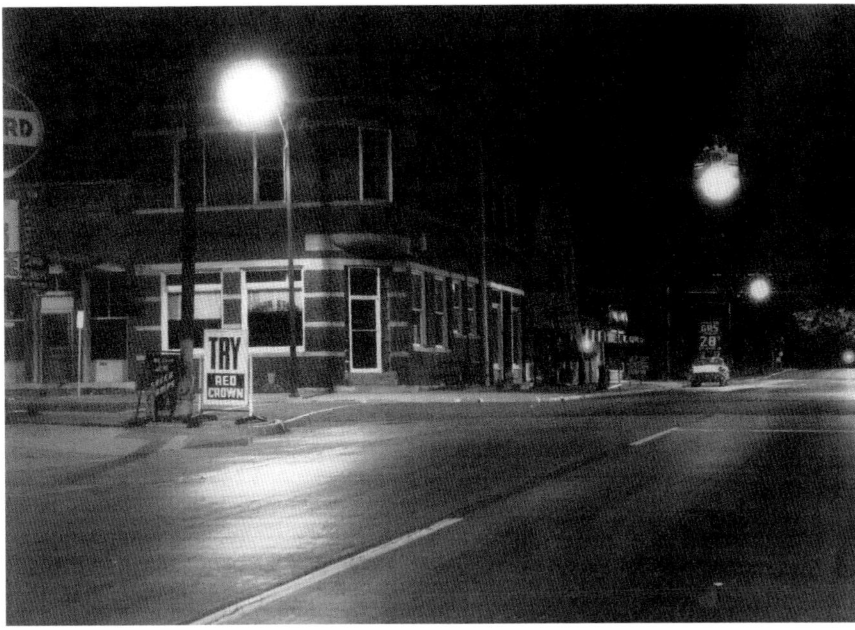
TRY
RED
CROWN

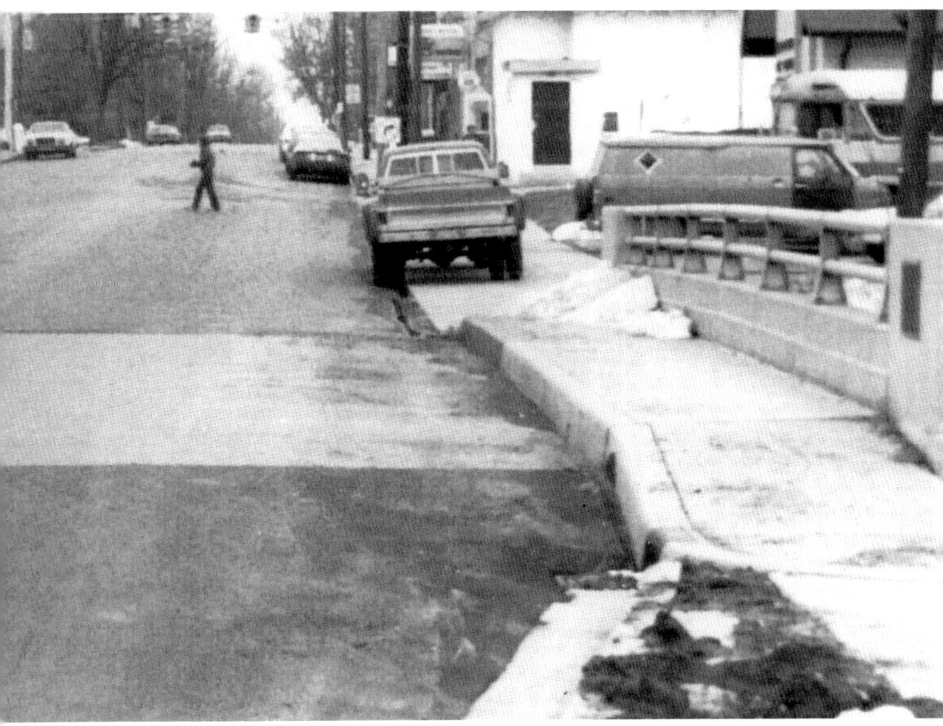

condition as a weed lot obscuring the few small remaining gravestones, many broken and aged, many beyond recognition. A few graves had been moved when the Friends Monthly Meeting sold a small portion of the ground to the Midland Railroad during the construction of the railroad right of way in the mid-1880s. A few burials were moved, but the details of that are obscure. Reportedly, "only a few buttons" were found in those graves.

Some hints of other changes are in the air—unhurried rural air that it is. In the spring of 1964, to the languid curiosity of dairy cattle grazing close by, a $277,000 sewer interceptor system is under construction at extended South Street, and the Street and Sewer Department, formerly one man and his part-time assistant, adds a few employees. Land is also being cleared for residential, commercial and industrial growth. A plant for producing Sacrete packaged concrete has recently been built off the southwest corner of town. And in town, the first commercial self-serve laundry opens, which includes a meeting room for women's clubs.

Many times in the history of this place the mention of an individual, such as in retirement, speaks of long-standing residence, and recollections flow in subsequent leisurely conversations. In 1966, postmistress Mary (Horton) Green retired from her familiar service window under the words "Resister, Money Orders, Postal Savings" after thirty years at the post office; she began there in 1927 as a rural mail carrier and was postmaster by May 2, 1936. Daughter of Westfield Meat Market owner Marl Horton of the Hortonville founding family, Mary had been a barber in town for six

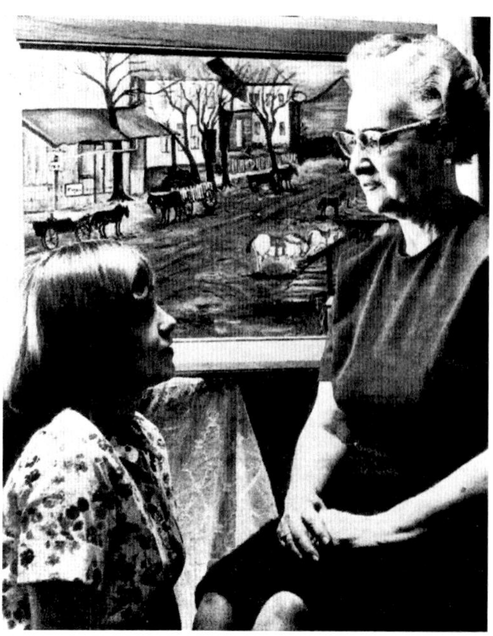

Mary Horton Green, showing one of her paintings (of East Main Street in Westfield from a photograph in 1865) to a high school student. Mary was Westfield postmaster from 1936 to 1966 after barbering and practicing chiropractic medicine in Westfield.

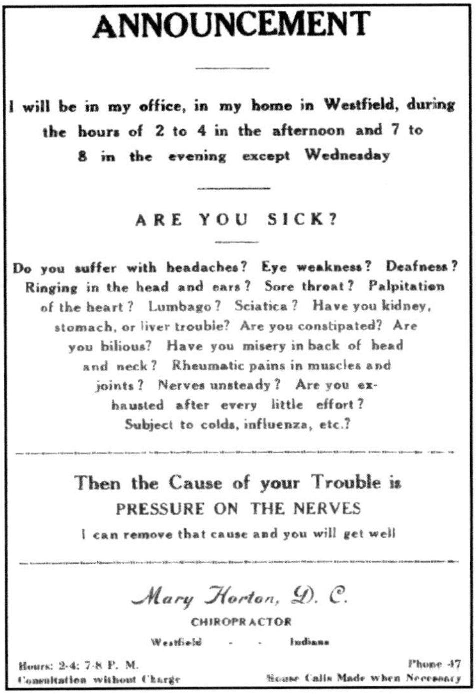

Ad For Dr. Mary Horton Green's chiropractic practice in Westfield.

years before being appointed postmistress. She had been trained in the barbershop of Lum Baker; her first customer was Ralph Erwin. Before that, she had become "Dr. Mary Greene, Chiropractor" while in barber school.

The next decade begins in vignettes suggested by the Westfield Lions Club's *Westfield Directory and Handbook* of 1970. This informative guide to the town lists husbands, wives and children, along with their phone numbers, occupations and postal addresses. But this helpful publication offers much more when reading between the lines. A town such as Westfield can be described in many ways, but a significant one is by its commercial environment.

The careers of several townspeople are reminiscent of earlier times. There's Donald K. Barker at his Shell station still under the "Barker Bros." banner above the door though he is the sole owner now. The business enterprises of the progeny of the pioneer Barker family grew with the advances made in personal transportation, beginning with Samuel F. Barker in about 1900 repairing bicycles when they were rather expensive and for young men and women and not children. Young suitors rode to court their sweethearts, also to jobs and for remarkably long jaunts in the country and to other towns. If they joined organizations of "wheelmen," they were issued guides giving road conditions, where bicycle repairs could be made, available town water pumps and even where vicious dogs had been encountered. Samuel Barker later serviced the first gasoline engines and installed the first gas pumps in town, and now Donald has been in his business for forty years. He says his goal is to be listed in the town directory of 1999, twenty-nine years into the future.

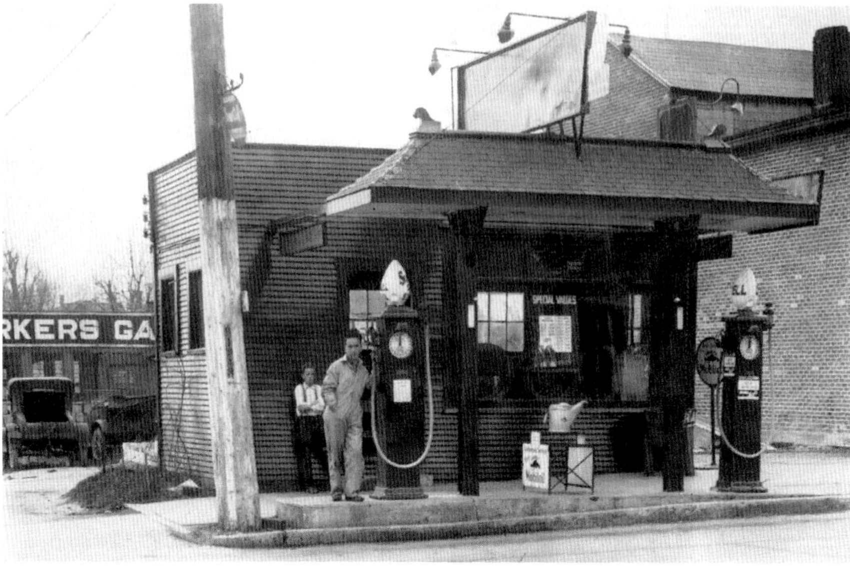

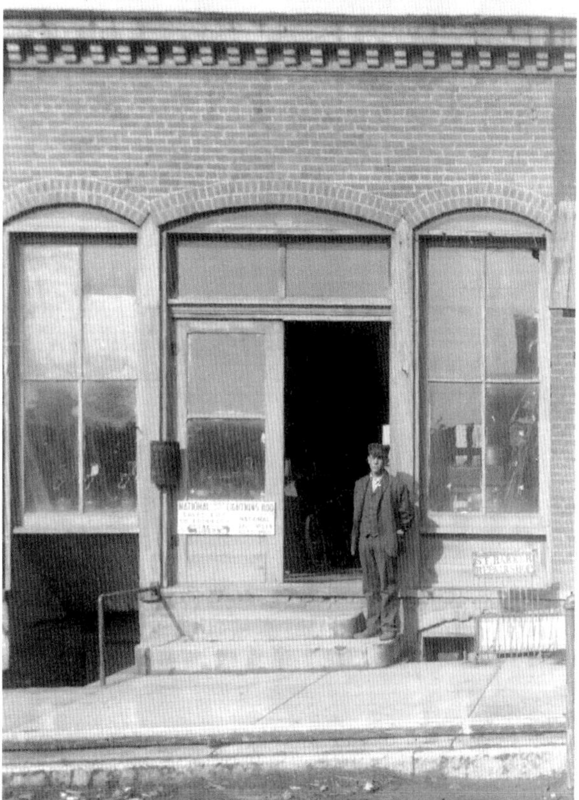

Above: Shell gas station, Westfield.

Left: Barker bicycle shop, Westfield, 1890s or later. With the coming of the first automobiles, the Barkers began repairing those as well at another location.

The grain elevator business in a town surrounded for miles around by farms has been vital for many decades. Fred Shole built an early elevator around the turn of the twentieth century. By 1902, it had been acquired by Goodrich Feed Co., which had many others in the state. In 1925, it was bought by Marcus Kendall but four years later sold back to the Goodrich Co. until 1946, when management was transferred to the Acme Goodrich Elevator. Now the Waitt Company has operated it for two years and added eighty-three thousand bushels of storage space, along with a complete remodeling.

Hometown girl Camilla Allen Axelrod, with a reputation for indefatigable energy and many acts of civic service, is enlarging her Camilla's Beauty Shoppe at the center of town. Known popularly by first name only (already arranged as such on her pre-purchased tombstone), Camilla, daughter of Nineveh and Barbara Allen, is ever ready to acknowledge her treasured local heritage and to work tirelessly to keep her community vibrant with the hometown spirit that she cheers on relentlessly. This WHS grad of 1947 attended beauty school and opened her first shop when she was eighteen. She has also managed restaurants, and she plans and guides bus tours.

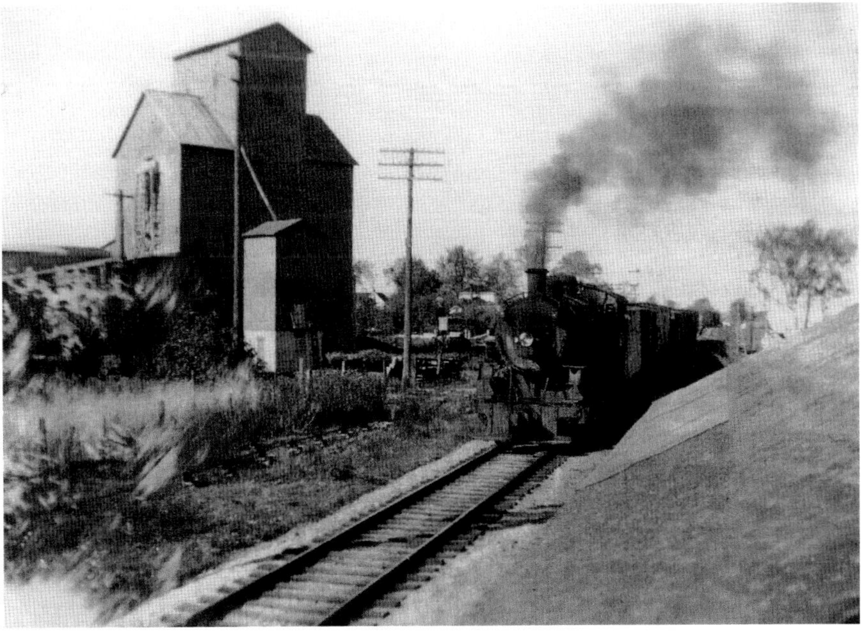

A Midland Railroad train passing the local grain elevator, a major freight customer of the railroad.

Camilla was born in 1929, grew up on the family farm and drove a tractor for disking and for baling hay, helped milk thirty-two cows and, when needed, drove the farm truck, with no doors, to town. In sixth grade, the janitor let her have a little room where she could fix girls' hair. At age fourteen, she worked in a town restaurant and was paid a bottle of chocolate milk and a bowl of chili and crackers. Her annual Christmas party in her home includes her six hundred ornaments; she hosts as many as one thousand people.

Five years ago, Floyd A. Carson and Les Wheeler formed the partnership Carson Wheeler Insurance Agency. Floyd, a Methodist, is a lifelong resident of the township and taught in the public schools for thirty-two years. He started his insurance business in 1946 part time and became a full-time agent in 1956. He has been a county commissioner. He is also director and vice-president of the Savings and Loan Association and a member of lodges and service clubs, including the Westfield Letterman's Club, raising funds for a new high school football field. Les Wheeler attended WHS and Purdue and worked with his father in farming. Les's son Joe, an Indiana University business school grad, has recently become partner.

James W. "Bill" Wood, another Methodist and WHS graduate of 1924, has farmed for thirty years, been a leader in 4-H and has been on the town advisory board for twelve years. He is also a well-known real estate dealer. John P. Furnas, another hometown boy born in 1915, began working for Standard Oil Company in 1949 and still delivers fuel oil to area homes; when not working, he can still be found hunting, fishing and camping. John, a Friend, is a fan of the Indianapolis Indians and a faithful supporter of WHS sports.

Roy Hadley's insurance business began in 1931, and since 1959, he has partnered with Ike Jones in their Hadley and Jones Agency with offices in the Westfield Savings and Loan Building.

Alton Hoard, another WHS graduate, learned cement block work from his father; his own business dates from 1950. That work and carpentry financed his college years. Al's Hoard Construction Company builds custom homes as well as remodeling, but recently he has also worked on airport hangars, vacation homes, warehouses, barns and post buildings.

Horace and Ruthanna Kirkman, both WHS grads, were married in 1930 and began their current greenhouse and flower shop business in 1964 as a retirement venture. Ruthanna also still works in Indianapolis.

Harry E. Lunsford came here in 1938 to operate the former Standard Oil station on the northwest corner of Main and Union Streets. He started with Standard Oil in 1929. He moved to a new station farther west on Mill Street in 1962, with son Bob as his partner.

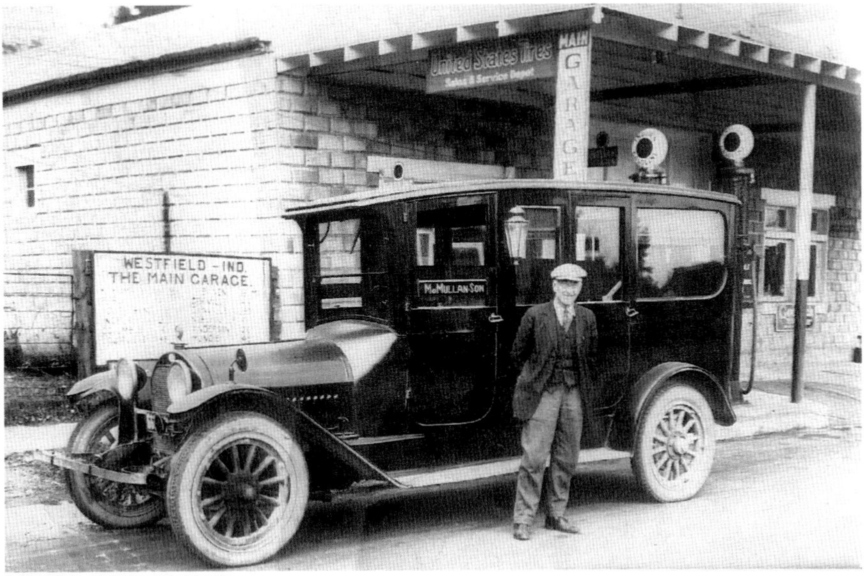

A McMullan & Son Funeral Home car.

The third generation McMullan and Son Funeral Home was founded in 1924, when Jeremiah C. McMullan came from Kempton, where he had prepared the bodies and received the callers in the homes of the deceased. He began here in a store building on the south side of Main Street. His son J. Richard McMullan worked with him. The business included a haberdashery. In 1930, they bought the old Hayworth Hotel on the north side of Main Street and in 1940 built a new building on the site. In 1967, they had the current building constructed on the south side of the street. Richard passed away last year, 1969, and the management was assumed by son Jerry C., so now it is a third-generation business.

Pickett's Cafeteria opened in 1958, anchoring the southeast corner of Route 32 and Union Street. Bernie and Mary's opening day saw fifty customers, and the business has thrived and is a popular fixture in the town's restaurant, cafeteria and lunch stand tradition, drawing people from neighboring communities. They now average 409 dinners per day, with fifty pies for weekdays and sixty for Sundays.

Westfield Savings and Loan began in 1923 with twenty original subscribers, a capital of $200,000 and has occupied several office spaces in town. It opened its current location in 1959 after four old buildings were razed at the site. Its capital is invested conservatively and securely in U.S. government bonds and first mortgages on real estate. In its forty-seven years

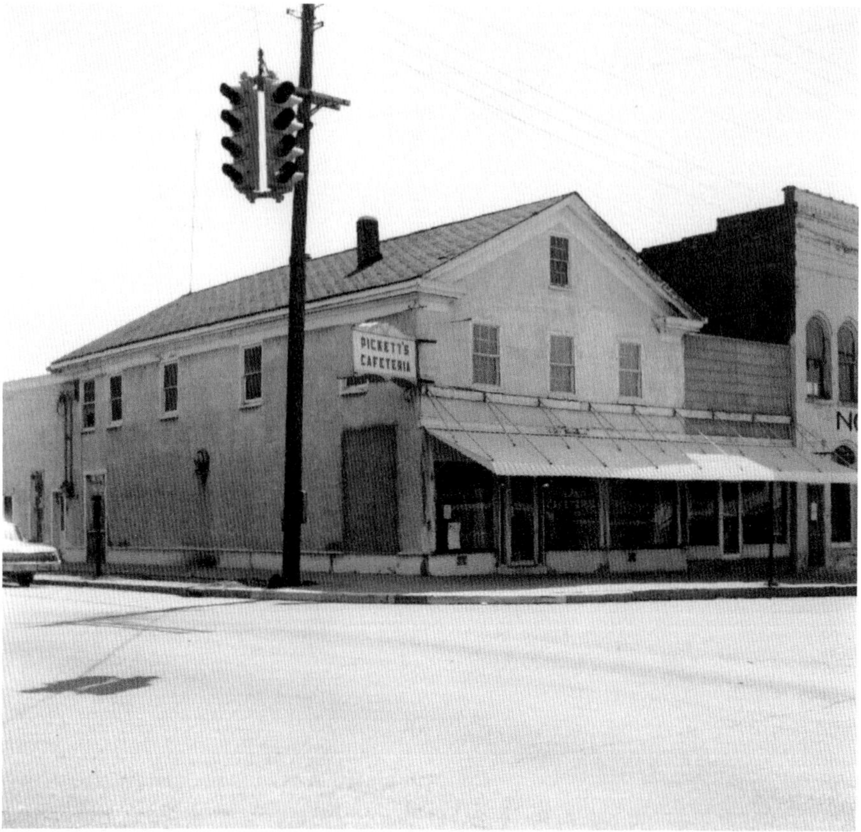

Pickett's Cafeteria, local landmark familiar to those who traveled U.S. Route 31 north and south through Westfield for many decades, as well as a local favorite for miles around.

of operation, the business has never foreclosed a mortgage, a compliment to the financial stability of its borrowers.

The Westfield Gas Corporation has 275 natural gas customers and services 1,000 liquefied petroleum gas customers in a twenty-five-mile radius. The six service trucks are fueled by liquefied petroleum gas. In 1966, the Federal Power Commission granted a first allotment from Panhandle Eastern Pipe Line Co. A second allotment is anticipated. The town sold its municipal gas company in 1948 to a private owner who installed much larger storage tanks and later a thirty-thousand-gallon tank located by the Monon Railroad line. The additional use of gas for purposes other than home heating has grown greatly.

The American Legion Post 318, now with thirty members, was named for George R. Hochstedler in 1920, shortly after the close of World War I during which its namesake was killed and buried in the American Cemetery at Is-sur-tille in France and later moved home to Summit Lawn Cemetery in 1922. Town marshal Earl Watkins spent four years, 1942–46, in the army and started a tree service four years ago.

Many of these men were away from their families during lengthy military service in World War II: Carson during 1942 and '43; Wheeler, three and a half years overseas as an air force pilot of B-24s; and Furnas, fifty-seven months in the army, three years of that in the South Pacific. Glenn McNealy, of McNeally's Cities Service gas station where Routes 31 and 32 cross, is also a veteran.

Other businesses in town include the Art and Decorating Shop of taxidermist Floyd A. Young; Bowden Tree Service; Budget Fabrics; and Burgher Hardware, where Henry Burgher delights in showing the large double doors of the former blacksmith shop built in 1890 that his hardware now occupies. Carmel Enterprises, Inc., named for where it began, fabricates fiberglass parts and sailboats. Carmel Chemical Corporation is located in Washington Township, and Curtis Dyna-Fog Products Co. makes insecticide and other fogging products. Bill Dennis's Barber Shop includes barbers Ken Foland and Clyde Slater. Ken and Bill talk sports; Clyde talks fishing and hunting mushrooms. Bill bought the shop from longtime barber Byron "Doc" Ross, whose shop was adorned with his hunting trophies. Montgomery's Antiques is owned by Phillip Montgomery, also a partner in Jones and Montgomery Electrical Co. in Indianapolis. Lewis Realty and Auction Service was the first realty office in town in 1952.

Westfield Plumbing and Heating Co. dates to the early 1950s. Meehan Real Estate's building at 301 West Main Street is said to be among the oldest in town, believed to have been used as an Underground Railroad station. Phillips Cleaners is now one year old. THRIF-T Building Supply, with its own railroad siding track, is the county's newest lumber company and successor to the Talbert-Roessler Building Supply, a name from long ago. Westfield Pharmacy (since 1953), the business established in 1897 by William W. Mendenhall and succeeded by sons Chase H. and Emmet J., who had the present corner location built in 1923, is now owned by Ray and Geannie Thompson. The Gee-Nee Drive In and Restaurant opened this year (it was the former Dog and Suds Restaurant) and is owned by Mr. and Mrs. Paul Tirey; he was formerly head of Sam Technical Institute in Indianapolis. Truss Manufacturing Co. relocated from Indianapolis in 1963 and sells custom-made gang-nail trusses to over 1,700 lumber companies in the state and elsewhere. Union State Bank, originally in Jolietville but here now for the past forty years, occupies the original corner bank building. The bank plans a new building at Main and Mill Streets. The Westfield Lions Club and the Westfield Jaycees meet for their civic purposes. The churches in town are the Westfield Friends Church and the Union Friends, the United Methodist, the Wesleyan Methodist and Westfield Missionary Baptist Church.

In March 1972, an important preservation project was completed when the mid-nineteenth-century Doan family home at the southeast corner of U.S. 31 and State Route 32 was moved ten miles to Conner Prairie to become part of the outdoor pioneer museum there where it would represent a period structure. Most other homes in Westfield and the township remain, speaking of historic times, styles and families.

But it is not all ancient history here. New construction in town is all the go now with $3.5 million in development, $1 million of that in light industrial initiatives and the rest in residential construction. Building permit fees in 1971 brought in $4,000 to the town coffers, three times that of the previous year. The population of Westfield in 1970 had been 1,835. It is now over 2,000.

Now meetings of the town board are lengthy with the number of construction applications and all that relate to expanding residential, commercial and industrial construction. The plan commission is similarly busy. The quarter-million-dollar sewer project includes a new water tower on the west side of 31.

By 1973, the push for new buildings and infrastructure is extending outside town and into the township. But there are few restrictions on land outside the town limits two miles from the center of town. Looking to the county commissioners for action is not an option; their zoning function was voted out in the 1950s.

Some new subdivisions have been built recently, for which the developers had to submit plans to the town, but for nearly the entire township, there is no such review required. In 1970, a group of township residents tried to join with the town to create some zoning, but an injunction was filed against the zoning proposal, and after a frustrating delay, the case was dropped. Recently, similar petitions are again being circulated. Residents north and northwest of Westfield, insulated at present from the need, they believe, of such precautions, do not want zoning. But those living south of town are being pressed by developments there; Carmel's northern city limit is now 146th Street, the township line between Washington and Clay Townships.

The year following the local celebration of the nation's 200th anniversary in 1976, the Westfield Business Association began the Westfield Historical

Central Business District Improvement Study, which "determined that the commercial activity of the Central Business District has the potential for economic improvement and growth by uncovering, restoring and extending the rich historical character of the business district" in this "small but dynamic community." This was an updating of a 1965 town board of trustees' Master Plan and Zoning Ordinance. The central business district is defined as "compact and centered at Main and Union Streets, the immediate area as Union Street from the railroad track on the south to East Street on the east." In the specific area now outlined, "there are historical structures dating from 1850 to the 1930s."

Several structures in particular have been closely observed. The building jointly occupied by the town grocery store and Marlow's Café is "nicely proportioned" Classical Revival style, as are some features of the former inn at Main and Walnut Streets. The Ehmans Hardware Store's "very well-proportioned three-bay statement with arched openings" and "brick corbelling" is an example of the Romanesque Style. The frame buildings at 311 South Union and 120 North Union have "restrained pseudo-Italianate detailing." The old bank building at its prime spot at the northeast corner of Main and Union has significant potential for reconstruction of the conical roof of the round cornering over the main door.

The Carnegie Library is its own statement of "restrained eclecticism" of the early twentieth century. And the small Arco Service Station on Main Street is "quite unique" with its sloped chimney and steeply pitched gable roof—a true find in historical architecture. That style of the early 1930s elsewhere has largely been demolished or modified beyond recognition.

The Westfield City Building at 143 South Union Street is said to be "well proportioned" but "has suffered from over modification," though its broad overhang of the low-pitched hip roof "is suggestive of the Prairie School…a significant period of development in the Midwest early twentieth century." Even the little arts and crafts shop across the creek from the city building, though with paint peeling, "is structurally adequate and worthy of renovation." (An accompanying "after" illustration shows the little structure with its raised false-front façade looking like a small frontier town store building of the 1890s.)

Building interiors must also be considered, to carry through on the historical theme of the preservation yet be adapted for current functional space. But in all, the buildings of the business center offer "a series of features such as size, good human scale, massing, rooflines, brick corbelling, simple fenestration, a good use of materials that gives a distinctive quality of design about the turn of the twentieth century to the business area."

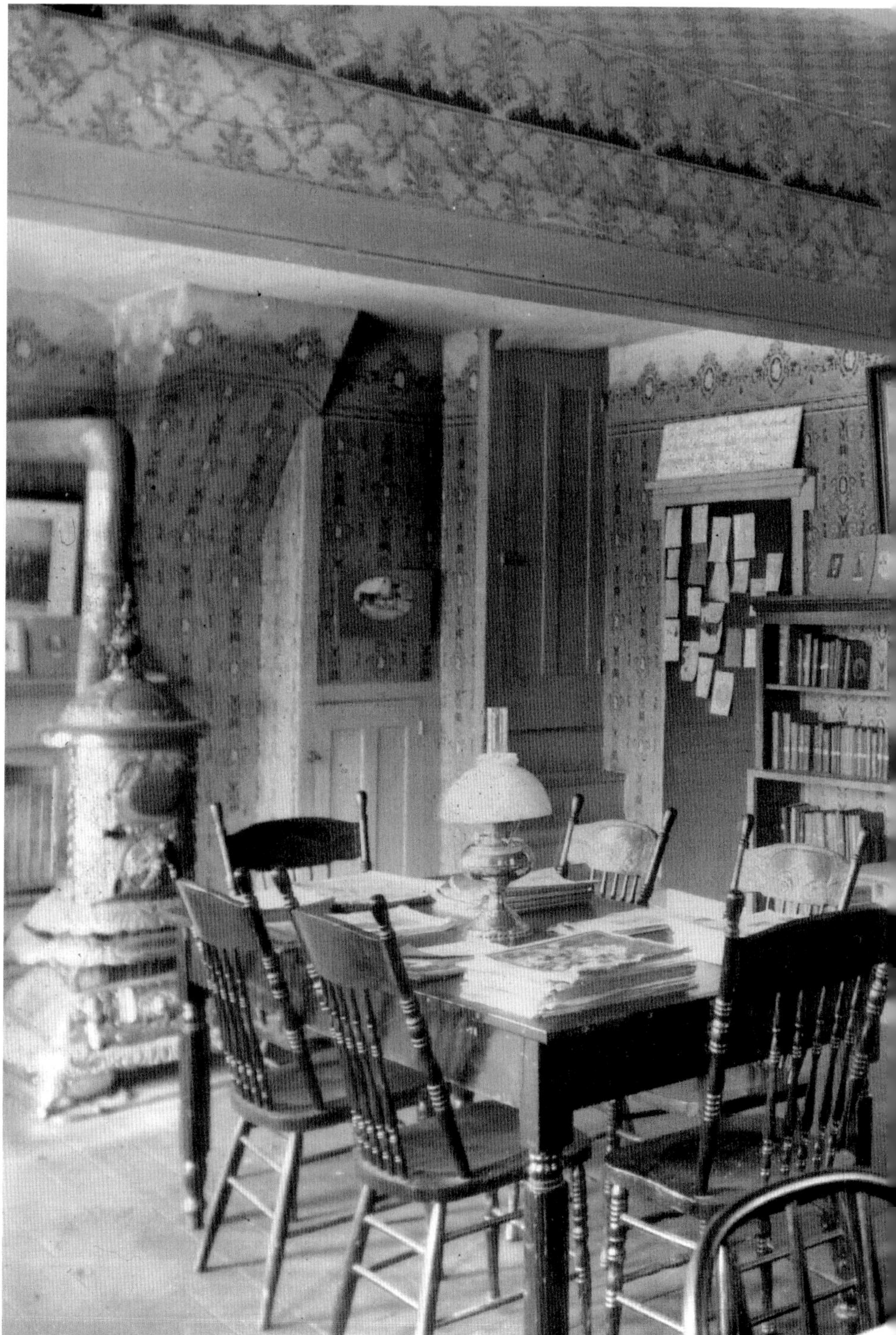

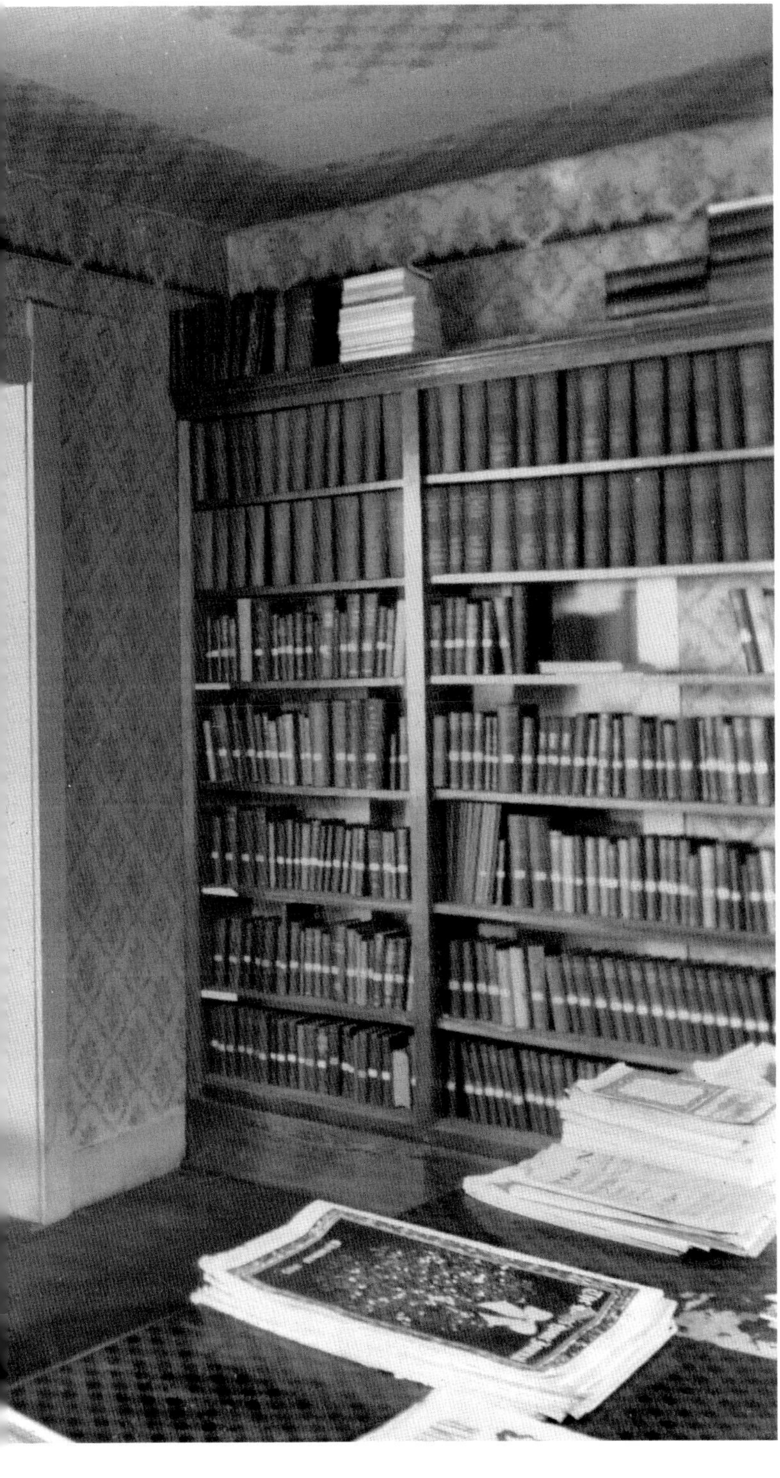

Westfield Carnegie Public Library opened in 1911 near the center of town as Westfield's third public library. The present library is near the school campuses.

No single building style predominates, a situation in which each distinctive style is a statement in itself, a variety of styles of the late nineteenth and early twentieth centuries. Most of the town's older residences are all well worth preservation.

The front elevations are not the only important side of the most notable buildings. The sides and rear entrances, if parking is there, get public attention. (Parking overall is insufficient, the study states.) The study pointed to the Cool Creek as "an integral part" of any revitalization efforts; its length could be landscaped with trees, shrubs and footpaths or walkways leading to the shops, along with places "to pause and relax."

The study also shows that several residences adjacent to the business center and those on Penn Street "are among the finest historic residences in the community." Even those in poor condition are "most worthy of restoration," particularly those on the south side of Penn Street nearest East Street. The residence at 123 East Main is "a nice…Gothic Revival Style; the decorative barge board is an interesting feature." The former inn at 201 East Main "is unquestionably one of the most significant historic buildings" here. The two-story "five-bay frame building is a fine expression of the Federal Style and is most worthy of restoration." Other buildings are "structurally sound," "solid," "in good physical condition," "excellently scaled," "nicely detailed," "having great potential" or "well proportioned."

The study found original architectural details of the Italianate, both Greek and Gothic Revival styles, many ornate "gingerbread" carpentry trims, brackets and "dental" moldings above doors and windows. Residents have given their homes new coats of paint and new paint on stucco exteriors.

Pickett's Cafeteria is said to be "one of the most significant historic buildings," "well proportioned and [with] a nicely scaled raking cornice." Others were "in poor condition and of considerable modification and alterations." And the unadorned square bulk of the "Telephone Building," built after World War II, is "the most unsympathetic addition to the streetscape."

The study closes with a few cost estimates, a list of potential business occupants of the restored buildings and a detailed list of things to do to achieve the study's final illustration. The study is, in large part, a history review in which buildings are the personalities, and it is all definitely relevant to the present task of planning for the future.

In partial response, the town council passed a zoning ordinance for North Union Street to allow only single-family residences, a move that would preserve the charm of the neighborhood with protections such as for the circa 1850 Levi Bowman house, a treasure not to be renovated as multi-family housing. There are cast-iron gates, flower gardens designed and maintained by master gardeners, porch swings and other atmospheric amenities illustrating the kind of overall look the town could preserve. Some homeowners in town come from lineage of note. Ann Van Camp, a longtime Westfield resident, still lives in her family's home on North Union Street.

The 1970s departed like a lion in March, only much more so. Memories of 1978 will long be dominated by the overwhelming winter blizzard that brought nearly everything to a halt for a few days. But the year will be remembered for something other than snowbanks and cancelations.

The few town officials are now in place in a much larger facility: the former Methodist church on Penn Street. The previous year, the Methodists in town and the congregation in Eagletown had combined to form the Christ United Methodist Church in its new location around the corner on North Union Street.

The town council purchased the former church and the parsonage. Now the original sanctuary, pews intact, has become an assembly room for monthly meetings of the town council, plan commission and the board of zoning appeals. The town's two police officers have set up in the church parsonage next door.

Now the fire department has the entire space in the former town hall on South Union Street in which to house its coming needs as its vital responsibilities also grow.

During town election year 1979, Westfield did not go the expense of holding an election; by state law, none was required when there were no opposition candidates. The Democrats, long the small "m" minority, did not slate any candidates. The most recent challenge to the Republicans was from a few independent candidates in 1963. Following the Civil War, Friends were of Lincoln's Republican Party; the choice stuck locally for many people, even though the party itself changed in many ways.

Meanwhile, work on Westfield's $277,000 sewer interceptor is ongoing with the building of levees seven feet tall around the lagoons the sewer plant will use. Residential construction is also occurring on the south side of South Street.

One new structure at the west edge of town gained attention for its new solar energy system. Indiana governor Otis Bowen attended the opening of the "world's largest" Dairy Queen restaurant during the spring of 1979, showcasing the new building across Highway 31 at the west edge of town.

14

The 1980s: True Modernity

The landmark Mendenhall Drugstore closed in February 1980. That long-familiar family name had been on signage since 1924, when Chase and Emmett Mendenhall built the store here on the southwest corner of the main intersection. The store's original popular soda fountain had been used until two years earlier.

But the next spring, a young pharmacist, David Weiss, a graduate of the Butler University School of Pharmacy, reopened the drugstore in May with a variety store atmosphere in addition to filling prescriptions. For his signage, he chose an antique, nineteenth-century script for "Westfield Pharmacy."

Therein is an image symbolizing the decade of the 1980s, many consequential changes being made here are heavily influenced by the rapid and large-scale growth of this locale. One landmark store closes and is reopened by a younger member of the same necessary profession who equips it for a new age of consumerism.

And the trend continues, as with the much-heralded arrival of a new corporate presence, which set a trend for the kind of similar arrivals desired now, corporate headquarters of non-"smokestack" industries. The largest independent telephone company in the nation, GTE, formerly General Telephone and Electronics Corporation, chose Westfield for its Midwest regional operation to be built on U.S. 31 North between 196th and 202nd Streets. This would be the beginning of the end for the township to be characterized chiefly by agriculture, though that result would not be immediate.

The first telephone in town had been installed in the home of Irvin Stanley in 1884 on Park Street by the Bell Telephone Company. The second was put into the Funderburgh Grocery Store, and later, Henry Barker put in a private line joining three families. The Barker line grew to include thirty-eight telephones. In 1901, the White Star Telephone Company was incorporated, with Irvin Stanley as director. Adding the Barker line, White Star served the community until 1928, when it was bought by the Commonwealth Telephone Company. When automatic dial was installed in early 1956 throughout by General Telephone Company (successor to the original local ownership), customers learned the new dial system from a film shown by the company in the high school auditorium.

In 1981, the Westfield Business Association dissolved to form the Westfield Chamber of Commerce. One of the first official acts chose Camilla Allen Axelrod as "Citizen of the Year" for her many civic activities, many of her own creation, such as this year being her seventeenth Christmas party for the residents of the Hamilton County Home. Among the chamber's many functions to promote commerce, its annual directory and handbook would become a one-stop source of vital statistics about the town and township.

As described in the chamber of commerce's 1981–82 handbook, the Westfield Washington school system is situated in a campus concept, with elementary, middle and high schools located on one campus. The overall enrollment has increased in the past ten years to a current total of 1,600 students. Two new buildings have been constructed: a new high school and middle school. The existing elementary school will soon have additions for the special areas of media service, music, physical education and art. Growth now includes expanded curriculum, a gifted program at the elementary, an orchestra for the middle school and microcomputer courses in high school, where college calculus is offered in the math department.

In 1983, the Monon Railroad had passed through Westfield for exactly a century. But this year, the Seaboard Railroad System petitioned the Interstate Commerce Commission (ICC) to stop rail service to Westfield—actually to abandon its tracks from Delphi, Indiana, to Indianapolis. The Hamilton County Farm Co-op, the Truss Manufacturing Co. (which had its own sidetrack) and others would lose their major freight transportation. The newly formed Monon Shippers Association waged a successful campaign to keep rail transportation available. Wanda Lockrem, executive director of the chamber of commerce, filed a protest.

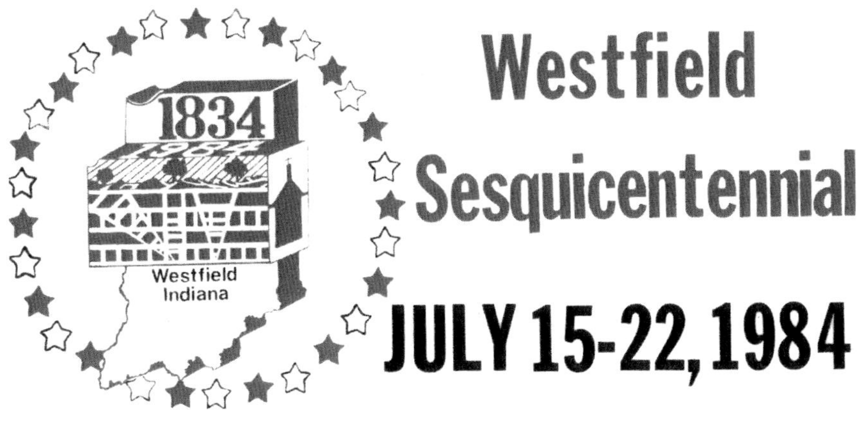

A commemorative Westfield Sesquicentennial license plate, 1984, was also designed.

But even after the shippers' association gained another stay and encouraged the railroad to consider changing to commuter and tourist travel, the death knell sounded when the tracks were taken up for roadwork on Route 32 west of town, and that break of a few yards came to symbolize the improbability of future rail service for Westfield.

At least commuter travel would get a boost when a local bus service with the hopefully suggestive title of the Indianapolis & Suburban Railroad began running under company president and Westville resident Thomas Evans, with twenty years of public transportation experience. From the bus station on South Union Street, the route extends to Home Place in Clay Township to the south and then becomes an express route to downtown Indianapolis. A week ticket is two dollars; the bus leaves town at 6:25 a.m. for an hour's ride to the capital city and returns by 6:00 p.m. The first run has begun with about a dozen riders, collecting more as it proceeds south through Carmel.

In November 1983, the new, much larger Westfield Washington Public Library opened. The possibility of a new public library had been sparked by a recent windfall of $160,000 from a former patron, a bachelor farmer who spent many free hours completing his family genealogy. Dairy farmer Joe Sumner died and left the money to the library as seed money for new construction. One facet of the planning was for a Sumner Room for genealogy and local history to memorialize the donor's long-abiding and productive interest. The original Carnegie Library opened in 1911 on West Main Street, and additions were made in 1917 and 1965. The new library, on Hoover Street at the north edge of town and next door to the school campus, is an impressive example of the

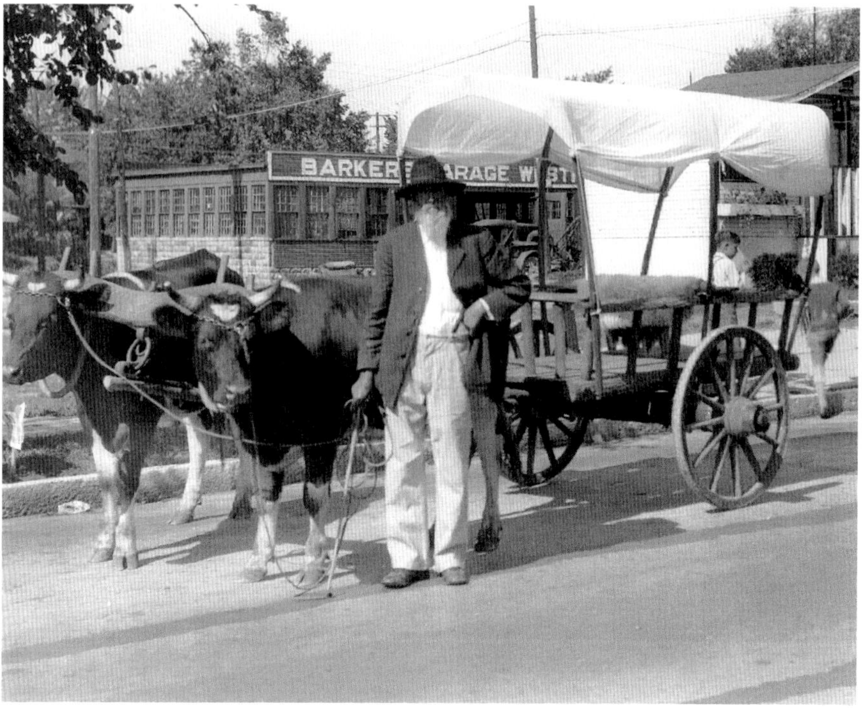

Reenacting the mid-1830s migration of Quakers from the South to Westfield for the town's centennial, 1934.

new age in public libraries with eleven thousand square feet in which adult and children's services have been increased greatly in space and programming. There is also a catering kitchen and a large public meeting room. Few other structures can say "community" like a local public library, as this new one does.

The planning for the town's 150th anniversary in 1984 had begun two years ago. Students at the high school had earlier designed a town flag with "Westfield Indiana 1834" forming a circle divided into three equal parts, for a cross (religious faith of the founders), a lamp and book (education) and an entrance to a tunnel (the Underground Railroad). The design has been used on the town's trucks and cars, letterhead and other places. The design would now be used in the promotion materials for the big celebration.

The chamber of commerce erected four large signs announcing the weeklong event, July 15–22, at the four entrances to town. Each day of the event had a theme: "heritage, farm and home, nine to five, youth, senior citizens, family and 'welcome home.'" Since the town had been founded

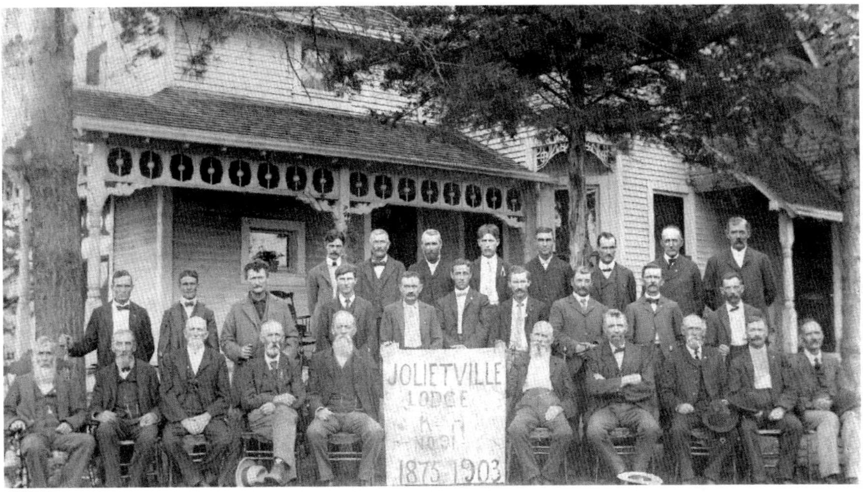

Lodge in Jolietville, Washington Township, Hamilton County, Indiana.

on religious principles, the celebration began officially on Sunday at the churches in town for "old-fashioned preaching, praying and praising." Then came an ice cream social, baking contests, a ham and bean and pioneer cornbread supper, a salad luncheon, a fish fry, parades, street dances, a quilting bee, pioneer crafts and displays, demonstrations of antique farming equipment, horseshoeing, a variety show, an art and antique fair and guided activities for small children. And, of course, a guided tour of the storied Underground Railroad stations here and out in the township.

A new history, *Our Westfield*, was for sale; 350 copies had been prepaid, and nearly that many more were still available at the Westfield Washington Historical Society. There were still some residents who could remember the grand centennial in 1934. Theirs was a worthy and admired perspective.

The editorial committee—Leanna and Joe Roberts, Stuart Neal and Byron Barker—took their deserved bows. The book was organized in two major sections: a history compilation and many pages of recollections, including some that had been prepared in the past by persons no longer living. It is a time also for recollections of the few villages out in the township. Eagletown, unincorporated, with perhaps one hundred residents now, was platted in 1848 by Jesse Waller and Ephraim K. Stout on Little Eagle Creek, which powered a sawmill and flour mill. There had been an all-grades school once, before the upper grades were transferred to Westfield, and some students rode the old Midland into town. The brick former Methodist church still stands, though it has served as the First Baptist Church.

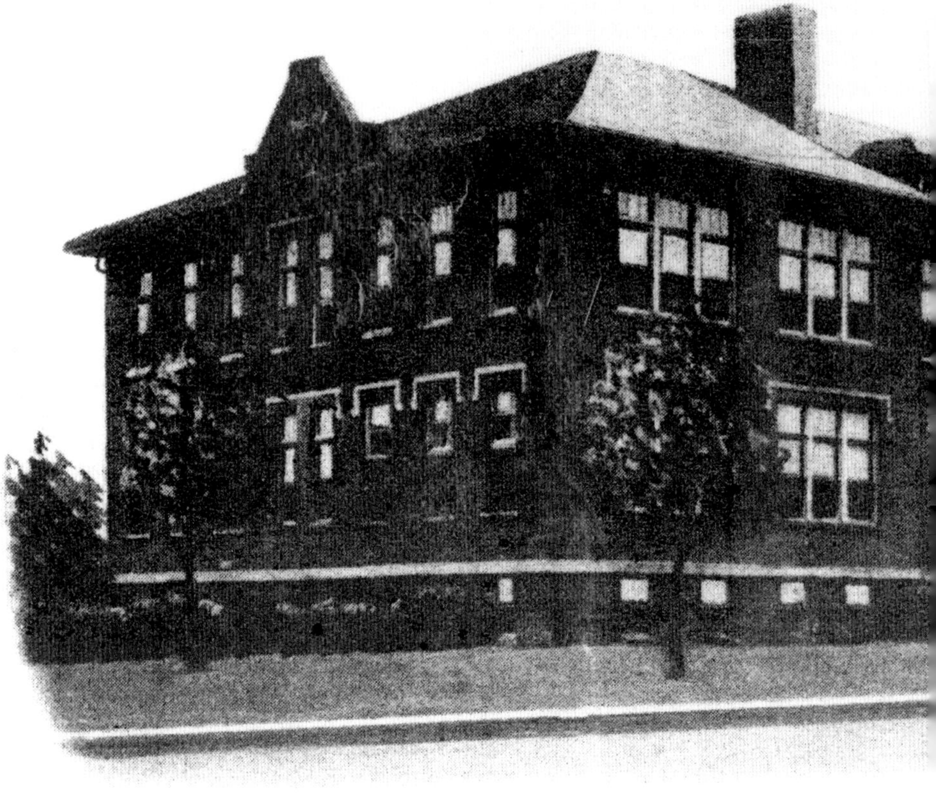

Westfield High School, showing the original portion built in the middle and later additions (photo early 1980s).

Remnants of Jolietville ("Joliet") are still on Route 32 west of town, a village once with a thriving dry goods store, a couple of grocery stores (one dating to 1910 still stands) and a bank that was later moved to Westfield.

On Wednesday, Senior Citizens' Day, two "Citizens of the Century" were named. Elsie Moon Cox, the great-great-granddaughter of Simon and Hannah Moon, is of direct lineage truly to the first days of the town. For many years, Elsie taught Latin and business and physical education and is known to generations of residents. The school yearbook for 1964–65 was dedicated to her. The second centennial citizen to be named was Roy O. Hadley, born on a township farm in 1906, WHS graduate in 1923, a resident all his life and well known in the insurance and banking business in Westfield and as a permanent promoter of all that is good about and for Westfield.

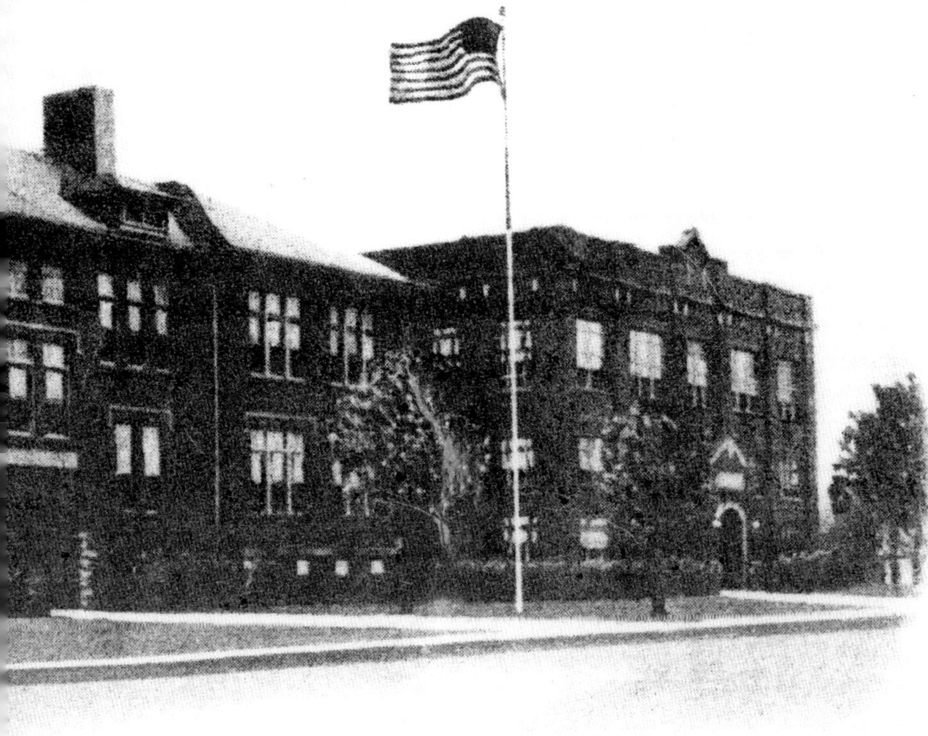

The sesquicentennial was yet another time to hear passages from *In the Days of My Youth*, a lightly disguised fictional account of the childhood of pioneer progeny James Baldwin (1841–1925), published in 1911, writing as "Robert Dudley." His father, Isaac Baldwin, had purchased one of the very early claims in Washington Township. This member of the impressive Baldwin family of educators had been a school superintendent in Indiana schools and had established one of the first grade schools in the state after the Civil War. He was an expert on children's literature with Harper & Brothers in New York City, where he also wrote school texts for the American Book Company, publishing over fifty books on a variety of subjects. When his fictionalized account of his early years in Westfield was first published, there were many complaints by those who were certain that the less than perfect characters he "created" were themselves or close relatives, lightly and ineffectively disguised. There was even a list of characters and their real-life counterparts made available by someone who claimed to know just who appeared in the book.

The big historical event, the town's 150th birthday, was deemed a success: another instance of local residents turning to the past, and inward, to celebrate their heritage.

The demolition of the former high school on West Main Street in the summer of 1984 changed the long-familiar landscape there. Though used for purposes other than classes and school activities, the building held many memories for hundreds of residents. A large portion of it had been destroyed in an immense fire in 1971. The demolition company estimated the number of bricks of the old school to be about 350,000 total, with 175,000 cleaned of old mortar and sold for sixteen cents each. The bricks would be used in new construction in the area. Westfield residents were offered a special price.

In 1984, the Westfield Economic Development Corporation organized with offices in the new school administration building. Members are a town board member, the school superintendent, a lawyer, bankers and representatives of GTE North. The group will develop a strategic plan for the Greater Westfield community to promote development "consistent with the current life style and traditional values of the area." The most pressing need is to address the growth toward Westfield from the township line to the south.

Also this year, the Indiana Mills Company moved from Carmel to a twenty-seven-acre site on U.S. 31 at the north edge of town. The company makes seat belts and associated items and now has land for a new factory, office complex and warehouse. Also, Ervin Ball's Ball Systems, manufacturer of high-tech measurement computing and control equipment, relocated its offices and laboratories to a twenty-acre, twelve-site development at 169th and U.S. 31 named the Ball Industry Park, Westfield's first industrial park, where the Ball company would be the prototype for others to follow.

The matter of growth has both proponents looking to a future of economic boom but also those who advise a slower "more managed" process, one of comprehensive discussions of permit requests. Some advise that more affordable housing be created. The population has grown from 1,217 in 1960, to 1,837 in 1970 and to 2,783 in 1980. The new Westfield Regional Interceptor Project, a vastly improved sewer system, came into use the fall of 1986 and improved on that basic utility for the community. In August 1989, bids were sought for extending a major sewer line west across U.S. 31 where growth has occurred and seems to be the future in that regard.

The call for residential construction got a good boost. The third-quarter 1987 report of the town building commissioner cites $6 million being spent on new construction in single-family and other family dwellings. The previous three months had seen seventy-three building permits granted, meaning receipts of nearly $9,000 for the town.

The new library has been open for four years. Nearly five thousand residents have library cards now. State statistics show that the library has more registered borrowers than most libraries its size. Circulation has risen over 200 percent in the past two years; the library is open twelve more hours each week. The library's wide-ranging reference services recently include a new computer system called "Infotrac" for finding research articles in many magazines and journals, another tool to save time in locating information requested about a wide range of topics.

The cover illustration of the chamber of commerce's handbook for 1983–84 favored a minimalist illustration to make a point: a simple outline of Indiana with two lines crossing in the middle, one labeled "U.S. 31" and the other "State Route 32." The phrase "within minutes of Indianapolis" had been used repeatedly in promotional materials. Westfield is fifteen minutes' travel from access to four of the state's interstate highways.

The P.L. Porter and Company, based in California, making seat-reclining mechanisms for the auto industry, moved here from California and will employ about 130 people

Urban planning is an overriding responsibility now. In preparation for more of these new light industry arrivals, an "overlay" to the township zoning ordinance has been created, adding restrictions for development along U.S. 31, for setbacks, landscaping, lot sizes and prohibiting some kinds of businesses.

In April 1988, the plan commission approves several developments and addresses issues of drainage brought by neighbors of the proposed projects. The commission's meetings have increasingly full agendas.

By 1988, the growth pattern north from Indianapolis is so apparent that the Westfield Economic Development Corporation is formed to work at managing the changes to come in land use. The town, along with the school district, local banks and developers, with representatives of GTE, will work together in this linkage organization to plan for the future, touching on all the affecting matters of chief concern.

The term "public safety" refers most often to the services of fire and police departments. How they worked together locally was shown in August 1987, when the Pan Am Games' opening torch run made an early morning detour into town from U.S. 31, as requested by the chamber of commerce. Indianapolis had won the hosting honors for this western hemisphere event held in advance of the World Olympics, and the runners and the support staff came down North Union Street and turned on State Route 32 and back to U.S. 31 to continue to Indianapolis. The chamber managed to alert enough people for a crowd of well-wishers to assemble to welcome the runners to town and urge them on. Dan and Julia Palko of Dan's Farm Kitchen gave all runners and caravan officials a complimentary breakfast. Jim Spelbring's fire department helped town marshal Ken Peters with traffic control. The two safety departments working together was a common reassurance to residents that such essential cooperation was characteristic here. One runner needed a tube of Ben-Gay shortly after leaving town; pharmacist Davis Weiss provided the cure, and Marshal Peters made that once-in-a-career official delivery run.

Volunteer fireman Bob Mikesell had joined a twelve-man volunteer force in 1937; he was sixteen years old. By 1968, he had become the first full-time paid chief. By 1981, the department had three full-time firemen and seventeen volunteers with new personal pagers to receive the alarm to answer. The department is equipped with two ambulances, three pumper trucks, one tanker, one rescue truck and one grass-fire vehicle. A "quick attack pumper," a compact vehicle with numerous pieces of equipment for firefighting and emergency health equipment, was soon acquired, and a new vehicle was also obtained for the chief's own use.

In late 1980, the police department had moved to the city building at 143 South Union Street, one block from the primary intersection in town and in the same facility as the fire department. In 1982, police chief Kenneth D. Peters headed a force of four sworn officers and seven reserve officers. All sworn officers had completed training at the Indiana Law Enforcement Academy in Plainfield, Indiana. In three years, the crime rate in town was reduced 50 percent.

When the police department was moved to the new town hall, the fire department acquired a new aerial ladder truck with a seventy-five-foot ladder and a 1,840-gallon-per-minute pumping capability and a new ambulance.

In midsummer 1987, Westfield fire chief Jim Spelbring began his campaign for a second fire station to keep up with growing demands. The department of four full-time firemen, twenty-one volunteers and the chief had made some seven hundred runs over the previous twelve months. The chief estimated the cost would be $500,000 for the new station with another $100,000 for six more full-time fire crew members. The town and township would share the cost. He recommended the new station be placed west of town, across Route 31, to accommodate the residential and other growth in that direction of late. The department has two ambulances, two pumpers, one mini pumper, one grass-fire truck, one tanker and a snowmobile since the intractable blizzard emergency of 1978 was still well remembered.

The department raised $5,000 to this end at the 1988 FireFest, officiating at the event's arts and crafts fair on town streets, mainly on the reputation of its barbecue on North Union Street.

School fundraisers are increasingly utilized now for specific school expenses. In 1988, the WHS band introduced the "Westfield Monopoly Game" to raise funds to send school music students to competitions. The game went on sale in mid-August. Produced by the Power Play Company, "the Game of Westfield" sells for ten dollars. The goal of the players is to own the real-life businesses in town that are shown on the playing board, each costing $250.

On Friday, September 4, 1987, Westfield was introduced to all who watched the regular "Live at Five" feature on Indianapolis TV Channel 13. The segment was broadcast from Westfield from the northwest corner of Route 32/Main Street and North Union Street. And it is the site itself that is the real slice of life story. When the chamber of commerce got the call for the opportunity, a location was needed in a hurry, and the corner property, hardly the most scenic in town, was empty and prominent. Could a mini "park for a day" be created almost immediately? The property owners agreed to allow the town to spruce up the corner. Perhaps it was the location, next door to the old Carnegie Library of 1911, that helped raise some major volunteer spirit. Adam Strong's Construction Company began the first stages of transformation; Wilfong Construction came also. Jim Gapinski of Heartland Growers, the immense greenhouse operation north of town, came through with live plants, flowers and even a few trees. Ron Passwater of Pickett's Cafeteria across the street added split rail fencing, and Jim Steckley's catering service fed the entire Channel 13 crew. Steckley also brought a post hold digger for the fence posts. Jones Trucking brought in concrete benches, Delello Electric Company brought outside lighting and Curley's Building Materials of Carmel and Keever's Hardware in town provided sundry needs. Jim Spelbring brought a pumper from the fire station down the street to keep the instant plantings watered. The police department had the most visible responsibility of safeguarding a very busy highway intersection.

There were others, of course, each of whom contributed his or her own essential service. The WHS band played, familiar TV weatherman Bob Gregory and TV host Kim Hood were, indeed, "Live at Five" at the main intersection of town for the instant crowd to gawk at. The overall cooperative, nearly immediate "coming together" of the affair was impressive. And as an afterthought, some remember that "it rained some."

One of the few references of late to the broad subject of agriculture now appearing in the local newspaper is about the threatening effect of the current drought on the farms. It was announced, though, that farmers in all ninety-two counties in the state are eligible for drought relief.

On June 22, 1988, the Westfield Economic Development Corporation hired an executive director, Jeffrey T. Shaw, and a deputy director. Shaw came from the Indiana Department of Commerce and the Indianapolis Department of Development. The collective attention of the Westfield community was well trained for forward looking. The future and the present were intertwined in a way that seemed to defy a singular focus on time.

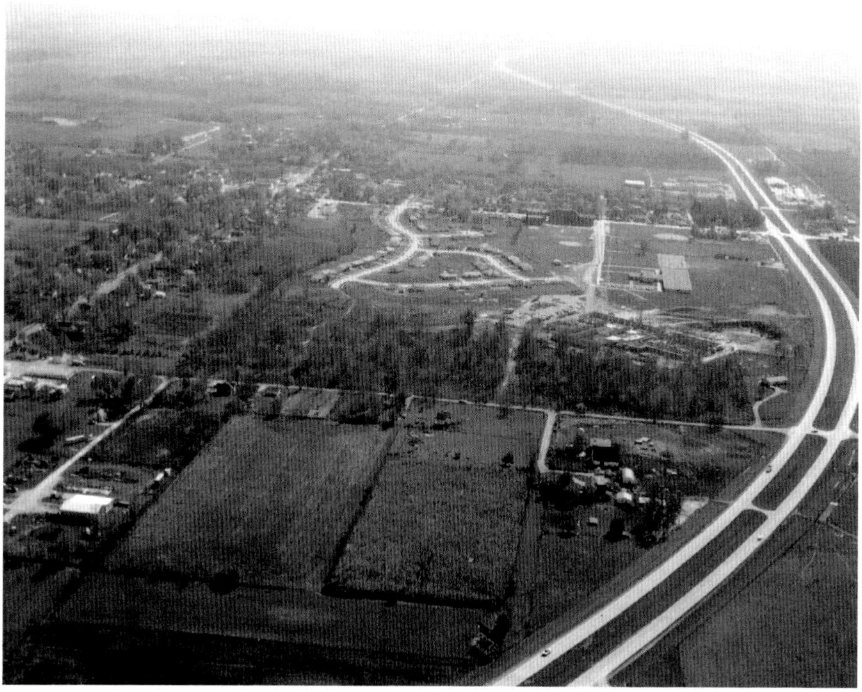

The new U.S. Route 31, view to the south, bypassing the center of Westfield (left center). State Route 32 crosses the new highway (top right) and still passes through Westfield. This common bypassing of towns changed their commercial futures dramatically.

15

The 1990s: New Promise, New Scale

The federal census of 1990 shows Westfield with a population of 3,304. The largest age group is young adults between twenty-five and thirty-four, with a median income of $33,486 ($44,892 in the township, $51,167 in the county and $34,082 statewide). High school graduates made up 85.1 percent of the residents (75.6 percent statewide).

Unemployment here is at 5.7 percent, which is the same as the statewide average. The numbers speak for an educated employee resource suitable for the kinds of positions the recent corporate arrivals need. Several employers have already profited from that resource. The largest, GTE, employs 1,200; Indiana Mills, 200; Aero Drapery, 175; Curtis Dyna-Fog Products, 75; and Heartland Growers greenhouse complex, 70. In addition to these employees, over 50 percent of the workforce traveled over twenty minutes to work, as in Indianapolis, Noblesville and Kokomo.

The former Regal Grocery Store closed in the summer of 1990. Libby Hadley worked there for thirty-three years. The large rectangular sign was removed in June 1991. The former store will be razed so the pharmacy next door on the corner can be expanded. With few exceptions, the neighborhood and small-town grocer is extinct; the grand supermarkets prevail, and one is usually minutes away by car.

Recently GTE, GTE North and Westfield Washington schools formed an education-technology partnership to build a state-of-the-art "smart campus."

GTE has its own Educational Network Access Division, and the company has invited other businesses to participate, including Epson and Hewlett-Packard. The new Shamrock Elementary School, a $9 million construction project, is being built about three miles from the main school campus at 161st Street and Springmill Road to open for 1993 school year. It, too, will be wired into the new information age system

The 100th commencement at Westfield High School was held in June 1991, and in September at the homecoming game, the school's new football stadium was dedicated, named the Allan Stanley Memorial Stadium by request of the student council. "Red" Stanley had been on the school board for twenty years, was a well-known sports supporter and fan and was among the first of a group of former grads, the "Lettermen," who had provided a playing field from their own resources and through fundraising on land adjoining the high school but not owned by the schools.

The latest groundbreaking at GTE North is for a company subsidiary GTE/Sylvania, which will consolidate operations from nearly two dozen sites across the nation to a new structure here and will also hire about 120 to 150 workers. The nationally known manufacturer of lighting products is building a national distribution center, a fifty-thousand-square-foot facility. Sylvania chose cornfields over palm trees; the company had also considered Tampa, Florida, before coming to Westfield to thirty acres at East 169th Street. Indiana Mills & Manufacturing is also expanding into a new warehouse.

GTE's company headquarters also broke ground in September 1991 for a facility to be called GTE Supply, a $10 million investment to support telephone operations in the company's areas of business, as well as provide products and consulting services to customers in twenty-one states. GTE "areas" include the Caribbean, Dominican Republic and South America. The new facility will employ seventy-two to one hundred people.

The former bus line based in Westfield a couple of years ago ceased after the City of Carmel refused to allow the bus to travel its city streets. Now company owner Tom Evans has resumed operation by acquiring another bus run between South Bend and Indianapolis.

In April 1992, the Town Council announced its "Westfield 2000 Plus" initiative for addressing the growth already underway. A recent survey by students at Ball State University in Muncie, Indiana, has begun with the twin inquiries "Who are we?" and "Who do we want to be?" for Westfield to remain relevant amidst the immense change occurring all around. The survey students first looked to the religious community. The number of church denominations has increased over the years. The ready choices now include the First Baptist Church of Westfield, the Catholic Church, the Christian (Disciples of Christ), the Church of Christ, the Church of the Nazarene, the Society of Friends (four meetings total in the township), the United Methodist church, and the Wesleyan Methodist church.

Overall, the survey respondents credited this place with small-town atmosphere, proximity to a large city, an excellent school system, being near major transportation corridors, friendly people, historic background and for safety and cleanliness. The most significant needs of the community were found to be an updated and revised master plan, recreation facilities, solutions to some traffic problems, maintaining a competitive downtown and establishing a mutual relationship between town and township. The historic dependence of the town businesses on the farm families' Saturday night purchases had been equally balanced with those outlying families needing the products and services offered in town. Some are asking how to regain a similar, updated version of that historic equilibrium. There is also a need to enhance quality of water supply and to develop a community identity.

The Westfield Streetscape and Revitalization Corporation received an Indiana Heritage Research Grant in June 1992 to record local oral history from 1900 to the present with aid from the Kiwanis Club. The recorded interviews will be conducted by a history student from the Indiana University/Purdue University public history department in Indianapolis.

For over sixty years, the landmark water tower has stood a block and a half north of the singular intersection of historic consequence in town and about one hundred feet to the west of North Union Street.

Looking somewhat like a rotund comic strip rocket on four spindly legs, it was launched in 1929 and reached 122 feet into the stratosphere at its topknot. It was equipped with two ladders, the longest from the ground to the circling catwalk, a much shorter one from there to the very top. Built to hold 60,000 gallons of water, it has been used until this year, 1992. It has been replaced by another nearby, a modern air-streamed silhouette with space age curved surfaces. In size, this one is truly majestic, with a capacity of 300,000 gallons of water.

Few have climbed the height of the old water tower with its outside ladder—those for its periodic maintenance and a few just for fun, fewer still pulling along some object large enough to be seen from afar and left sitting on the catwalk. Once it was a few school desks. Bill Dennis tried the climb

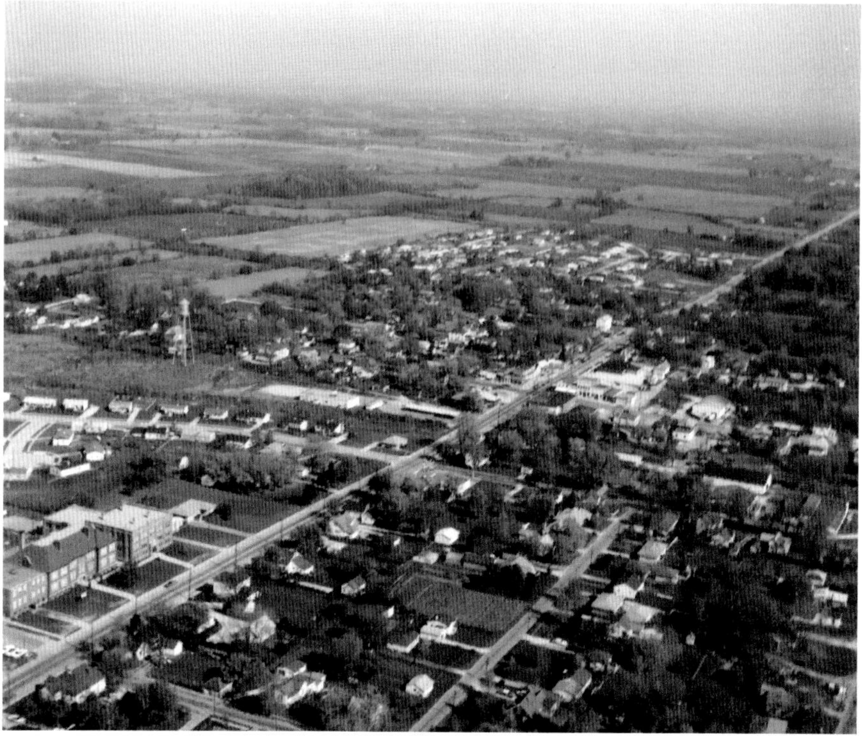

Westfield water tower and Westfield High School (lower left), 1970s.

once. He got to the catwalk but decided not to go the extra steps of the little ladder to the very top where he had intended to hang a T-shirt. The view was literally overwhelming, he remembers, and he stepped gingerly back down "real easy," he says. Someone else intended to paint a message or whatnot with blue paint at the top of the rocket, but the paint bucket dropped just as the artwork of intended consequence began.

When it was announced that the old tower had to come down, there was genuine protest as from a collective sense of ownership, as for an antique with value in the abstract for many. The old familiar tower was a symbol of memories of growing up here, marrying here, of looking for the first sight of it when coming back home from traveling.

The Westfield Washington School System's participation in "The American School 2000 Project: The Technology Initiative" gained the notice of the *Christian Science Monitor* on March 2, 1993, for the kindergarten to twelfth

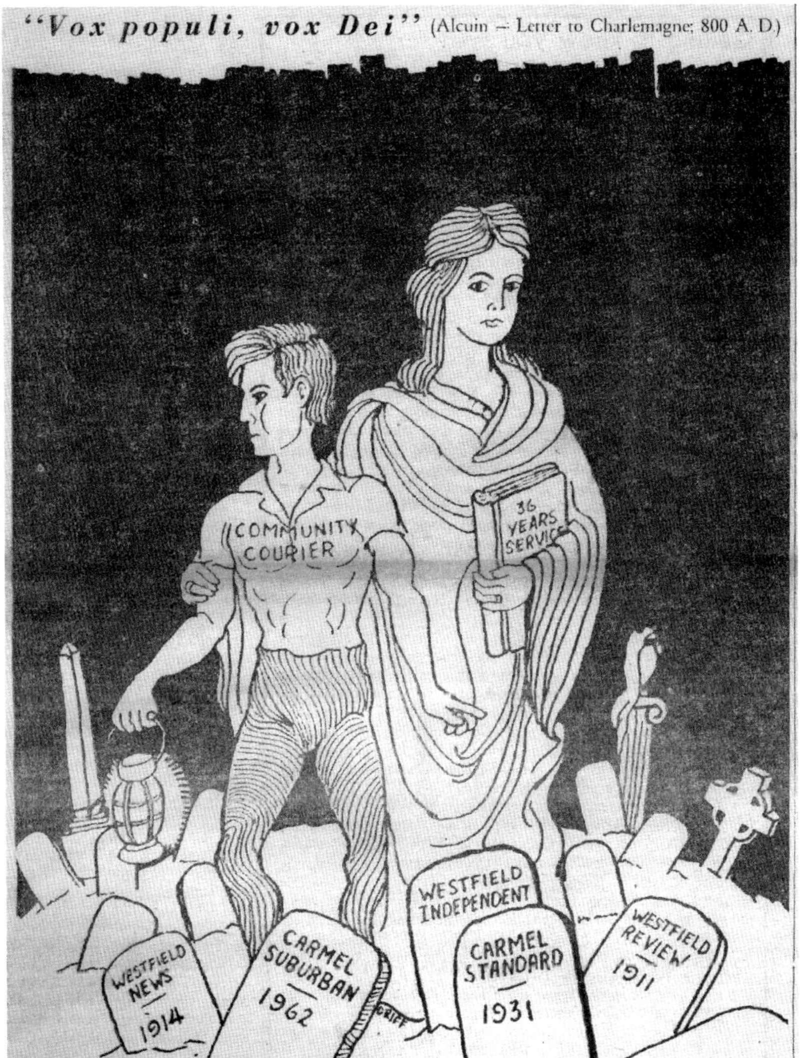

The *Community Courier* newspaper begins publication in Westfield in 1964, designed to serve all of southwest Hamilton County (it replaced the *Booster* advertiser).

grade installation of voice, data and video technology. Local schools, the article reports, are "wired for the 21st century" with "miles of copper and fiber-optic cables connecting each classroom with a main technology center at the school." The all-school voice mail system invites parents to communicate with teachers, as but one of the new uses. Teachers can call up audio-visual programming for the televisions mounted in the classrooms, including video tapes, laser discs, CD-ROMs, motion pictures and programming by satellite. Being a "national showcase as a learning environment of the future...the information age," Westfield Washington schools have joined about one hundred other schools in the nation in this up-to-date learning method, a trend growing more in public schools than in colleges and universities, the article states. What was needed yet was software directed to disadvantaged students who are having trouble learning to read and complete basic assignments. The estimated $1 million cost has been carried by the capital projects budget and by arrangements with corporate vendors who reduce the prices of their wares to the school.

Westfield has an impressive record of local newspapers beginning in 1884 with the *News* published by W.P. Houk and Ferdinand W. Taylor and later owned by A.P. Howe from about 1889; the name was changed to the *Hamilton County News* by new owner Edward E. Neal fourteen years later. Lamont Cressen bought the paper in about 1911 and changed the name back to the *News*. It ceased publication for a while and then was continued by Arthur E. Pinkham until 1914. Jasper Manlove brought out the *Westfield Gazette* in 1885, later called the *Air Line* by his daughter Olivia C. Manlove in 1889. Also beginning in 1885, the *Index* was the local temperance and women's suffrage paper for about five years. The *Patriot* began about 1892 by J.F. Beals for a short run. The *Westfield Review* came out in 1917. Daily M. Hudler brought out the *Westfield Independent* in 1918. The later two were of short duration. In 1926, the weekly advertising *Booster* began with Charles and Roger G. Ervin and ended in 1965, said to be the longest-running "shopper" paper in the nation. Its printing operation was destroyed by fire in 1947, but the father and son team managed without missing printing a single issue. It became the *Courier* in 1964, though published in nearby Carmel for all of southwest Hamilton County. The Westfield High School published the *Green and White* of general importance from 1923, named for the school colors. In more recent times, newspaper consortiums have published papers directed to individual communities; for Westfield, it was the *Topics* and then the *Westfield Enterprise*, "the weekly that's read daily."

The *Westfield Reporter* came out on February 4, 1987, with Wanda Lockrem as publisher and editor. The introductory issue listed fifty-two commercial charter subscribers; the paper could be purchased at Butch's Market, the

Eagletown Grocery, Jan's Flower Café, the Westfield Grocery, the public library, the Westfield Pharmacy, the "Pop-In" and at White's Donuts.

In 1993, the *Westfield Reporter* was acquired by John R. Holmes. The paper continues to enhance the quality of life in advice columns by three local doctors, by being the go-to place for school sports news and with announcements of public interest and importance. The paper announces meetings of organizations of special interest with each having some civic or social reason for being, including the Lions, Masons, Kiwanis, Eastern Star, Job's Daughters, Fun for Folks over Fifty, the VFW Post 19207, Westfield Youth Soccer Association, the Westfield Public Library Board of Trustees and the Westfield Washington Chamber of Commerce.

Each list of contents shows current interests, the needs, responsibilities and opportunities of living in the community, such as the "Funwalk" for literacy, the church directory, entertainment announcements, crossword puzzles, fire and ambulance runs, real estate, cookbook recipes, health articles, classified ads, money management and news of students and the schools.

The variety of topics is as varied as readers of the paper: the community moves toward additional water supply; the Lifeline emergency air transport

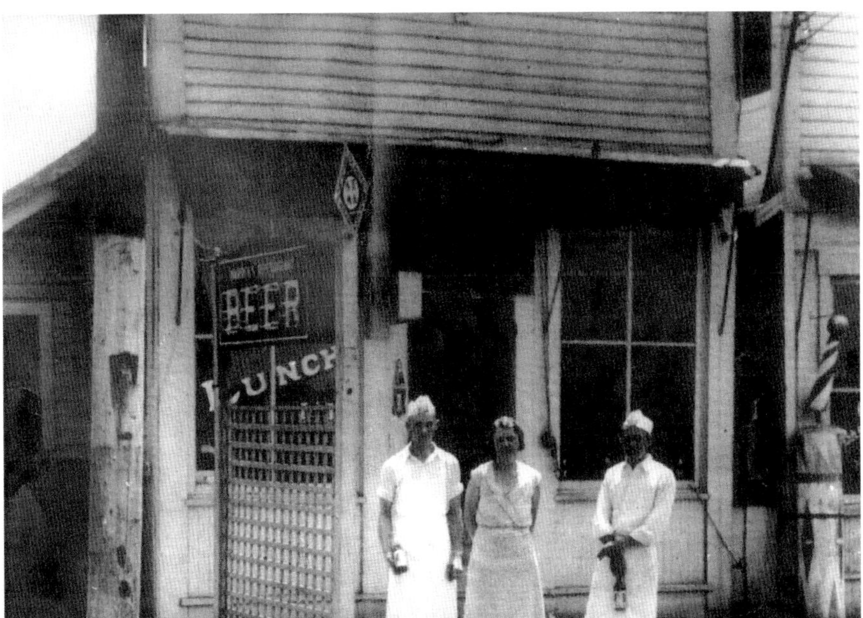

Warren's Lunch Shop, North Union Street, Westfield, Indiana, with an early beer sign in town.

assists Westfield Fire Department during one harrowing emergency; and the Westfield Washington High School Shamrocks continue a winning streak. On "Our Page" for the children, local artist Julie Sole creates puzzles, cartoon characters and a weekly calendar of events of benefit to kids, a mini newspaper of its own on one page. Both editors have featured detailed front-page articles regarding some issue facing the community.

In his "Our Opinion" column, editor John Holmes continues his predecessor's emphasis on the importance of a citizenry that knows the facts about current local issues: town budgetary matters and public funding, public services, public education, the nuts and bolts of local infrastructure, matters affecting employment, taxes and more. Holmes, as had Lockrem, cites the "far too small" turnout for town council meetings, which leaves the council unsure about public opinion and the public unaware or unresponsive about such daily matters as mandatory recycling, water supplies, school construction, traffic congestion, business development, planning and zoning and more.

The description of the recent Newby Family Reunion, with a photograph of the sixty-one family members attending from near and far, speaks volumes about the connectivity of large families in one place with common roots so compelling that members come from long distances for even temporary companionship.

The new Bank One opens, and staff members of three existing local banks—Union State Bank, First Indiana Savings Bank and AmeriTrust Bank—attend "incognito," wearing comic black-rimmed glasses with attached bushy eyebrows, nose and mustache, the kind of interaction that mollifies somewhat the strict competition each bank must pursue.

The "Stetho-Scope" health articles by Dr. Robert D. Habig raise important concerns such as "can the farm be made safer?" In what the doctor still calls "a great rural community," farm accidents do happen from fatigue, time pressures because of seasonal weather, equipment breakdowns and environmental factors, and there is the need to ensure the safety of children on the farm. Other medical doctors and health experts also contribute information of vital importance.

In the summer of 1993, Jeff Benton's Eagle Scout project cleaned the old Friends Cemetery grounds. He led a group of helpers in repairing broken stone benches, trimmed vegetation so the plaque for the Martha Doan Memorial Garden, installed in 1977 by the Westfield Women's Club, could be seen again, along with the large polished stone monument for the numerous pioneer families listed in 1966.

On July 14, 1993, Fire Station "82" was dedicated on U.S. 31 at East 151st Street. V.J. Macy, fire chief in 1953, watched with current chief Bob Smith. By 1995, the department had grown to fourteen firefighters including the chief and seen a 13.8 percent increase in activity with runs within the city limits nearly double that of the township and some runs out of the township as well. Ambulance runs account for 75 percent of the total.

In June 1993, the chamber of commerce has a new executive director. Julie Sole is a Hamilton County native, and she has volunteered with various educational and support groups. A freelance artist, Julie has worked in the art department of an Indianapolis publishing company and has done feature graphics for the *Westfield Reporter*.

In July, bonds are issued for a $2.9 million public library expansion project of more than twenty-four thousand square feet, nearly doubling the present space. The parking lot will increase in size as well.

The U.S. Census Bureau estimated the town population in late 1995 grew from 3,304 in April 1990 to 4,211 in July 1994. A special census in 1997 showed population growth of 63 percent from 1990, 3,264 to 5,341; an immediate result was additional state cigarette and alcohol revenues based on population.

During 1995, a full-time investigative division was added to the police department, bringing the total number of police officers to fourteen, with two experienced officers assigned to active criminal cases.

On January 1, 1995, pioneer progeny Mildred Williams Stalker (Mrs. Myron Stalker), born on October 15, 1895, will wait nine months and fifteen days before celebrating and commemorating a full century of life here among others who trace their lineage to the founders. Mildred cast her first vote in a presidential election in 1921, not only because she had reached voting age, but also because it was the first time any woman got the vote. Mildred voted for Warren G. Harding seventy-five years ago, and she says, "I have never, ever, missed a chance to vote yet."

Mildred well knows that the women's voting issue had long been a local concern, along with the intertwined temperance issue. Mildred's female relatives locally had spoken, debated, marched and otherwise protested their unjust barring from the voting booth. Born of a devout and historic Quaker lineage, Mildred believes she has attained this remarkable age by eating more vegetables than meat, and following the advice "tend to you own knittin'."

Tom Gifford, another local centenarian, was born on May 12, 1895, six months before Mildred. His family lived on a farm near Jolietville. He rode the Midland Railroad to Westfield to high school; the ride cost a dime a day. But before boarding, Tom milked cows and fed the horses. The family raised most of their food and raised their own beef and pork. In winter, the beef carcass was hung from a rope from the hay track in the barn; for breakfast, Tom would slice off a piece of the meat. He stayed on the farm until he married Jean Hershey and took a job at the Talbert Lumber Yard in town in the early 1920s. When he had earned enough, they bought a 140-acre farm and lived there for forty years and reared two daughters. In the 1960s, they moved to a house in Westfield, where he still lives; his wife died in 1980. Tom knew Mildred Stalker from when she worked in the office at the lumberyard and from their school years. Now he cares for a large garden and his strawberries on the farm that is now operated by his son-in-law. He attributes his longevity to not smoking or drinking and eating rolled oats for breakfast every morning. Tom advises saving some money, especially if you live to be one hundred.

The town council has decided wisely and conscientiously to keep the town administrative offices of town hall within two blocks of the very center of historic Westfield, around the corner of North Union at Penn Street. The council purchased a parcel of land on the east side of town hall for potential expansion. The town now has forty-seven employees, two of whom are part time, and an addition of seven new hires. Mary Lou Thatcher, clerk treasurer, retired after twenty-eight years in the office. Both she and Camilla have streets named for them. New residential development is trending to the west, across U.S. 31. But the council's choice to keep an official presence in "old town" speaks to the sense of community and the historical perspective that many feel is characteristic here.

And reasons for revisiting the past occur with appreciable frequency here. The high school homecoming in 1996 honored members of the 1946 football team during halftime. In September 1996, the Westfield Woman's Club celebrated its 101st anniversary. The last remaining charter member of 1895, Alma Bray, died in 1953. The club initiated the first grant of funds from Andrew Carnegie, who responded personally, for the first Carnegie Library in the county in 1911. Over many years, the club title has been affixed to numerous benefits for individuals, education and the town overall. Another charter member was the much-admired Martha Doan, academic educator, amateur botanist, Quaker and daughter of a prominent pioneer family.

In 1996, the utility department planned the new Westside Wastewater Treatment Facility to provide wastewater services to the growing community west of U.S. 31, expected to be in operation by April 1998. An old water main was replaced running nearly the entire width of town along State Route 32, as the lead project to replace old water mains throughout the town.

The building permits issued within the township in 1996 by the community development's increasingly busy staff of four was more than ever: 459, 87 more than last year, a jump of 23.3 percent. The value of the previous annual construction activity was $87,775,591. Permits for single-family residences were 297, 60 more than in 1995. There are now sixteen "active" subdivisions in the township, for a total of 2,148 lots platted for planned construction. The total tax rate of the township is the second lowest of the ten towns and cities in the county. The increase, in graph form, of commercial permits issued from the lowest number in 1981 to that of 1995 is the silhouette of the Midwest terrain climbing to a Rocky Mountain peak—quite impressive.

Some new actions address quality of life matters, such as the town establishing the Westfield Parks Advisory Board in August 1996, which began the Westfield and Washington Township Community Parks and Recreation Survey in April 1997. By December, the town council has approved the funding mechanism for new parks, the Town of Westfield Parks Impact Fee Ordinance. Some involved are looking to tourism to attract visitors to Westfield. One concept is a large park of several sports playing fields, an exercise track, suitable parking and a retention pond for aesthetics. They are wondering if this can be created on the school campus at the northwest corner of town. As of yet, the concept is in the initial discussion stage.

In 1997, contractors have begun the renovation of the high school, an improvement costing $1.8 million. This building is being readied for the fifth and sixth grades. The new high school is taking shape; it is entirely new construction at $34.5 million. It will open for the 1997–98 school year and will house nine hundred students its first year. The two elementary schools, minus the fifth grades, will use the vacated space for a rapidly growing school district and the increased number of new elementary students. Westfield Middle School will lose the sixth grade for an increase of middle school–age students.

A comprehensive planning process has begun with public meetings about land use in the township as a whole, with an engineering consultant facilitating the meetings and a target date of mid-1998 for completion, with updates planned for every three to five years ongoing.

If "publish or perish" haunts authors, then it's "annex or die" for town government. Beginning in 1990, the town began the process of annexing the land extending south of town to 146th Street, the southern township line. Another 283 acres, including a subdivision, a cemetery, an enclosed industrial property and a commercial property, are annexed. And in 1997, another 32.65 acres with a single parcel zoned industrial and with two new businesses there now are annexed as well.

During 1997, the employment of town government personnel grew to seventy full-time employees, ten more than the previous year. New hires were mainly in the police, fire and utilities departments

Now the town considers majorly upgrading the city's public safety facilities. Both the fire department and the police department have grown more in the past few years than in the fifty years preceding. Fire chief Bob Smith listed space needed for firefighters' quarters, an administration office, equipment storage and training. Police chief Bryan Foster says police lack space for interviews, lockers, evidence storage, conferences, impounded vehicles, exercise equipment, weapons and far larger public areas.

The town council and the Township Advisory Board had set in motion the plans for a new thirty-five-thousand-square-foot public safety building, and the location decided on said much about the matter of growth in general. The new facility will be built west of U.S. 31, on West State Route 32, positioned amidst the newest growth of the town that is already underway. Some expansion could still be expected south of town to the township line at 146th Street, but presently the physical growth of the city is to the west, onto former farm fields. Westfield and the township will share the cost of the new public safety facility proportionally.

The ribbon cutting for the new public safely building was on September 20, 1997. The impressive multi-use facility houses the police department, fire department and the third township-wide fire station #81. These functions had moved in earlier in the summer. The total cost for the facility on fifteen and a half acres was $5,875,500, including financing cost. The design with the two departments in one facility had been chosen as a cost savings said to be "significant." Seventeen of the department's twenty-eight firefighters were at the new site. The architecture was called "colonial with the simplicity of the Quaker influence" and "brick Shaker style with a white cupola."

A new ambulance was added in January, and in February a new aerial ladder truck called "Ladder 81" was also added. Manning the new equipment requires many hours of training for the fire crew, all of whom

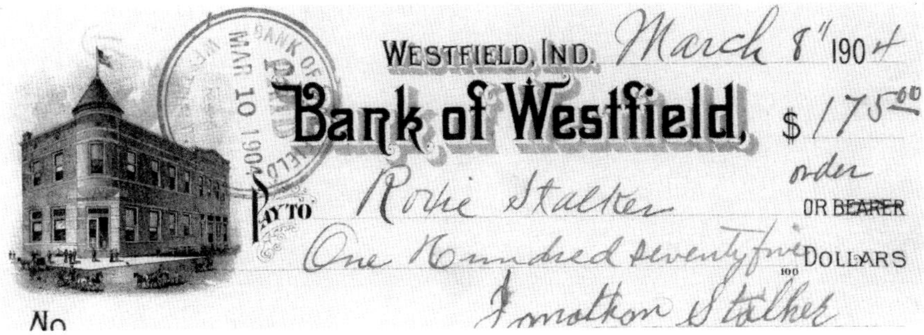

Check from the Bank of Westfield, 1904, showing a grand drawing of the landmark bank building, northeast corner of the primary intersection in town. The building is said to be haunted by the ghost of former night watchman Frank West, who grew up in the children's home in Westfield.

are working toward certification in a nationally recognized training program of the National Fire Protection Association. Accreditation means successful completion of seventy hours of classroom study and hands-on experience in all facets of their profession. The department's other fire stations are #82 on 151st Street and #83 on South Union Street.

In the spring of 1998, the new Westfield Post Office opened next door to the new public safety building. Truly the future of Westfield would see much more development well west of the center of "old town." At least in primary function, the new facility was a continuation of postal service to Westfield first begun in the spring, 161 years ago in 1837. More former farm acreage was being put to new use. Before long, U.S. Highway 31 will be back at the center of the town, now a full-blown city grown west of center to surround the highway, about to resume its role as a major thoroughfare through the community.

With room to spread into the former farm fields of the township, Westfield can still retain enough of its small-town feel in and around the now historic structures still existing to claim that as one of its growing attributes. In the studious realm of preservation are the memories told and retold that add character to sites like the old bank building with its own relatively magisterial presence on the northeast corner of, now formerly, the primary intersection in town, the former Bank of Westfield. It was built in 1900 and occupied for its original purpose for the next seventy years. Its later occupants have been an art gallery, a mortgage company, a spa salon and a boutique bakery, all while some would have it that the ghost of Hank West, a former town night watchman hired after a break-in during the early years of the bank, is present also. In the 1930s and 1940s, Hank boarded close by with Camilla Axelrod, and their demonstrative arguments about the proper heat in the residence are legendary. He had been reared at the orphanage in town and never married. Hank West died in 1984, but true believers are sure he is still on duty, in his own ethereal fashion.

16
The New Millennium

Ever Forward: The Third Millennium

To ponder the novelty, to greatly understate the process, of entering the third millennium of human calculated existence can be viewed here in Westfield as if in time-lapse photography with a space age soundtrack, a distinctive vibratory whir of mechanical exuberance. Back in "real time," the static view here from about any vantage at about any time from at least the mid-1980s forward has been of changes just made, in the process of being made or of impressive changes already announced in the planning stages.

One handy and hardly relatable statistic is that from a population of 1,837 in 1970, there has been a 548 percent increase by 2004. What this place once was with a traditional stability, dependability and security, it is now a "place to be" for planners of commerce, educational frontiers, upscale family residence and even matters of profitable public entertainment.

One of the major changes in progress here has been talked of and planned in part for some time, but by late July 2003, the Indiana Department of Transportation and the Federal Highway Administration announced specific designs addressing the increased traffic flow on U.S. Highway 31 at the west edge of Westfield. The town's chief concern has been that the reconstruction of the highway not divide the original town site from the major growth on the west side of the highway, especially the vital runs of the police and fire departments. But that, at its worst, is a temporary matter. At the moment, the immense mounds of earth moved and the enormous machinery involved are well-understood stage props for the developing grand show to come.

In the early years of the 1990s, transportation of a more primitive, say, first millennial form is in the works with a federal grant of $950,000, paired with $190,000 from the town and township as required, for building of the first portion of an exercise trail on the old Monon track bed beginning at the southern township line, a new linear walking and biking path that will intersect and join together the growing number of parks in town with more of the same to come. When that first portion of the extended Monon Trail is built, Indianapolis, for the hiker and biker, is 15.7 miles south on an adjunct trail that passes the new museum of art, a destination of its own increasing significance. The construction in Washington Township is overseen by the Westfield Parks Department for not only the standard twelve-foot-wide walking path, but also for several other common amenities such as restrooms, drinking fountains, picnic shelters, landscaping, parking at trailheads, bicycle racks and more. A similar exercise trail will be built on the former Midland Railroad route.

"Westfield Stands Its Ground," said a headline in the *Indianapolis Star* of May 1, 2004, about the southern portion of the township and Westfield's

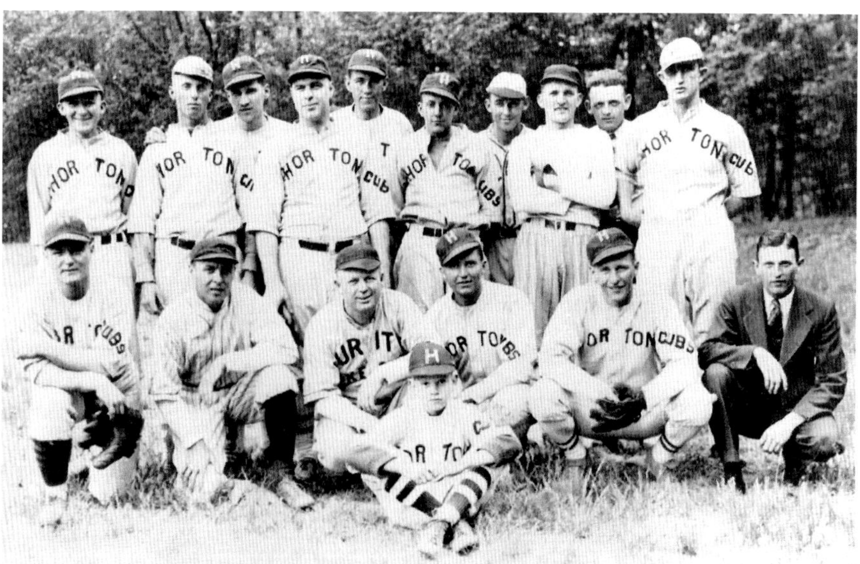

Men's baseball team of Hortonville, Washington Township, Hamilton County, Indiana, 1920s.

determination to keep all of Washington Township for its twenty-three thousand or so strong and continually growing population. The town had recently annexed another nine square miles in that southwest portion of the township, increasing its then population of 11,182 by 105 percent. And being Westfield, the historical perspective in all regards is not entirely out of mind.

The front page headline of the *Noblesville Daily Times* on June 22, 2005, "Special Census Initial Report: Population Exceeds Expectation," tells of Hamilton County being twenty-second in the nation for recent and rapid growth. School demographics and other matters complicated by rapid growth challenge planners of all sorts.

Then below the fold on the front page, "Stillness in the Midst of Growth" focuses on little Hortonville on 203rd Street west of U.S. 31 and northwest of Westfield. The wide-angle news photograph featured is a view from atop the four one-hundred-foot-tall grain silos, three concrete and one steel, beside the county co-op's grain elevator in Hortonville. The view is pure Americana: a small wooden United Methodist church with a steeple and three long windows on the side shown and a steep-roofed entry shelter at the front door, and close by is a nineteenth-century farmhouse with a proper midwestern barn of the same century. It is Tuesday, and the few cars at the church are of members of the Westfield Washington Historical Society who are listening to reminiscences about the history of the town. Inside, Mary Jane Carey, who has played the church organ for fifty years and has lived here for eighty years, addresses those assembled, and then they all look at period photographic views of the past in town and its surroundings.

Mary Jane "was a Horton," they all know, so her remarks are given due attention. June Millikan Cordell, also in attendance, was born on "Horton Hill" to the southeast; her grandfather Lemuel Venable was a carpenter who helped build many of the local structures still standing. Across the street from the church was a grocery store, and June lived above the store when young. Both women remember the church bells of the Friends and the Methodist churches on Sundays. The churches held many joint services, including many extended revivals, which usually added members to each church. The only thing "recently" of any note in Hortonville has been the theft of some candy money from the co-op's office trailer by the grain elevator: "That was in '95." Ten years ago.

Hortonville resident Ellis A. Wells wrote in 1936 that this was "a thriving place" when he arrived there as a child in 1899. There were two factories: E.J. Roberts and Will Pearce made drain-tiles, and William McCain made cheese. Lon Jones and Henry Rogers each had general stores. Levi Cain was postmaster. Chester Tingle was the railroad agent on the Monon, built through town thirteen years earlier, inspiring the first Horton family to set stakes and begin a town. Drs. Aldred and Baldwin "kept folk in fairly good physical condition." Just east out of town on Horton Hill was School No. 2. Later the school was moved into town and became the Hortonville Friends Meeting, first called the Mt. Zion Meeting. The bell installed had "a tone midway between an ordinary dinner bell and the sweet tones of "Old Union High in Westfield." A combined revival meeting in 1899 swelled the congregations of both churches. As John Hinshaw was known to say, "I tell thee, the Lord is in it." The renovated school meetinghouse had a long bench on the rostrum for the Quaker "worthies," with the pastor in the middle. One, John Keys, was often critical but would then lapse into his Quakerly philosophy of "well, it won't last always." Keys's farm was just east of town, and he drove his one-horse wagon with some barrels to the cheese factory for the whey after the cheese curds had been strained out, added some yellow corn and said "it helped stretch the pigs' hide some."

Though it was not a silent meeting in the English Friends tradition, the pastor did assume his place in the every-member-a-minister tradition; he was boarded by a member for whom he milked the cow, mowed the lawn and tended the

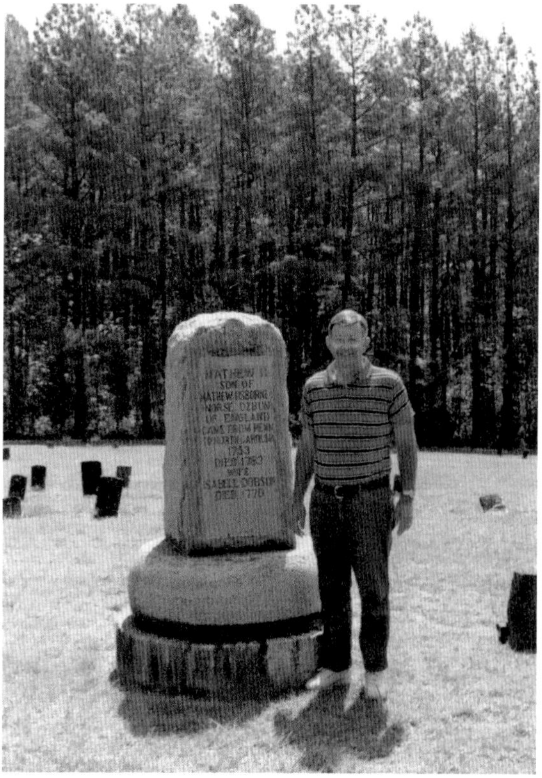

Westfield Washington Township resident Steve Osborn at the ancestors' grave marker in North Carolina. The family came to Indiana to buy land in Washington Township in the early 1830s. They were among the Quaker Migration leaving in protest of slavery (Quakers were eventually forbidden by southern state laws from aiding slaves, even from purchasing their freedom). In the pioneer era and two or three generations thereafter, the largest concentration of Quakers in Indiana lived in Washington Township.

garden. When, in 1940, a renovation of the meetinghouse cost $600 more than had been "subscribed," the members helped operate a small thirty-six-acre farm and paid the debt with the fall harvest. Eventually, a new meetinghouse was built.

The *Westfield Community Guide* get-acquainted newsprint publication of 2005 is headed "Boomtown," depicting the latest large-scale development at 156th Street and Springmill Road to be called "Centennial" for its build-a-nearly-complete-new-community design concept on something of a historical theme like the colonial towns in the East that grew around a central "green"; this one is three hundred acres with a community church near the center, a pool, sports courts, three lakes, a dog park and a sledding hill for the residents of the new commuter village with the James Michenererian title.

In October 2006, the 170th anniversary of Hinkle Creek Friends Meeting is announced, as is a series of revival services, the combination of events illustrating

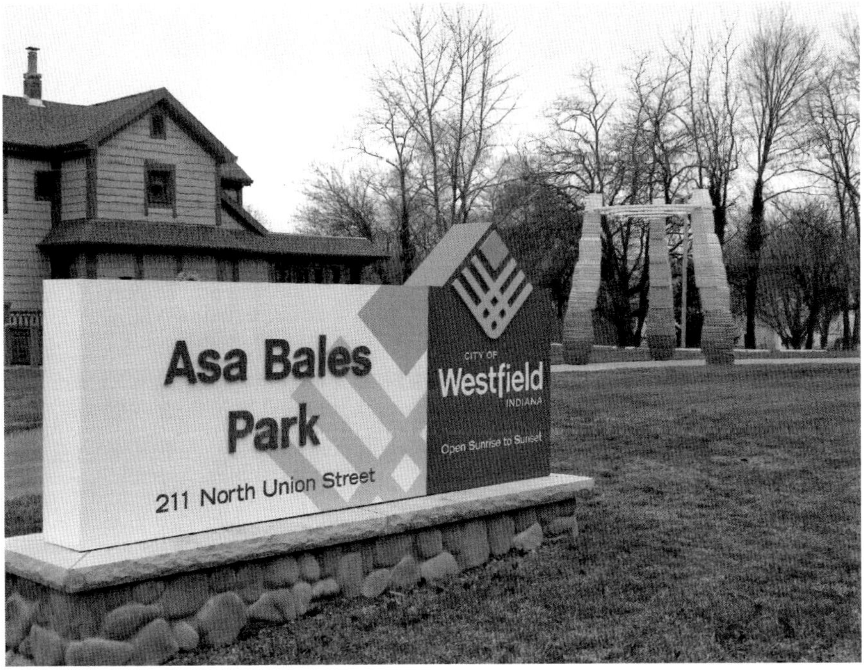

City park named for Asa Bales, cofounder of Westfield in 1834. Asa also cofounded an Anti-Slavery Friends Meeting of "separatists" from the "body (orthodox) church." Bales and many others were willing to break the fugitive slave laws to hide and transport escaped slaves north. Asa and his wife, Susannah, are buried in that group's cemetery nearby. After the Civil War, the Anti-Slavery Friends were welcomed back into the original Friends meeting. But Asa and Susannah died suddenly in late 1845. Their son Riley took his place aiding slavery escapees on the Underground Railroad.

a relevant matter of local history. This Friends meeting was organized soon after the first founders arrived, and some of them chose land claims farther out from the village then aborning. Now the same site is 445 East 206th Street. In the 1870s, the widespread popularity of religious revival campaigns attracted some Friends to worship in that manner, led at first by the revival preacher and then by paid ministers for the first time in Quaker history and anathema to old-style Quakers based on the multiple offenses of the paid clergy (the "hireling" ministry) of the 1650s in the English Lake Country where Quakerism began.

Yet another physical reminder of things as they were a century and three quarters ago, another alluring memento has been uncovered, this time at 220 North Union Street in the very center of the original village of Westfield, a one-story log cabin, seventeen by twenty-one feet, with seventeen-foot hand-hewn (how else?) beams, that emerged during renovation of the home that had grown as need be around the historic structure. While trying to date its original use, the logs are being dismantled, marked for restoration and stored. The best guess so far is that it could have been the first home of the William Osborn family; it was at the southwest corner of his original eighty-acre claim purchased in 1832 and was prime real estate when the village was first platted in 1834.

But newly discovered log cabins are few. Eight of the fifteen largest subdivisions in the Indianapolis metro area are in Hamilton County. Indeed, things are booming here; the new high school stadium, the size of some at small colleges, is to be named Riverview Health Stadium, for the support of the Riverview Hospital satellite facilities, one of which will specifically serve the students and faculty.

By mid-November 2006, Westfield had added three new parks dutifully named for historical families of prominence. At 169th Street and Ditch Road in Maple Knoll subdivision is Osborn Park, thirty-five acres designed for youth athletics; Armstrong Park in the Countryside subdivision at Spring Mill Road is another seventeen-acre site for youth sports. (The Armstrong family was the most prominent black family in the town's long history of racial harmony.) The third new park, at the corner of 161st and South Union is Liberty Park, and then there is the Raymond Worth Park, which includes five acres of the Richardson Wetlands, accessible by a lengthy boardwalk for up-close observation.

The Roy O. Hadley Community Park is on the northwest corner of Route 32 and North Union Street. Another larger area has been set aside on Hoover Street just east of the public library, and there is more public space with Quaker Park, Simon Moon Park and Old Friends Cemetery Park. Now another Eagle Scout project has built a disc golf course.

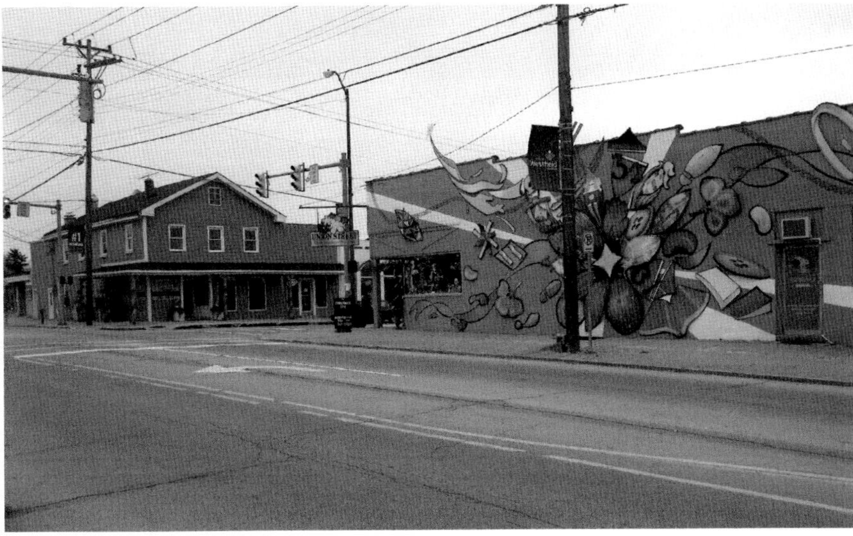

Former Mendenhall Drugstore (right) with colorful outdoor artscape and Pickett's Cafeteria (left) at the central intersection, Westfield, December 2013.

The Martha Doan Memorial Gardens, then Park, and now the Old Friends Memorial Park are the incarnations through which the former original Friends Cemetery has gone near the site of the original meetinghouse. But it should not be missed that Ms. Martha Doan, a charter member of the Westfield Women's Club in 1895 and from a prominent pioneer family of staunch Quakers, is a prime example of the best Westfield has ever produced. Ms. Doan was a graduate of Union High School, and a dominant theme in her life was higher education; she had earned three degrees by age twenty-one (bachelor's and master's of science from Purdue and bachelor's of literature from Earlham) and a fourth (a doctorate of science) from Columbia University in 1896. She was reportedly the first woman to do so. She was also dean of women and taught chemistry at Earlham College, Iowa Wesleyan College and Vassar College. She died in 1960 at age eighty-eight. People here with long roots into the past still speak of her with pride as a fellow resident in spirit.

During 2007, residents thought about the change coming in the town's status as a new full-fledged city and its first mayoral race. The candidate elected in November, Andy Cook, has lived here with his family for many years and has a useful background as a state public health official and knows about the environmental challenges involved with large population growths.

The "Party on the Patio" has been meeting beside Cool Creek on South Union Street to discuss and advance plans for the "Grand Junction" concept of urban revitalization. The city's recognition in the July 2013 issue of *CNN Money Magazine* as a "Best Place to Live" encourages the "Party" members. The city has been declared one of the top fifty places to live in the nation and this year is the only one ranked in Indiana; it is fifth in the Midwest and eighteenth in the nation. The Party meetings have not only kept the Grand Junction concept alive but also have advanced the cause admirably. It will all come about, they have no doubt, an "old town" revamped to accommodate and entertain residents and tourists with a family fun theme.

In early June 2014, the town, without knowing it officially, greeted a U.S. Navy veteran, Kenyon Eastin of Utah, who had begun walking from Horsehoe Cove, New Jersey, on May 28 and passed through on his way to San Francisco, not to raise money or even any banner awareness of any single cause or purpose, but as a personal challenge. But he had gained a following for his social media communiqués about his travels.

Actually, it was Erin O'Rear, out doing some deliveries from her pottery shop, who stopped to take a relief stint at pushing Kenyon's cart of food and supplies for awhile. She had heard about him on the area NPR station. What the long-haul pedestrian may have heard about during his brief swing through town was the buzz about "Westfield's new industry": travel-team family sports tourism. The ambitious "Grand Park" of over twenty baseball diamonds and other sports amenities has already seen 300,000 people come to play the ballgames or attend as family members. And not only have major hoteliers shown interest, but also the growing sports medicine field is to be represented in major fashion. As Mayor Cook says, the state tourism department itself should thank Westfield for bringing thousands of visitors from all directions into Indiana heading for Grand Park. The city now has an official hospitality coordinator who also heads the "SuperService" training program for local residents interested in the new tourism industry.

The former highly valued and cared for farmland has now taken on a new value and purpose. The founders had no idea.

17

The Spoken History Perspective

When Westfield residents Hal and Caroline Montgomery are asked about the biggest change to come to Westfield since they came here over sixty years ago, they both say, "What is happening now!"

Before Caroline and Hal Montgomery graduated from high school they had already seen U.S. Highway 31 rerouted from the center of town to bypass it at the western edge, a major change to the center of town. Before that, the highway had always been the town's access to the outside world, and the world passing through benefited the restaurants, automotive and other services and those who "let rooms" for overnight travelers.

Caroline came here from Oklahoma shortly after World War II in 1946 with her parents and two sisters in a snug Ford coupe. Her father had come to operate the pumping station of the Mobile Pipeline Company's crude oil pipeline from the Southwest through Indiana and on to the East. The pipeline crossed the southeast corner of the township. She remembers her first winter in Indiana; she thought she had awoken in Alaska. She began the second semester, fifth grade, at the all-grades school in Westfield; the family lived on Spring Mill Road before building a house on Highway 32 west of town.

Hal and Caroline graduated from WHS in the class of '57. Caroline was a "twirler" with the high school band and remembers a band marching routine designed to form a champagne glass on the field was canceled due to complaints of those still holding to the town's strong temperance tradition. During one summer, Hal worked setting hundreds of tomato plants in an area farm field, and in the faintly cast shadows from the few dim streetlights on Halloween night, he and a few others threw rotten tomatoes off the roof of the Standard Station in town. How else to personify growing up in a small town?

Hal worked with his father, an electrician, after high school wiring some houses on Westlea Drive in town. He and Caroline married in 1958 and moved to West Lafayette, Indiana, for him to study electrical engineering at Purdue University. After college, he was hired by International Harvester (IH) on the west side of Indianapolis; he drove a '46 Chevy coupe with one window broken out to work. He was with IH for the next twenty-five years, though driving cars with all windows intact. Caroline assumed the common role of housewife and mother of their three children and joined several homemakers' clubs in town.

When Hal piloted his father's two-seater Cessna 150, he took many aerial photos of Westfield in the 1970s, and their historical value increases by the year; he has "thousands," he says. The photos provide a plane's-eye view of Westfield in the late '60s and early '70s.

The changes to which the two refer include the present-day uses of those historic buildings at the center of town, usage befitting these times. One fine

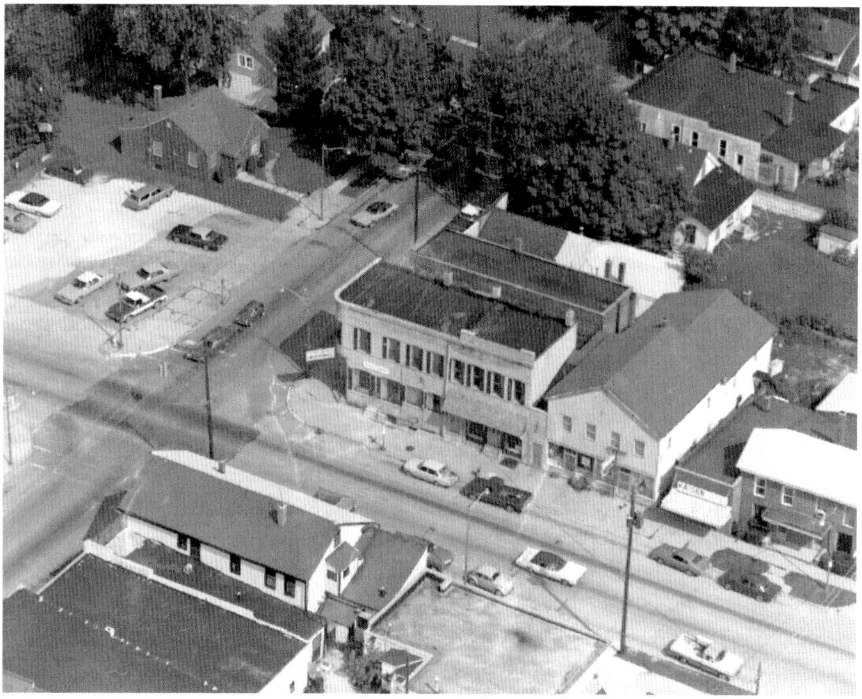

The center of Westfield with State Route 32, left to right, and former U. S. Route 31, lower left to upper right (also called Union Street and Range Line Road), 1970s.

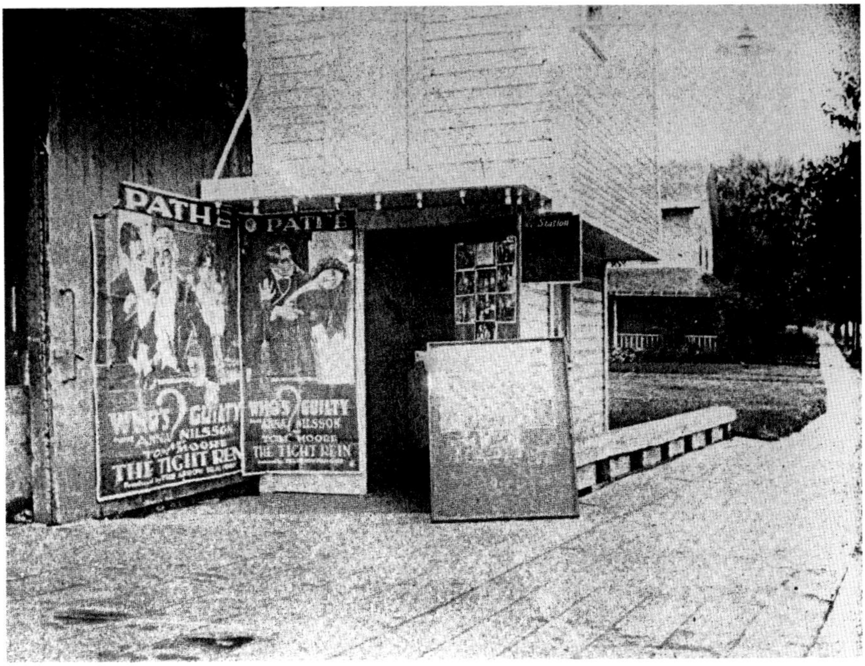

Entry to Samuel F. Barker's Gaudium movie theater, Westfield, circa 1914.

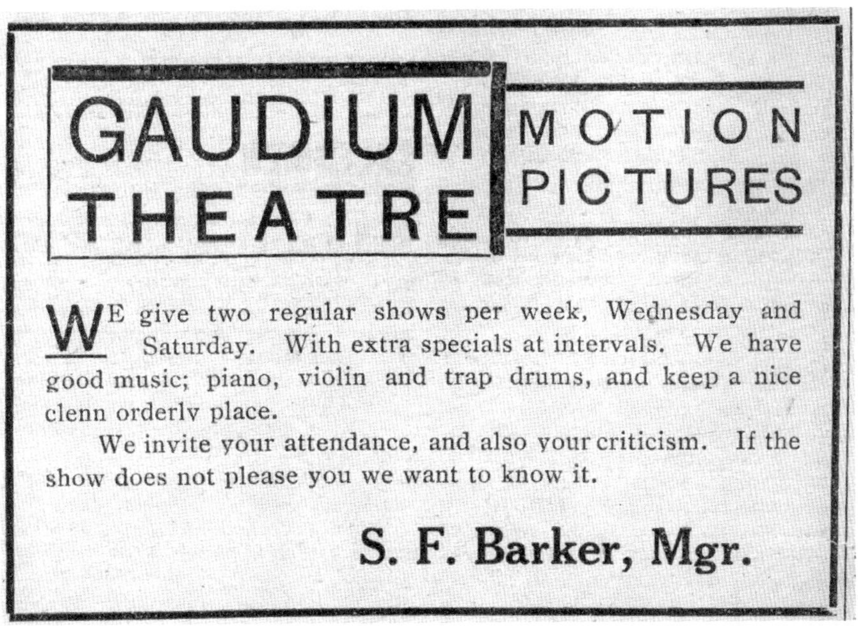

Ad for the Gaudium Theatre in Westfield.

old building now houses a boutique brewery, one of many in the area of wide popularity for those who appreciate tinkering with tinctures of taste for individually crafted brews.

In 1971, Hal Montgomery and a partner opened a package liquor store near the crossroads in town and stocked it with ten cases of the familiar amber bottles with the bold Pabst Blue Ribbon labels. "We'll never sell ten cases," Hal said at the time. The store was in a historical little building with a decided tilt to it, Hal says; it seemed to be "held up by leaning on Bill Dennis's barber shop" next door. Hal and Caroline managed the nascent business, soon moved and enlarged, for the next thirty years. The only observation Caroline will submit about selling liquor in a town long known as a temperance stronghold: "We had a front door and a back door." They sold the store to a new owner in 2001. They also operated a busy restaurant, Monty's Place, on West Main Street next door to the public library. Hal is a charter member of the Westfield Jaycees, and he and Caroline are proud of the park the club built on Hoover Road back when parks were not so plentiful here.

Now the Montgomerys, along with WHS grad Terea Skelton and others, have formed a likely popular entry, the Main Street Productions (now housed in a former historic church in Eagletown), as one of the places "to meet, eat and greet" in the center of old town, as an integral part of the coming "Grand Junction" of family attractions. At its present location, Westfield Playhouse was granted $5,000 for a new façade and has been newly painted. And in addition to staging ambitious plays (their Civil War drama is Ken Burns live), the group works with the "Voices of the Past" presentations held occasionally for tours of Westfield history.

Westfield barber ("We need your head for our business") Bill Dennis has a barber's common avuncular side for his small customers and is a local sports oracle for older patrons. Bill has been involved in every aspect of local youth and young adult sports as player, coach, umpire, referee and faithful fan. He transferred from the former Union High School to begin the sixth grade in the public school to play sports. Throughout his school days, he played on teams with the same boys until graduating in 1957.

From those small-town sports memories, Bill speaks with amazement about the capacity of Grand Park for hosting more than twenty youth baseball teams at once, that many more when the first games are over and repeated for as long as the park is open each day. He remembers when baseball gloves were "more like a small leather rag" than the pro player–

autographed models seen at Grand Park now where teams from all over the Midwest and beyond come for championship competitions.

In his day, the Westfield High School rivals were the close-by towns in the county and maybe one or two across the county line—Carmel, Kirkland, Sheridan, Walnut Grove, Fishers, Lapel, Cadiz, Markelsville, Shirley in Henry County and the much larger Noblesville. Sheridan dominated basketball, winning the "sectional" competitions eight times in a row in the 1950s.

Now in semiretirement, Bill, a southpaw and a former shot putter, has a "hitch" in his left arm, can't raise it above his shoulder, due, he says, to pitching in cold weather without proper warm-ups—not in his boyhood the finely tuned training, the exacting science of kinetics and sports medicine clinics at Grand Park for today's athletes.

Indeed, the finely manicured and maintained sports fields of Grand Park are a sports Valhalla, no mere 1950s school diamond or sandlot. Bill says that back then the basketball courts in some of the smaller and older schools had waves in them, making dribbling difficult, and some school gyms had structural columns in the middle of the floor. At Carmel's gym, a modern marvel when that all-grades school opened for the 1921–22 school year, making an overambitious layup could land the player in the furnace room immediately beyond the goal. There also, players putting the ball in play from the sidelines had to dodge the overhanging feet of fans sitting on the edge of the balconies on both sides of the court. And when kicking the football through the goalpost uprights at Kirklin's field, the ball then had to be retrieved from the neighboring cornfield. When not in school, summer swimming was at a spring-fed pond, a discarded board rigged for diving, out west of town near the Midland train tracks back of the new Westfield Public Safety Building.

Westfield teams were truly competitive, Bill remembers, winning their share of games in all sports. He is proud of having played in the last basketball game ever held in the old WHS gym in 1956. "We lost, but we took Windfall High School to a double overtime." It was a grand effort fully realized and nearly as grand in recollection. Glory days. Retold for the price of a no-nonsense haircut.

Thirty acres of former farmland west of town, now within Grand Park, was part of the Bill Wood farm where son Craig Wood went to farming after studying agricultural sciences at Indiana's famous "cow college," the mighty Purdue University. Where once the two worked in relative solitude on spacious fields, now thousands of youth ballplayers, parents and fans attend games, visitors from others states near and far.

Craig Wood's farming career is a prime example of how that calling has changed in his lifetime; he is the only one in his high school graduating class of 1973 who has gone into farming full-time, the only one of seventy-three other graduates. He took over farming from his father with the "no till" preparation of fields; far fewer passes over the fields using less diesel fuel as a major advantage. He still farms about 240 acres of the typical Brooks and Crosby clay loam of the township.

Ten years into his farming career in 1988, Craig faced one of the most memorable droughts in decades. "We harvested about a third of what we might have had," he says. He was featured on the front page of the *Indianapolis Star* newspaper as a young farmer facing extreme, ruinous weather conditions in an occupation so dependent on the vagaries of the weather. So he knows from experience how to survive in the business because of good planning. "The guy who is pushing his pencil," planning ahead and taking all the elemental aspects of farming into careful consideration ahead of each new growing season can succeed. But the farmer who does not lay some back for the unexpected will surely suffer for it, he says.

Craig is conversant with computer applications, of course, for planning, recording and reporting on farm operation. He plans for four harvests of alfalfa each season, a hay crop far less common than before, and he still grows some wheat. He still raises hogs, cross breeds of Hampshire, Chester White, York or Duroc, and beef cattle, Angus, Hereford and two Charolais calves at present, for the family's "freezer meat" customers.

Craig knows numerous farmers in the state from his leadership roles in agricultural organizations. He has lobbied both the state legislature and the U.S. Congress. His sociability for one whose life's work is often solitary is well rounded; he credits his parents for being involved with many social activities off the farm. The Woods are a musical family; all play instruments, and there's a third-generation trombone succession going on now. Craig and his wife, Sandra, both are involved with the music program at the Westfield United Methodist Church, and they have toured Europe with choral groups.

His tenure as president of the Indiana Soybean Association qualifies him to speak glowingly about that "wonder crop" and its many uses from the time of its introduction to midwestern farming to the present, including soy diesel fuel and soy ink; the list is endless and in nearly every instance an improvement, including environmentally, over whatever the new product replaces.

Craig is at work at other activities off the farm. But he still "has the soil under my fingernails," he says, and farming will remain a prime interest, one with a long heritage here in the midst of rapid change.

Afterword

The Bread Bowl

Inside the gentle sweep of a hand-carved bread mixing bowl believed to date to 1631 is painted a picture of Simon Moon's second home here. For the most recent 170 years of that time, the family heirloom has been called "Hannah's [mixing] bowl" since her death in 1844. The much earlier date associated with the bowl predates the founding in the early 1650s of the Society of Friends (Quaker), of which town founders Hannah and Simon Moon were birthright members. The picture was painted with fine primitive talent by Lula Moon, wife of Wyman Moon, son of Riley and Susanna Moon, son of Simon and Hannah.

Simon and Hannah purchased a 70-acre claim in 1832 at the crossroads where the village of Westfield developed. Simon set aside a few town lots, along with Asa Bales and Ambrose Osborn from their claims adjoining his, to plat the village. Then, shortly before the town plat was filed at the courthouse in Noblesville on May 6, 1834, Simon purchased a 160-acre claim four miles north of the village and there built the home that, later covered with sawn lumber, appears in the painting.

Not far from the farm was the "Dismal Swamp," where the family knew the few secret safe trails through the quicksand and the few safe high ground spots where they could hide escaped slaves until escorting them at night northward to the next station of the Underground Railroad.

The faithful preservation of the bowl from such an early date proves great affection for it. But it was also useful. Brought here in the extended Quaker Migration from the Southland with the few belongings that could fit in a

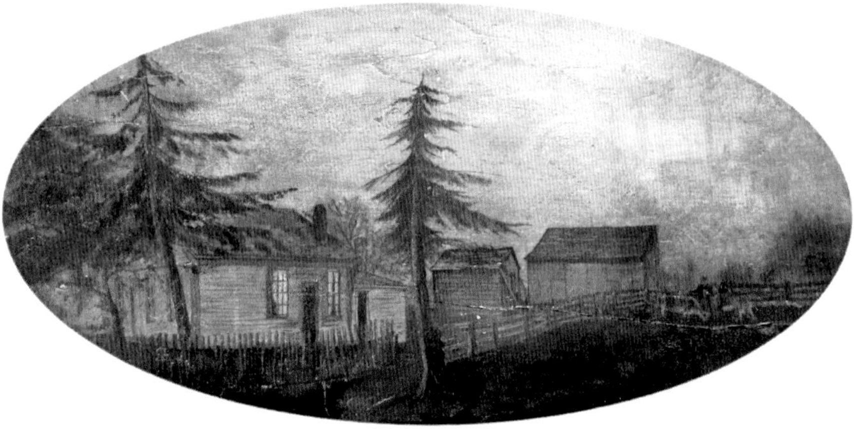

Painting in a bread mixing bowl of the Simon and Hannah Moon home north of Westfield close by the Dismal Swamp where the family hid escaped slaves on secret high ground before transporting them by night north to freedom. The home dates to the mid-1830s. Painted by Lula Moon, a fourth-generation Moon wife, the bowl is said to date to 1631, a Quaker Moon family heirloom.

wagon or cart, it saved Simon from making another from one of the many trees he felled in clearing land for farming.

The family heirloom now belongs to Carol Cox Daubenspeck, daughter of Elsie Moon Cox, named a Citizen of the Century at the town's sesquicentennial in 1984. An active member of the Westfield Washington Historical Society, Carol's home in the township, still surrounded with some vestige of the country life of her ancestors, contains neat shelves of thick notebooks of family history compilations. She has given many talks to all age groups about the Moon family.

To those for whom "know thyself" is an important notion, the painting offers a peaceful yet enlivening two-fold opportunity, first to watch oneself entering the painted scene (who is this person truly desiring transformation into the past?), and second, once truly inside the scene to experience a panoramic presence, an evocative total environment in which to move, touch and commune, a holographic *knowing* of such a realm. To say a picture was painted "after the fact" belittles the malleable nature of fact.

Bibliographical Essay

The earliest record evoking a real *felt* beginning of the story was written with quill pen and boll ink in practiced, flowing calligraphic script by two literate Quakers on behalf of those gathered inside a newly built log "meetinghouse" in a densely forested wilderness.

Reading the handwritten record of that first official gathering of "founders" in December 1835 is to see the hands of the "recording clerks" form each letter in turn almost worshipfully without the slightest blurring or errant ink blotch, recording "the will of the meeting," likely knowing, without hint of pride (a Quaker insistence) that their handwriting would be read these 179 years after. They knew because they were creating records similar to those written by others of their kind two centuries before them with similar lasting importance.

There is renewable energy in viewing such a scene, even this far removed in time. Energy to pursue similar discoveries, to make many inquiries, to visualize and understand the succession of events, of eras, begun at that early gathering of founders. In this regard, the Friends Archives at Earlham College in Richmond, Indiana, hold many more similar materials for understanding the larger order of things in which the story begins.

The same enlightening resides in the many letters, diaries, journals, early account books, more recent newspapers and clippings and similar sources cited in this work at the archives of the Westfield Washington Historical Society (cited in this work). The random nature of these records makes for an episodic story narrative; each item adds its own priceless insight to the whole, sometimes showing a new cast of characters. And each item deserves an appreciative nod to those who located, donated, catalogued and used proper conservation materials and methods to preserve these invaluable records.

It is particularly fortunate to have available a county newspaper first published just as the founders began their first minute book. Two newspapers published in Noblesville during two short runs, the *Newspaper* (1836–39) and the *Little Western* (1842–45), include references to Westfield and Washington Township. The ephemeral nature of weekly or daily newspapers draws the reader into the events among the people found there for a distant familiarity that further inspires the search for yet more such information. These and many other newspapers of Noblesville have been viewed at length and are in an impressive accumulation of like treasures in the light, roomy Noblesville Public Library history and genealogy department.

Directories published for special purposes and times, especially those that appear between federal ten-year census years, are particularly important. Some such sources acquire an affectionate moniker such as "The People's Guide" of 1874, referring to its wordy complete title common in its day, or simply "Helms" for the 1880 atlas of Hamilton County and its lengthy self-aware title. And there is "Shirts," the county history published in 1901 written by the son of a founding family, elsewhere in the county titled *A Primitive History of Hamilton County* by Augustus Finch Shirts.

The Map of Hamilton County, Indiana, "drawn by C.S. Warner" and published in 1866 with its inset of Westfield, invites an imaginative stroll through town, passing structures represented by dark squares and rectangles in which those in that year following the war are working at their trades and others are present conducting business transactions. Listening with an expectant, engrossed attention, the true believer walks the village streets and hears all the sounds of the times—anvils ringing, the random rhythm of horses' hooves on the dirt streets, wagons creaking, street-side chatter and the occasional spoken remark from a voice rising above all the sounds and listening for that one voice of a singular resident the visitor has just read about in one of the records being compiled here, just now. A few of the entrepreneurs are listed in the short "business directory" of prominent professionals, merchants and "mechanics" within the map inset. (The map, which belonged to a Civil War soldier, was discovered rolled in an attic one hundred years and three months after it had been published and has been restored by the county surveyor's office.)

The suggestion by President Ulysses Grant for publishing local history all across the nation during the approach to the nation's centennial celebration in 1876 helped bring about numerous foundational works, county atlases, county histories and so forth. The timing was of importance also. The centennial publications preserve the recollections of many more eyewitnesses, of course, and the segments of the larger story they have heard from their parents and, at least within families, what is remembered from those of a generation during the Revolution.

The Westfield Public Library's Sumner Local History Room contains relevant publications, along with donated original and secondary source materials, family histories and ready reference files of many titles and WHS annuals.

During the Great Depression, the publications funded by the Federal Works Progress Administration sustained more than just the livelihoods of authors, teachers and others. These *People's Guides* of each state contain brief histories of numerous locales in each state, as well as descriptions of towns and cities, natural and human constructions and much more in the 1930s and '40s.

Among county plats of more recent production but of historical interest, the original land grant map created by the office of Hamilton County surveyor Kent Ward is a one-stop view of that development in all the county providing not only a ready reference tool but a visual impact as well.

Many other necessary works, though said to be "secondary" sources, have over time acquired their own individual significance. A prime example is *Our Westfield* published during the Westfield Washington 150th anniversary in 1984. The book includes treatments of a wide variety of topics over a great number of years and recollections of many current and former residents. There is also a wealth of photographs and other illustrations. (Near the beginning of this volume is a transcription of a letter dated "9th month, 14th, 1827" sent from Westfield, North Carolina, by Jacob and Mary Bales to their son Asa Bales before he arrived in Hamilton County.)

Information collected by all levels of government is always of great use to the historian, and especially for this work, the nineteenth-century federal agricultural and manufacturers censuses. Other local government records include the volumes of estate probate records, cited in this work, that contain useful lists of personal possessions upon the deaths of the former owners, along with important family genealogical data. Original long-form deed abstracts are also fascinating finds with the first page showing the original purchaser of each claim followed by numerous pages of details about how that original claim has been divided for sale over a century and more; and there are occasional notations attached for legal reasons but also giving genealogical and other information, even the occasional small, hand-drawn map also attached showing original names of creeks and other natural features. The pocketsize field notebooks of the early surveyors all across the state are useful introductions to that work during an especially important era. The Indiana State Archives houses many of these technical treasurers.

Township trustees' school records include teachers' contracts and, sometimes, individual school and classroom records; the curricula listed shows what the students are learning. Pride in public schools produces helpful sources such as school annuals, a good source for photographs (and popular hairstyles), along with school newspapers, articles about school activities and more, as shown in what has been cited from the late 1930s in this work. These sources are alive with the exuberance of the daily school experience and the combined kinetic force of school extracurricular activities.

Sources such as the annual handbooks of the Westfield Chamber of Commerce provide vital facts for revealing analyses. Recorded interviews, oral histories, are of inestimable value, especially those filmed, showing telling nuances: facial expressions, voice inflections, dismissive waves of the hand, hesitations, even faux pas, which can inform about the prevailing social norms and customs or local rules of etiquette. Even voice modulation has its particular value, as it changes during the interview.

Numerous background sources have aided in the creation of brief contextual exposition in which to narrate the story's many facets. A superior example is *The Old Northwest Pioneer Period, 1814–1840* (Indiana Historical Society, 1950) by R. Carlyle Buley, an Indiana University professor who won a Pulitzer Prize for the monumental pair of volumes. Professor Buley's bibliographical travels are truly a wonder to behold, as when showing the value of period newspapers as but one source for his exhaustive work.

The wealth of annual compendiums by state government departments on agriculture, geology, botany and other topics are of great value to the historian, again for background information and terminology of use in the narrative.

The publications of the Indiana Historical Society and the Indiana Historical Bureau are also useful for the same kind of exposition that informs the events and persons of the story. The society has its own impressive history dating from 1830, along with its long list of unique definitive publications, and the bureau dates from the times when local history was required teaching in three grade levels of public education in the state. For this important work, the bureau has an impressive history of unique and essential publications. Both the society and the bureau have published many volumes of verbatim records, personal papers, journals, diaries, etc. of great value to the historian. The multivolume diary of Calvin Fletcher, particularly the first seven volumes (1817–62), has been helpful for this work. The diaries are published by the IHS (1972 forward); the Bureau's *Indiana Boundaries, Territory, State and County* by George Pence and Nellie C. Armstrong (1967) was similarly helpful.

The occasional erstwhile amateur historian who compiles a limited history of a church, a school or a business, most often to commemorate an anniversary, often becomes the default "authority" on the primary topic. A fine example is "Westfield Methodist Church 1850–1944, Ninety Years of Service," author unstated though likely Paul D. Brown, church historian. (A particular delight: a hand-drawn floor plan of the church in 1865 locating the "Amen Corner"—yes, it actually was a semiofficial adjunct to the services, not just a general worship service exuberance or condemnation—along with the other features of the interior.) Another example is a lengthy letter from former Hortonville resident Ellis A. Wells, Whittier, California, in 1936, published here, in which he reminisces in appreciable detail about growing up in his hometown.

Information about the short life of the Farmers Bank of Westfield was found in a highly specialized work, *Indiana Obsolete Notes and Script*, by Wolka, Vorhies and Schramm (1978). (Alas, no illustrations of the Westfield bank notes but alluring word descriptions instead.)

Other sources have been viewed, and enjoyed, as cited in the work.

Index

Y

Z

About the Author

Author, historian, former teacher and director of a state historical society rare book and manuscripts library, Tom Rumer (BS, MA, MLS) has written on a variety of topics, time periods and regions in American history, including migration (on the Oregon Trail, the Quaker Migration from the South to the Midwest), environmental, labor, agricultural, genealogical, veterans' and Native American and black history, as published in trade books, journals, magazines, newspapers and TV and radio scripts. Tom's publications have been awarded and called "definitive" by authorities in the fields in which he has written. Formerly from west-central Ohio, Tom and his educator wife, Barbara, live in an 1840s log cabin in central Indiana amidst native woodland and prairie plants.